Creating Readers

Dedication

To Bill Martin, Jr., who has touched us all with his love of language

Acknowledgments

My daughter, Richele Bartkowiak, for her clever, child-appealing illustrations of stories and poems

My daughter, Tiffany Markle, for her creative poems and tongue twisters in areas where few existed

My editor and friend, Kathy Charner, for her creative finishing touches and for her continuous support and encouragement

Creating Readers

Over 1000

Games, Activities, Tongue Twisters,

Fingerplays, Songs, and Stories to Get

Children Excited about Reading

Pam Schiller

Illustrations: Richele Bartkowiak and K. Whelan Dery

gryphon house

Beltsville, MD

Copyright

© 2001, Pam Schiller

Published by Gryphon House, Inc., 10726 Tucker Street, Beltsville MD, 20705
or P.O. Box 207, Beltsville MD 20704-0207.

Visit us on the web at www.gryphonhouse.com

Illustrations: Richele Bartkowiak and K. Whelan Dery
Cover photograph: The Stock Market

Library of Congress Cataloging-in-Publication Data

Schiller, Pamela Byrne.
  Creating readers : over 1000 activities, tongue twisters, fingerplays, games, songs, poems, and stories / Pam Schiller ; illustrations, Richele Bartkowiak and K. Whelan Dery.
      p. cm.
  Includes bibliographical references and index.
  ISBN 0-87659-258-2
  1. Reading (Early childhood) 2. Early childhood education--Activity programs. I. Title.
LB1139.5.R43 S35 2001
372.4--dc21   2001023799

The publisher and the authors cannot be held responsible for injury, mishap, or damages incurred during the use of or because of the activities in this book. The authors recommend appropriate and reasonable supervision at all times based on the age and capability of each child.

Every effort has been made to locate copyright and permission information.

Bulk Purchase

Gryphon House books are available at special discount when purchased in bulk for special premiums and sales promotions as well as for fund-raising use. Special editions or book excerpts also can be created to specification. For details, contact the Director of Sales at the address above.

Table of Contents

The Great Debate

Every few years we find ourselves in a debate over the systematic instruction of phonics versus some other less direct form of instruction. During the 1950s and 1960s, the language experience approach was in vogue. This approach relied heavily on sight word recognition and suggested that sound/symbol recognition would occur on its own.

During the 1980s and 1990s, the whole language approach took root and is still popular today. This approach is an attempt to blend the language experience approach and the use of phonics within meaningful context. This approach requires that the teacher be constantly surveying upcoming instruction for opportunities to point out phonetic connections. There is no systematic plan for teaching phonics in this approach. Phonics instruction is intended to spontaneously "pop up" in daily lessons and routines. It takes a skilled and practiced teacher to do this well.

As time has passed, it has become apparent that some children who are instructed using the whole language method later encounter difficulties in reading. It is evident that some children need more formal instruction in phonemic awareness. It is this recognition that has moved us to our current instructional approach to early literacy—the integration of language experience and the systematic teaching of phonics.

It seems that we may have finally hit a balance. We recognize that many children need more direct instruction in phonics and that all children need to experience phonics in meaningful context, as it pops up in daily routines and lessons.

Now the debate has turned from what to when. When do we begin a more systematic approach to reading instruction? How do we sequence instruction so that it is developmentally appropriate?

Looking to Brain Research for Answers

The crucial first few years of life lay a foundation for reading skills in later years. Between the fourth and eighth month of life, a child's brain develops what is called a "native language map." A neuron is assigned to every sound in the native language. So, argue as we may about when phonics should be introduced, it is clear from the research that infants are already way ahead of us. This is why talking and reading to infants is so important. The initial wiring for hearing is connected during the fifth month in utero. The baby begins to hear sounds at that time. So literally, we can start talking and reading at that point and know that we are contributing to an infant's development of auditory discrimination.

Continuing to talk and read to an infant will contribute to the development of syntax and vocabulary, but it will take matching this information with real life experiences to prepare a child for reading.

There is no absolute timetable for learning to read. Normal ranges vary by as much as three years. According to many experts, providing rich experiences for brain development and then leaving children to their own unique timetable is still the best practice.

First Things First!

What makes sense developmentally? First, we speak and then we read, but what happens between these two great human accomplishments?

It takes most infants two years to master speaking—two years filled with many maturational achievements and experiential opportunities. An infant's sense of hearing matures around the fifth month. Neural connections for the sounds in an infant's native language are assigned between the fourth and eighth month of life. Experientially, infants are spoken to, read to, saturated in language, and rewarded with many celebrations of small approximations of speech such as cooing and babbling along the way. The process for learning to read is dependent on similar maturational achievements and experiential opportunities.

Between the ages of two and six years, a child's wiring for vision matures, small muscle coordination is achieved, and critical thinking skills emerge. The child becomes capable of longer periods of attention and is rapidly developing a more sophisticated vocabulary. These maturational achievements make the years between two and six fertile ground for introducing reading.

Experientially during this time, children need multiple and repetitive opportunities to play with language (e.g., rhyming, singing, looking for patterns) before they begin the more formal process of mastering the mechanics of reading (e.g., matching sounds with symbols). Language is a relatively new accomplishment that will be perfected with plenty of exploration.

Before the formal process of reading begins, children need to experience language from the inside out. They need opportunities to talk and to write (in their own way, using invented spelling and drawings).

The list on page 12 outlines developmental stages and skills, sequential and overlapping, that children need to experience and master on their reading journey.

As children practice using language, they need to receive feedback. They also need time to reflect on and evaluate their own progress. And don't forget to celebrate the many milestones they achieve as they navigate the road to reading. In short, children need time— time to experience language and time to practice and evaluate what they experience; time to reflect; time to develop and time to grow; then, time to reflect and grow some more.

Stages of Development	Skills
1. Getting Ready Listening Falling in love with sounds	Auditory memory Auditory perception
2. Comprehending Enacting, dramatizing, and recreating stories Answering multi-level questions	Language development Conceptual development Critical thinking
3. Developing Oral Language Extending and enriching vocabulary Matching words to thoughts and actions	Language development Auditory perception
4. Understanding Functions of Print Understanding spatial orientation Recognizing part/whole relationships Putting thoughts on paper	Visual perception Visual memory Motor coordination Conceptual development
5. Acquiring Reading Skills Reading predictable text Recognizing sight words Developing phonological awareness	Auditory memory Auditory perception Visual perception Visual memory Visual motor coordination Language development Conceptual development Critical thinking

Basic Principles of Emergent Literacy

What is emergent literacy? It is a term used to describe the beginnings of oral and written language proficiency. According to research, here are the basic principles of emergent literacy.

1. Literacy is a social process. It occurs in the context of children's interactions with other children and adults.
2. Literacy begins at birth. From an infant's first observations of human behaviors and her resulting imitations of adult sounds and social cues, literacy is developing.
3. All aspects of literacy—listening, speaking, reading, writing, and thinking—develop interdependently.
4. Literacy develops along a continuum just like intellectual and physical growth. Children will develop literacy at their own pace. Slow times are often times when internalization is occurring.

Realistic Expectations

No two children are alike. Each is uniquely individual, based on both genetic makeup and environmental influences. However, there are some general expectations for specific age-related accomplishments that have emerged from years of observation and study.

Below is a list of age-related accomplishments, reprinted with permission from *Preventing Reading Difficulties in Young Children* (National Academy Press, 1998). Keep in mind the timing of these accomplishments are contingent on maturational and experiential differences among children.

Birth to Three-Year-Old Accomplishments

- Recognizes specific books by cover.
- Pretends to read books.
- Understands that books are handled in particular ways.
- Enters into a book-sharing routine with primary caregivers.
- Demonstrates enjoyment of rhyming language and nonsense words.
- Labels objects in books.
- Listens to stories.
- Requests adult to read or write.
- Begins to show attention to specific print, such as letters in names.
- Uses increasingly purposeful scribbling.

- Begins to distinguish between drawing and writing.
- Produces some letter-like forms and scribbles with some features of writing.

Three- to Four-Year-Old Accomplishments

- Knows that alphabet letters are a special category of visual graphics that can be individually named.
- Recognizes print in the local environment.
- Understands that different text forms are used for different functions of print (e.g., a grocery list is different from a menu).
- Recognizes separable and repeating sounds in language (e.g., in "Peter, Peter, Pumpkin Eater": p, e, -er, Peter, and eater).
- Uses new vocabulary and grammatical constructions in his or her own speech.
- Understands and follows oral directions.
- Is sensitive to some sequences of events in stories.
- Shows an interest in books and reading.
- When being read a story, connects information and events to real-life experiences.
- Demonstrates understanding of literal meaning of a story being told. Uses appropriate questions and comments.
- Displays reading and writing attempts.
- Identifies some alphabet letters, especially those from own name.
- Writes (scribbles) messages as part of playful activity.
- Recognizes beginning and rhyming sounds in familiar words.

Five-Year-Old Accomplishments

- Knows the parts of a book and their functions.
- Begins to track print when listening to a familiar text being read or when rereading own writing.
- Reads familiar texts emergently (i.e., not necessarily verbatim from the print alone).
- Recognizes and can name all uppercase and lowercase letters.
- Understands that the sequence of letters in a written word represents the sequence of sounds (phonemes) in a spoken word.
- Recognizes some one-to-one letter/sound correspondences.
- Recognizes some words by sight such as the, I, my, you, is, are.
- Uses new vocabulary and grammatical constructions in own speech.
- Makes appropriate switches from oral to written language styles.
- Notices when simple sentences fail to make sense.
- Connects information and events in text to life and life experiences to text.

- Retells, reenacts, and dramatizes stories or parts of stories.
- Listens attentively to books the teacher reads to class.
- Names some book titles and authors.
- Demonstrates familiarity with a number of types or genres of text (e.g., storybooks, expository texts, poems, newspapers, and everyday print such as signs, notices, labels).
- Correctly answers questions about stories read aloud.
- Makes predictions based on illustrations or portions of stories.
- Demonstrates understanding that spoken words consist of sequences of phonemes.
- Given spoken sets such as pan, pan, pen, can identify the first two as the same and the third as different.
- Given spoken sets such as ran, pat, did, can identify the first two as sharing one same sound.
- Given spoken segments, can merge them into a meaningful target word.
- Given a spoken word, can produce another word that rhymes with it.
- Independently writes many uppercase and lowercase letters.
- Uses phonemic awareness and letter knowledge to spell independently (i.e., invented spelling).
- Writes (unconventionally) to express own meaning.
- Builds a repertoire of some conventionally spelled words.
- Shows awareness of distinctions between "kid writing" and conventional writing.
- Writes own name (first and last) and the first names of some friends and classmates.
- Writes most letters and some words when they are dictated.

Celebrating Milestones

Just think how we celebrate children's first words and even their first sounds. We pick them up and hug and squeeze them. We laugh with glee. We have them say the words over the telephone to a distant relative or friend. We can't stop celebrating and reinforcing these remarkable achievements.

Think about how we celebrate children's first steps. Again we are exuberant. We have them demonstrate this new skill to everyone. We are happy at first just to see them stand with balance. Then one step delights us. Two steps is even more exciting. And when a child takes several steps between two loving parents, he or she receives support from start to finish.

Reading needs this same attention to celebration. It is equally as complex a task as speaking and walking. Find ways to celebrate each tiny accomplish-

INTRODUCTION

ment along the way to mastery. Bring in other children and teachers to listen to the group story your class has written. Build and develop class cheerleaders. Children are very interested in peer approval. Be sincerely enthusiastic about children's ability to hear rhyming sounds. Encourage children to use a checklist to check off skills as they accomplish them. Have a Green Eggs and Ham Party when children become competent at injecting the predictable lines in the story.

A Road Map for Instruction

How to Use This Book

This book is written following a developmental sequence that ensures children develop both the desire and the skills necessary to read. It is filled with listening activities, songs, stories, finger plays, and rhymes that allow children to play with and fall in love with language. They become acquainted with and accustomed to the rhythm and patterns of language.

As children develop more refined auditory and visual skills, you will be able to focus more specifically on individual letter sounds and other mechanics of reading. It is important that children develop a disposition (desire) to read. As a matter of fact, disposition is equally as important as skill because no matter how well you may be able to read, you will not read if you haven't got a desire to read. The activities in the first chapters of this book help develop disposition and teach children the joy of reading.

Reading successfully requires having the big picture of what reading is all about. Children need to understand that words have meaning and that words can be represented by printed symbols (letters). They need motivation and desire to tackle the challenge of distinguishing similar sounds and seeing discrete differences in letter shapes.

This book offers activities and suggestions to help children develop both the big picture (Getting Ready, Chapter 1) and the skills (Acquiring Reading Skills, Chapter 5) they need to read. It is also filled with suggestions for celebrating milestones along the road to mastery.

Take it slow. Consider reading a journey—a journey with many sites to explore, stops to enjoy, and milestones to celebrate. Let the children be your guide. As Daniel Greensberg says, "When the brain is ready, you can't stop a child from reading." Happy journey!

Getting Ready

Listening Games and Activities

Group Games

Where Is That Sound?

Sit children in a circle. Ask them to close their eyes. Walk to a corner of the room and use a rhythm band instrument to make a sound. See if the children can point in the direction of the sound they hear. (If you don't have a rhythm band instrument, tap a pencil or just whistle.)

Gossip

Sit children in a circle. Ask a child to select a word or a phrase and whisper it into the ear of the child sitting on her right. That child then whispers what he heard into the ear of the child to his right. Continue around the circle until all children have heard the word or phrase. Invite the last child to say what he heard out loud. Is it what the first child said? Continue the game for as long as the children show an interest in playing.

It's Time to Celebrate

Clap and praise everyone when a word or phrase comes back unchanged.

Find Me

Blindfold a child (IT). Select another child (no blindfold) to be IT's partner. Move somewhere in the room, a good distance from IT. Whisper IT's name. Can IT walk to the place where you are standing? IT's partner is to help only when IT is in danger of tripping or walking into something.

Head, Shoulders, Knees, and Toes; Hokey Pokey

Sing songs and play games that require listening for directions such as "Hokey Pokey (page 71)," "Head, Shoulders, Knees, and Toes," and "Open, Shut Them (page 206)." Here is a favorite to try.

Teddy Bear, Teddy Bear
Teddy bear, teddy bear, turn around.
Teddy bear, teddy bear, touch the ground.
Teddy bear, teddy bear, reach up high.
Teddy bear, teddy bear, touch the sky.
Teddy bear, teddy bear, bend down low.
Teddy bear, teddy bear, touch your toe.

Loud and Soft Hide and Seek

Select a child to be IT. Ask IT to leave the room. Hide a beanbag. When IT returns, tell her you and the children are going to sing a song while she looks for the beanbag. When IT is close to where the beanbag is hidden, sing louder. As IT moves farther away, sing more softly.

It's Time to Celebrate

Clap when IT locates the beanbag. Encourage children to clap with you.

Tick Tock

Hide a ticking alarm clock and encourage children to find it. You can also hide a musical toy and look for it.

Who Said That?

This is a listening game that requires recognizing a familiar voice without the advantage of sight. Children will be asked to recognize a friend's voice just by hearing one spoken word. Select a child to be the listener. Have her sit in a special chair in front of the group. Blindfold her or ask her to close her eyes. Point to another child in the group who will be the mystery voice. He can simply say "Hi," or use another greeting. Does the listener recognize the voice? If not, let the speaker say something else. Continue until the listener recognizes the voice.

Copying Sound Sequences

Ask children to close their eyes and listen to a sequence of three sounds. (Rhythm band instruments work well for this activity because you usually have duplicate instruments, one set for you and one for the children.) See if children can open their eyes and repeat the sequence of sounds using the same three instruments. Play variations of this game by changing the source of the sounds. You can tap a pencil, crumple paper, shake a rattle, and so forth.

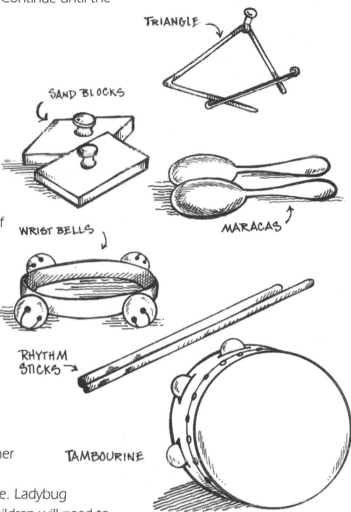

TRIANGLE

SAND BLOCKS

MARACAS

WRIST BELLS

RHYTHM STICKS

TAMBOURINE

Clapping Syllables

Teach children to listen carefully to their name and then clap out the syllables they hear. Once they get good at listening, you can move onto clapping out the syllables of other words.

Simon Says

Play Simon Says. You can change Simon to another name that fits with your theme. For example, Brontosaurus Says fits well with a dinosaur theme. Ladybug Says works with an insect theme. In any case, children will need to listen carefully to directions to make sure they follow only those directions that are preceded by (Chosen Name) Says.

Marco Polo

Play this game outdoors in an open area. Select one child to be IT. Ask the rest of the children to close their eyes. IT chooses a spot to stand. Start the game by asking the children to call out "Marco" to which IT answers "Polo." Children use their listening skills to try to find IT with their eyes still closed. The first child to locate IT becomes the new IT.

Clapping, Snapping Patterns

Encourage children to create a clapping and snapping pattern. Record their patterns on an audiotape. Play the tape back. Are the children able to identify their patterns? Can they repeat them?

CHAPTER 1

Center Games and Activities

Create a Listening Center

Designate an area of the room as a Listening Center. You'll need a cassette player, two to four headsets, and some books on tape. Other accessories for this area include music tapes, a tuning fork, and sound canisters.

Following Directions

Tape record the directions (keep them simple) for a learning center activity. Have children listen to the tape before doing the activity. Are they able to follow the directions?

Taped Stories

Encourage children's parents and siblings to record a story and use it in your listening center. Are children able to recognize the voices of their parents when the tape their parents recorded is played?

Sound Canisters

Fill film canisters or potato chip cans with items that make distinct sounds such as paper clips, gravel, pennies, and nails. Make two canisters with each item so they can be used for matching. Glue lids on securely. Invite children to shake the canisters and match the two that sound the same.

Tone Bottles

Fill several glass bottles with varying amounts of water. Start by filling four bottles ¼ full, ½ full, ¾ full, and full. Provide a stick for tapping the bottles. Challenge children to arrange the bottles according to the pitch of the sound they hear (from highest/least water, to lowest/most water) when they tap the bottles. Now fill additional bottles with water levels in between the levels that you already have. Challenge children to arrange the bottles again by the pitch. After a little practice, cover the bottles with construction paper so that children are unable to see the water level and try this game again. Are they still able to get the right order?

It's Time to Celebrate

Distinguishing pitch is a big accomplishment. Let children know you recognize their developing skill of auditory perception.

Bell Bags

Place two, 4" (10 cm) squares of felt together. Glue three sides together (around the perimeter) to make a bag. Make four more bags. Place one jingle bell in the first bag, two in the second, three in the third, and so forth. Use Velcro on the top of each bag to seal it. Invite children to arrange the bags by listening to the sounds they make, from the loudest to the softest sound.

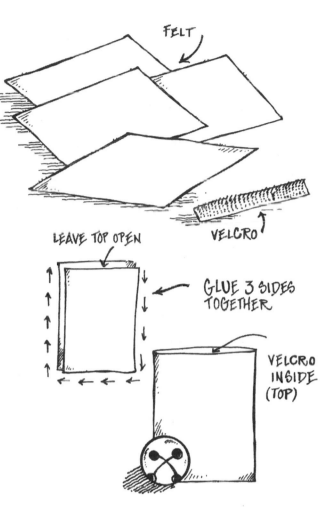

FELT

LEAVE TOP OPEN

VELCRO

GLUE 3 SIDES TOGETHER

VELCRO INSIDE (TOP)

Animal Sound Match-Up

Record animal sounds on a tape. Provide plastic animals or use the animal pictures on Appendix page 375. Invite children to match animals and sounds.

Sound Match-Up

Record several routine sounds such as water running, paper tearing, blowing, scratching, door closing, walking, chewing, coughing, clapping, and snapping fingers. Use the Sound Cards on Appendix page 411 and challenge children to identify the sounds they hear on the tape by matching them to the Sound Cards.

Field Trips

Listening Walk

Take children on a listening walk. Instruct them to be very quiet and to concentrate on using their ears more than their eyes during the walk. When you return to the classroom, record on a chart or chalkboard all the sounds that the children report hearing during their walk. Classify the sounds. Which sounds came from animals? Which sounds came from nature (e.g., wind whistling, leaves rustling)? Which sounds were human-made sounds (e.g., laughing, horns honking)?

Seventy-Six Trombones

Take children to a local high school to visit the band or orchestra during rehearsal. Have children listen from different seats in the auditorium, then invite them to sit on stage and listen. What a difference a seat can make!

Transitions

It is important that children focus their attention and settle down before they are expected to listen. Generally children respond better to games, songs, and fingerplays than they do to commands. You can use strategies such as blinking the lights or holding up two fingers like rabbit ears (when children see your fingers up, they hold their fingers up) to signal that it's time to listen. You can start a clapping rhythm, such as clap once, clap twice, clap three times (when children hear the clapping, they join in). All of these activities help the children make transitions from play to listening.

Here are some songs and fingerplays/action rhymes that can help set the climate for listening.

Songs

This the Way (Tune: "Mulberry Bush")
This is the way we get ready to listen,
Ready to listen, ready to listen.
This is the way we get ready to listen,
To listen to our story.

You can substitute other words or phrases. For example, you might change get ready to listen to perk up our ears; you might change story to directions or our teacher.

Come and Listen (Tune: "Are You Sleeping")
Come and listen,
Come and listen,
To my song,
To my song.
Happy children singing,
Happy children singing,
Sing along, sing along.

Oh, Do You Know What Time It Is? (Tune: Muffin Man)
Oh, do you know what time it is,
Time it is, time it is?
Oh, do you know what time it is?
It's story time right now.

Fingerplays/Action Rhymes

I Wiggle My Fingers (suit actions to words)
I wiggle my fingers.
I wiggle my toes.
I wiggle my shoulders.
I wiggle my nose.
Now no more wiggles are left in me.
So I can sit still as I can be.

Quiet Time
Let your hands go clap, clap, clap. (*clap*)
Let your feet go tap, tap, tap. (*tap*)
Fold your hands in you lap. (*put hands in lap*)
Don't go to sleep. It's not time to nap. (*shake head no*)
Do you know what time it is? (Answer: Quiet Time)

Be Very Quiet (suit actions to words)
Shhh—be very quiet,
Shhh—be very still.
Fold your busy little hands,
Close your sleepy little eyes.
Shhh—be very quiet.

Books about Listening

Books that focus on listening:
Daydreamers by Eloise Greenfield
Fancy that! by Pamela Allen
Hattie and the Fox by Mem Fox
The Mystery Beast of Ostergeest by Steven Kellogg
The Other Way to Listen by Byrd Baylor
The Snail's Spell by Joanne Ryder
Listen to the Rain by Bill Martin, Jr.

Brain Connections

- Children begin to listen while they are still in the womb. The wiring for hearing is mature enough to determine and respond to sounds during the fifth month of prenatal life.

- Hearing is fine-tuned as children listen carefully to the sounds of everyday language. The more we talk to them, read to them, and sing to them, the greater the ability to discriminate sounds and enlarge their vocabulary.

● Sound discrimination and adequate vocabulary are critical factors in the development of literacy.

Falling in Love With the Sounds of Language

Children fall in love with language when they are exposed to all the wonderful ways language can be used. They enjoy hearing words sung. They enjoy hearing their own names presented in a variety of ways. This section will provide activities that explore some of the delightful aspects of language.

Onomatopoeia

Onomatopoeia occurs when a word imitates or sounds like the thing it names. Onomatopoeia occurs in songs, poems, stories, and everyday speech. Here are some examples.

Songs

Six White Ducks

Six white duck that I once knew,
Fat ducks, skinny ducks, they were, too.
But the one little duck with the feather on his back,
He ruled the others with a quack, quack, quack!
Quack, quack, quack!
Quack, quack, quack!
He ruled the others with a quack, quack, quack!

Down to the river they would go,
Wibble-wobble, wibble-wobble all in a row
But the one little duck with the feather on his back
He ruled the others with a quack, quack, quack!
Quack, quack, quack!
Quack, quack, quack!
He ruled the others with a quack, quack, quack!

Hear the Lively Song

Hear the lively song
Of the frogs in yonder pond.
Crick, crick, crickety-crick,
Burr-ump!

Old MacDonald Had a Farm

Old MacDonald had a farm, E-I-E-I-O.
And on this farm he had a cow, E-I-E-I-O.
With a moo, moo here,
And a moo, moo there.
Here a moo, there a moo,
Everywhere a moo, moo.
Old MacDonald had a farm, E-I-E-I-O!

Additional verses:
Pig—oink, oink
Cat—meow, meow
Dog—bow-wow
Horse—neigh, neigh

Poems

The Rain

Splish, splash,
Splish, splash.
Drip, drop,
Drip, drop.
Will the rain ever stop?

The Wind

Swoosh, swirl, swoosh, swirl,
Watch the leaves tumble and twirl.

A Thunderstorm

Boom, bang, boom, bang,
Rumpety, lumpety, bump!
Zoom, zam, zoom, zam,
Clippity, clappity, clump!
Rustles and bustles,
And swishes and zings!
What wonderful sounds
A thunderstorm brings.

The Squirrel

Whisky, frisky,
Hippity hop.
Up he goes,
To the tree top!

G E T T I N G   R E A D Y

Whirly, twirly,
Round and round.
Down he scampers,
To the ground.

Furly, curly,
What a tail!
Tall as a feather,
Broad as a sail!

Where's his supper?
In the shell?
Snappity, crackity,
Out it fell!

The Big Bass Drum

Oh! We can play on the big bass drum,
And this is the way we do it.
Rub-a-dub, boom, goes the big bass drum,
And this is the way we do it.

Oh! We can play on the violin,
And this is the way we do it.
Zum, zum, zin, says the violin,
Rub-a-dub, boom goes the big bass drum,
And this is the way we do it.

Oh! We can play on the little flute,
And this is the way we do it.
Tootle, toot, toot, say the little flute,
Zum, zum, zin, goes the violin,
Rub-a-dub, boom goes the big bass drum,
And this is the way we do it.

Clickety, Clack

Clickety, clickety, clack.
Clickety, clickety, clack.
Clickey, clickety, clickety, clickety,
Clickety, clickety, clack.
Here comes the old train along the rickety track.

Stories

Read books that are rich in onomatopoeia. Here are a few suggestions.
Barnyard Banter by Denise Fleming
Bertie and the Bear by Pamela Allen
Listen to the Rain by Bill Martin, Jr.
One Duck Stuck by Phyllis Root
Ordinary Albert by Pamela Allen
The Snowy Day by Ezra Jack Keats
Where the Wild Things Are by Maurice Sendak

Alliteration

Alliteration occurs when a group of words with the same beginning sound
are used. It occurs in songs, stories, and everyday speech. It is at the heart of
tongue twisters, which children adore. Here are some examples of alliteration.

Tongue Twisters

The Baker

If a baker bakes for another baker,
Does the baker who bakes,
Bake the same way as the baker she is baking for?

Activity Connection: Can you write the same rhyme for a teacher, a
doctor, an actor?

Peter Piper Picked a Peck of Pickled Peppers

Peter Piper picked a peck of pickled peppers.
A peck of pickled peppers Peter Piper picked.
If Peter Piper picked a peck of pickled peppers,
Where's the peck of pickled peppers Peter Piper picked?

Or this short version:

Peter Piper picked a peck of pickled peppers
How many pecks of pickled peppers did Peter Piper pick?

Activity Connection: Try some pickled peppers for snack. Make up a simi-lar rhyme for another alliterative name like Silly Sally.

She Sells Seashells

She sells seashells by the seashore.
The shells she sells are surely seashells.
So if she sells shells on the seashore,
I'm sure she sells seashore shells.

Or this short version:

She sells seashells by the seashore.
By the seashore she sells seashells.

Activity Connection: Provide a collection of seashells for children to exam-ine. Give them a magnifying glass for a closer look.

How Much Wood Would a Woodchuck Chuck?

How much wood would a woodchuck chuck
If a woodchuck could chuck wood?

Activity Connection: Ask children what they think a woodchuck is. Try to find a picture of a woodchuck to show them.

Clickety, Clack

Clickety, clickety, clack,
Clickety, clickety, clack,
Clickey, clickety, clickety, clickety,
Clickety, clickety, clack.

Activity Connection: Invite children to form a train. Challenge them to join in, one at a time by first stating what kind of car they want to be—engine, caboose, freight, tanker, etc.

A Skunk

A skunk sat on a burning stump.
The skunk thought the stump stunk,
And the stump thought the skunk stunk.

Stories

A My Name Is Alice by J. Bayer
More Bugs in Boxes by D. Carter
Six Sick Sheep by Joanna Cole
"The Three Billy Goats Gruff" (traditional)
The Z Was Zapped by Chris Van Allsburg

Rhyme

Children take to language more readily when it is "jinglely" and "rhymey." It's just more fun and it's predictable. Because detecting rhyme requires that children listen for likenesses and differences in sound, it is great preparation for phonological awareness. This section is filled with rhyming fun. There are songs, poems, games, and activities that are especially "rhymey." Have fun!

Poems

Fire! Fire!

"Fire! Fire!" said Mrs. McGuire.
"Where? Where?" said Mrs. Bear.
"Downtown!" said Mrs. Brown.
"What floor?" said Mrs. Moore.
"Near the Top!" said Mrs. Kopp.
"What a pity!" said Mrs. City.
"Here I come!" said Mrs. Plumb.
"Water! Water!" said Mrs. Votter.
"Get out of my way!" said Mrs. Lei.
"Let me see!" said Mrs. Chi.
"Break down the door!" said Mrs. Orr.
"Well, I declare!" said Mrs. Wear.
"Oh, help us and save us!" said Mrs. Davis,
As she fell down the stairs with a sack of potatoes.

Activity Connection: Invite children to make up new rhymes, using the same pattern as "Fire! Fire!" and using names they know.

Monday's Child

Monday's child is fair of face;
Tuesday's child is full of grace.
Wednesday's child is full of woe;
Thursday's child has far to go.
Friday's child is loving and giving.
Saturday's child works hard for a living.
But the child who is born on Sunday
Is fair and wise and good and gay.

Activity Connection: Encourage children to find out what day they were born on. Invite them to draw a self-portrait that illustrates the day they were born.

A Ram Sam Sam

A ram sam sam,
A ram sam sam.
Guli guli guli,
Ram sam sam.
A rafi, a rafi,
Guli guli guli guli guli,
Ram sam sam.

Activity Connection: Encourage children to make up their own nonsense chants.

The Purple Cow (Gelett Burgess)

I never saw a purple cow,
I never hope to see one.
But I can tell you, anyhow
I'd rather see than be one.

Activity Connection: Let each child make a Purple Cow Shake. Provide a small scoop of vanilla ice cream, 2 tablespoons (30 ml) of grape juice concentrate, and 2 tablespoons (15 ml) of milk in a baby food jar. Close the lid and shake, shake, shake. Enjoy!

Pudden Tame

What's your name?
Pudden Tame.
What's your other?
Bread and Butter.
Where do you live?

In a sieve.
What's your number?
Cucumber.

Activity Connection: Can you substitute other rhyming answers? Let children make some pudding. Put 1 tablespoon (10 g) of instant pudding mix in a baby food jar. Add ¼ cup (60 ml) of milk. Close lid and shake until thick. Enjoy!

I Asked My Mother

I asked my mother for fifty cents,
To see the elephant jump the fence.
He jumped so high he touched the sky,
And didn't come down till the fourth of July.

Activity Connection: Make up a hand jive to this rhyme.

The Owl and the Pussy-Cat (Edward Lear)

The Owl and the Pussy-Cat went to sea,
In a beautiful pea-green boat.
They took some honey, and plenty of money,
Wrapped in a five-pound note.

The Owl looked up to the stars above,
And sang to a small guitar,
"O lovely Pussy! O Pussy, my love,
What a beautiful Pussy you are, you are!
What a beautiful Pussy you are."

Pussy said to the Owl, "You elegant fowl!
How charmingly sweet you sing!
O let us be married! Too long we have tarried,
But what shall we do for a ring?"

They sailed away for a year and a day,
To the land where the Bong-tree grows.
And there in a wood a Piggy-wig stood,
With a ring in the end of his nose, his nose,
With a ring in the end of his nose.

"Dear Pig, are you willing to sell for one shilling
Your ring?" Said the Piggy, "I will."
So they took it away, and were married next day,
By the Turkey who lives on the hill.

They dined on mince, and slices of quince,
Which they ate with a runcible spoon;
And hand in hand, on the edge of the sand,
They danced by the light of the moon.

Activity Connection: Compare this poem to "Frog Went A-Courtin'."

Fuzzy Wuzzy

Fuzzy Wuzzy was a bear.
Fuzzy Wuzzy had no hair.
Fuzzy Wuzzy wasn't fuzzy,
Was he?

Activity Connection: Cut a bear shape out of fake fur. Cut clothes out of wallpaper scraps and let the children dress the bear.

I Had a Loose Tooth

I had a loose tooth,
A wiggly, jiggly loose tooth.
I had a loose tooth,
A-hanging by a thread.
I pulled my loose tooth,
My wiggly, jiggly loose tooth.
Put it 'neath my pillow,
And then I went to bed.
The fairy took my loose tooth,
My wiffly, jiffly loose tooth.
And now I have a quarter,
And a hole in my head.

Activity Connection: Invite children to draw a picture of what they would look like with a missing tooth.

Eletelephony (Laura E. Richards)

Once there was an elephant,
Who tried to use the telephant.
No! No! I mean the elephone
Who tried to use the telephone.
(Dear me! I am not certain quite
That even now I've got it right.)

However'er it was, he got his trunk
Entangled in the telephunk.
The more he tried to get it free,
The louder buzzed the telephee.

(I fear I'd better drop the song
Of the elephop and telephong!)

Activity Connection: Make tin can telephones for the children to use.

Whoops!

A horse and a flea and three blind mice,
Sat on a curbstone chewing ice.
The horse he slipped and fell on the flea.
The flea said, "Whoops, there's a horse on me."

Songs

Down by the Bay

Down by the bay, where the watermelons grow.
Back to my home I dare not go.
For if I do my mother will say,
"Did you ever see a pig dancing the jig?"
Down by the bay.

Activity Connection: Invite children to substitute other rhyming phrases
for "a pig dancing the jig." As children develop a better ear for sounds, try
focusing on repetitions of a specific sound. For example, you might use the
"at" sound and come up with variations such as, "Did you ever see a bat
wearing a hat," or "…a rat chasing a cat," or "…a gnat swinging a bat."

A-Hunting We Will Go

A hunting we will go, a hunting
   we will go,
Heigh ho, the dairy-o, a hunting
   we will go,
A hunting we will go, a hunting
   we will go,
We'll catch a fox and put him in
   a box
And then we'll let her go.

A hunting we will go, a hunting
   we will go,
Heigh ho, the dairy-o, a hunting
   we will go.
A hunting we will go, a hunting
   we will go,
We'll catch a fish and put him on a dish
And then we'll let him go.

G E T T I N G   R E A D Y

A hunting we will go, a hunting we will go,
Heigh ho, the dairy-o, a hunting we will go.
A hunting we will go, a hunting we will go,
We'll catch a bear and cut his hair
And then we'll let him go.

A hunting we will go, a hunting we will go,
Heigh ho, the dairy-o, a hunting we will go.
A hunting we will go, a hunting we will go,
We'll catch a pig and dance a little jig
And then we'll let him go.

A hunting we will go, a hunting we will go,
Heigh ho, the dairy-o, a hunting we will go.
A hunting we will go, a hunting we will go,
We'll catch a giraffe and make her laugh
And then we'll let her go.

Activity Connection: Make up some new verses with other animals to catch.

A Sailor Went to Sea

A sailor went to sea, sea, sea,
To see what she could see, see, see.
But all that she could see, see, see,
Was the bottom of the deep blue sea, sea, sea.

A sailor went to chop, chop, chop, . . .
A sailor went to sho-bop-sho-bop, . . .

Activity Connection: Tie a disk magnet to a string and then to a pole to make a fishing rod. Place bottle caps in a tub and invite children to do some magnetic fishing. Write the words sea and see on the bottle caps and let the children sort them as they "catch" the lids.

Hanky Panky

Down by the banks of the hanky panky,
Where the bullfrogs jump from bank to banky,
With an Eep! Eep! Ope! Ope!
Knee flop-i-dilly and ker-plop.

Activity Connection: Cut lily pads out of green felt and let children jump from pad to pad. Encourage them to make frog noises as they jump.

Mares Eats Oats

Mares eat oats and does eat oats,
And little lambs eat ivy.
A kid will eat ivy, too.
Wouldn't you?

Activity Connection: Make oatmeal and see if your "kids" will eat oats.

Catalina Magnalina

She had a peculiar name but she wasn't to blame.
She got it from her mother who's the same, same, same.

Chorus
Catalina, Magnalina, Hootensteiner, Bogentwiner,
Hogan, Logan, Bogan, was her name.

She had two peculiar teeth in her mouth.
One pointed north and the other pointed south.

Chorus

She had two peculiar eyes in her head.
One was purple and the other was red.

Chorus

She had two peculiar hairs on her chin.
One stuck out and the other stuck in.

Chorus

Activity Connection: Invite children to draw their rendition of Catalina Magnalina. Can they think of another peculiar characteristic for Catalina?

Michael Finnegan

There was an old man named Michael Finnegan.
He had whiskers on his chinnegan.
They fell out and then grew in again.
Poor old Michael Finnegan,
Begin again.

There was an old man named Michael Finnegan.
He went fishing with a pin again.
Caught a fish and dropped it in again.
Poor old Michael Finnegan,

Begin again.

There was an old man named Michael Finnegan.
He grew fat and then grew thin again.
Then he died and had to begin again.
Poor old Michael Finnegan,
Begin again.

Activity Connection: Let children finger paint with shaving cream.
Encourage them to make any letters they can.

Hinky Dinky "Double D" Farm

Oh it's beans, beans, beans that make you feel so mean,
On the farm, on the farm, on the farm, on the farm.
Oh it's beans, beans, beans that make you feel so mean,
On the Hinky Dinky "Double D" farm.
Mine eyes are dim, I cannot see,
I have not brought my specs with me.
Repeat:
...corn...that makes you feel forlorn...
...meat...that knocks you off your feet...
...pie...that makes you want to cry...
...soup...that makes you want to droop...
...peas...that makes you want to sneeze...

Activity Connection: Invite children to continue making up verses.

Rime Time (Tune: "The Addams Family")

Rime time, rime time,
Rime time, rime time, rime time.

There's can and there's pan,
There's fan and there's ran.
There's man and there's tan,
The "a-n" family.

Pet, jet, vet, net, let, set...
Like, hike, bike, mike, trike, pike...
Pot, dot, hot, not, lot, got...
Ball, call, hall, fall, tall, mall...
Sit, lit, hit, kit, fit, pit...
Book, look, cook, hook, took, nook...

Activity Connection: Help children come up with other same sound families.

Rhyming Games

Fill-in-the-Blank Rhymes

I like oranges, I like to feel them,
But I can't eat them until I _____ (peel them).
Peaches are juicy, peaches are round.
When you shake the tree, they fall to the _____ (ground).

A banana is yellow and shaped like the moon.
When it's in pudding you eat it with a _____ (spoon).

Pears are golden, juicy, sweet, yummy,
And round at the bottom like Santa's _____ (tummy).

Oranges are round, oranges are sweet.
Oranges are made for me to _____ (eat).
Corn has shucks and grows on stalks.
When you pop it, it jumps and _____ (talks).

Grapes and bananas grow in a bunch.
I like to have them with my _____ (lunch).

Fill-in-the-Blank Nursery Rhymes

After children have been exposed to nursery rhymes, try saying the rhyme
and pausing at the end of each line and letting children supply the missing
work. For example, "Jack and Jill went up the _____." (hill)

Say and Touch

Say "pup," now stand up.
Say "go," now touch your toe.
Say "neat," now touch your feet.
Say "real," now touch your heel.
Say "laugh," now touch your calf.
Say "bee," now touch your knee.
Say "high," now touch your thigh.
Say "paste," now touch your waist.
Say "yummy," now touch your tummy.
Say "best," now touch your chest.
Say "colder," now touch your shoulder.
Say "farm," now touch your arm.
Say "twist," now touch your wrist.
Say "sand," now touch your hand.
Say "crumb," now touch your thumb.
Say "check," now touch your neck.
Say "pin," now touch your chin.
Say "south," now touch your mouth.
Say "rip," now touch your hip.
Say "rose," now touch your nose.
Say "week," now touch your cheek.
Say "try," now touch your eye.
Say "clear," now touch your ear.

Say "bear," now touch your hair
Say "bread," now touch your head.

Rhyming Objects

Place several pairs of objects with rhyming names (e.g., hook/book, shell/bell, fork/cork) in a box. Let children take out an object, say its name, and then find the object with the rhyming name.

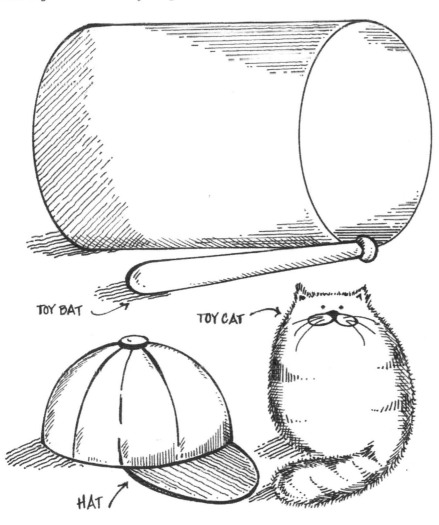

TOY BAT

TOY CAT

HAT

Rhyming Web Art

Have children draw an object on their paper and then draw as many things as they can think of that rhyme with that object. Help beginners so that they don't pick a beginning item with limited rhyming matches.

Rhyming Concentration

Play a concentration game with the Rhyming Object Cards on Appendix pages 409 and 410.

The Name Game

Let children make up rhymes that go with their names. Nonsense rhymes are okay.

Rhyme or Reason Game

Sit in a circle with children. Start the game by giving a word to the child next to you. Let's say the word is sun. The child must either provide a rhyming word or a connecting word. A rhyming word for sun might be bun. A connecting word for sun might be moon because the sun and the moon are in the sky. The next child in the circle must then provide a rhyming word or connecting word for the word the child next to you has given.

Rhyming Story in a Can

Place several rhyming objects or photos in a can. Have children remove the items and create a story that includes the items.

Rhyming Riddles

Say, "I am thinking of something that you wear on your feet. Its name rhymes with rock," (sock) or "I am thinking of something that you wear on your head. Its name rhymes with cat." (hat)

More Rhyming Riddles

Read *A-Hunting We Will Go* by John Langstaff. This is a collection of rhyming riddles. Challenge the children to create riddles that have answers made up of two rhyming words. For example:

What is big and furry and purrs? (fat cat)
What kind of dance happens in Autumn? (fall ball)
What do you call water that freezes, unfreezes, and freezes again? (twice ice)
Where do mice sleep? (mouse house)
What do you call a shoe with a sticky sole? (glue shoe)
What do you call a stamp that you lick? (damp stamp)
What is large and oinks? (big pig)
What's a carnival for hair? (hair fair)

Stories

Read books that are rich in rhyme. Here are a few suggestions.
A-Hunting We Will Go by John M. Langstaff
Anna Banana: 101 Jump Rope Rhymes by C. Chapman
Brown Bear, Brown Bear, What Do You See? by Bill Martin, Jr.
The Cat in the Hat by Dr. Seuss
Chicka Chicka Boom Boom by Bill Martin, Jr. and John Archambault
Chicken Soup with Rice by Maurice Sendak

Henny Penny by Paul Galdone
A House Is a House for Me by Mary Ann Hoberman
In the Tall, Tall Grass by Denise Fleming
Jamberry by Bruce Degen
One Fish, Two Fish, Red Fish, Blue Fish by Dr. Seuss
Quick as a Cricket by Audrey Wood
Spiders Spin Webs by Yvonne Winer

Here is a rhyming story children love.

Directions: Use a black sharpie pen to trace the patterns from Appendix pages 369 and 370 onto Pelon. Color with crayons and cut them out. Use them with the flannel board to present the Henny-Penny story below.

Henny-Penny

Once upon a time there was a little hen named Henny-Penny. She lived in a barnyard with her friends, Cocky-Locky, Ducky-Lucky, Turkey-Lurkey, and Goosey-Loosey. Every day the farmer would scatter seeds and grain for Henny-Penny and her friends to eat.

One day, while Henny-Penny was peck, peck, pecking the seeds and grains the farmer had scattered, something hit her right on top of her head. "What was that?" asked Henny-Penny. She looked up at the sky and, seeing nothing but sky, she began to cluck loudly.

"Something just hit me on the head. The sky is falling. I must go quickly and tell the king."

So off Henny-Penny went, walking as fast as she could. Soon she met Cocky-Locky. "Where are you going?" asked Cocky-Locky.

Without even looking back, Henny-Penny answered, "The sky is falling! I'm off to tell the king."

Cocky-Locky looked up at the sky. "The sky looks fine to me," he said.

"A piece of the sky fell right on my head!" said Henny-Penny.

"Oh, my!" said Cocky-Locky, and he joined Henny-Penny on her journey.

So on Henny-Penny and Cocky-Locky went, walking as fast as they could. Soon they met Ducky-Lucky.

"Where are you going?" asked Ducky-Lucky.

Without even looking back, Henny-Penny answered, "The sky is falling! We're off to tell the king."

Ducky-Lucky looked up at the sky. "The sky looks fine to me," she said.

"A piece of the sky fell right on my head!" said Henny-Penny.

"Oh, my! said Ducky-Lucky, and she joined Henny-Penny and Cocky-Locky on their journey.

So on Henny-Penny, Cocky-Locky, and Ducky-Lucky went, walking as fast as they could. Soon they met Turkey-Lurkey.

"Where are you going?" said Turkey-Lurkey.

Without even looking back, Henny-Penny answered, "The sky is falling! We're off to tell the king."

Turkey-Lurkey looked up at the sky. "The sky looks fine to me," he said.
"A piece of the sky fell right on my head!" said Henny-Penny.

"Oh, my!" said Turkey-Lurkey, and he joined Henny-Penny, Cocky-Locky, and Ducky-Lucky on their journey.

So on Henny-Penny, Cocky-Locky, Ducky-Lucky, and Turkey-Lurkey went, walking as fast as they could. Soon they met Goosey-Loosey.

"Where are you going?" said Goosey-Loosey.

Without even looking back, Henny-Penny answered, "The sky is falling! We're off to tell the king."

Goosey-Loosey looked up at the sky. "The sky looks fine to me," she said.

"A piece of the sky fell right on my head!" said Henny-Penny.

"Oh, my!" said Goosey-Loosey, and she joined Henny-Penny, Cocky-Locky, Ducky-Lucky, and Turkey-Lurkey on their journey.

Soon the five friends met Foxy-Loxy. "Where are you going?" asked Foxy-Loxy.

"The sky is falling. We're off to tell the king." The five answered together. "May I show you the way?" asked Foxy-Loxy.

The five friends suddenly realized that they did not know where the king lived. So they said "Oh, thank you, Foxy-Loxy."

Foxy-Loxy took Henny-Penny, Cocky-Locky, Ducky-Lucky, Turkey-Lurkey, and Goosey-Loosey straight to his den, and they were never seen again. Do you know what happened to them?

Read *Chicken Little* by Steven Kellogg, which is the story of Henny Penny without the rhyming names. Compare the two stories.

It's Time to Celebrate!

Celebrate children's mastery of rhyme by inviting them to create a rhyming book for the classroom library. Have each child make a pair of rhyming word pictures. Put the illustrations in a baggie book or some other form of book where they can be a lasting tribute to the children's reaching this milestone.

Brain Connections

- The window of opportunity for children to absorb language is between birth and six years of age.

- Children are particularly attracted to the patterns of sounds, such as the rhythm and cadence of a story, as early as the third month of life.

- Research consistently demonstrates that children who have rich language backgrounds have an easier time mastering reading

Reading Aloud to Children

Reading aloud to children should begin when the baby is still in the womb. An infant's hearing is wired well enough by the fifth month in utero to hear sounds outside the womb. Mothers, fathers, grandparents, caregivers, and teachers can help children learn about language and narrative by reading and enjoying good books with them. Below are some tips for reading aloud to children.

Tips for Reading Aloud

1. Get comfortable. Make sure children are comfortable.
2. Make sure children can see the illustrations.
3. Choose books that are appropriate for the age level of the child.
4. Read books on diverse topics and things of interest to children.

5. Build background knowledge. Let children examine the cover of the book. Encourage them to predict what the story might be about.

6. Use good expression as you read. Make your voice soft and quiet, excited, or surprised to fit the situation.

7. Promote higher-level thinking by asking questions that go beyond the comprehension level (see page 51).

8. Stop and talk about challenging vocabulary. Help children learn how to use the illustrations for clues.

9. Re-read favorite books.

10. Watch for cues that children are uninterested and stop. You don't have to finish reading a book that no one wants to hear.

Selecting Books for Listening and Loving

Infant Book List

Animal Crackers by Nancy Dyer
Baby Faces by Margaret Miller
Baby! Talk! by Penny Gentieu
Big Fat Hen by Keith Baker
Bounce Bounce Bounce by Kathy Henderson
Clap Hands by Helen Oxenbury
First Steps by Lee Wardlaw
How a Baby Grows by Nola Buck
Hush Little Baby by Sylvia Long
I See by Rachel Isadora
Itsy Bitsy Spider by Iza Trapani
Moo, Baa, La La La! by Sandra Boynton
Mother Goose Magic by Kay Chorao
Nighty-Night by Dawn Apperley
Of Colors and Things by Tana Hoban
Pat the Bunny by Dorothy Kunhardt
Pickle and the Box by Lynn Breeze
Sleepytime Rhyme by Remy Charlip
What's on My Head? by Margaret Miller
Who Says Moo? by Ruth Young
Yellow Hat, Red Hat by Basia Bogdanowicz

Toddler Book List

Animal Crackers by Jane Dyer

The Animal Orchestra by Scott Gustafson

Barnyard Banter by Denise Fleming

The Best Mouse Cookie by Laura Numeroff

Big by Keith Haring

Can You Guess? by Margaret Miller

Dots, Spots, Speckles, and Stripes by Tana Hoban

The Earth Is Good by Michael Demunn

Exactly the Opposite by Tana Hoban

Eyes, Nose, Fingers, and Toes by Judy Hindley

Five Little Monkeys Sitting in a Tree by Eileen Christelow

Flower Garden by Eve Bunting

Frozen Noses by Jan Carr

Good Day, Good Night by Marilyn Singer

Growing Vegetable Soup by Lois Ehlert

Have You Seen Bugs? by Joanne Oppenheim

Hello Toes! Hello Feet! by Ann Whitford Paul

Hey, Little Baby! by Nola Buck

Horatio's Bed by Camillea Ashforth

In the Small, Small Pond by Denise Fleming

Inside, Outside, Upside Down by Stan and Jan Berenstain

Is It Red? Is It Yellow? Is It Blue? by Tana Hoban

I Went Walking by Sue Williams

Let's Go Visiting by Sue Williams

Little Red Hen and the Ear of Wheat by Mary Finch

Lunch by Denise Fleming

Mrs. Wishy-Washy by Joy Cowley

My Five Senses by Margaret Miller

Nature Spy by Shelly Rotner

One Fish, Two Fish, Red Fish, Blue Fish! by Dr. Seuss

Planting a Rainbow by Lois Ehlert

Shapes, Shapes, Shapes by Tana Hoban

Snowy, Flowy, Blowy by Nancy Tafuri

Teddy Bears' Picnic by Jimmy Kennedy

These Hands by Hope Lynn Price

Time for Bed by Mem Fox

Toddlerobics by Zita Newcome

Up the Ladder, Down the Slide by Betsy Everitt

Wake Up, Little Children by Jim Aylesworth

What Makes Me Happy? by Catherine and Laurence Anholt

When the Teddy Bears Came by Martin Waddell

Where Does It Go? by Margaret Miller

While You Were Sleeping by John Butler
Who Hops? by Katy Davis
Who Took the Farmer's Hat? by Joan Nodset
Who Uses This? by Margaret Miller

Three's, Four's, and Five's Book List

Abiyoyo by Pete Seeger
Alexander and the Terrible, Horrible, No Good, Very Bad Day by Judith Viorst
Bedtime for Frances by Russell Hoban
Blueberries for Sal by Robert McCloskey
Bread and Jam for Frances by Russell Hoban
Brown Bear, Brown Bear, What Do You See? by Bill Martin, Jr.
Can I Keep Him? by Steven Kellogg
The Cat in the Hat by Dr. Seuss
Changes, Changes by Pat Hutchins
Chicka Chicka Boom Boom by Bill Martin, Jr. and John Archambault
Chicken Little by Laura Rader
Chicken Little by Steven Kellogg
Corduroy by Don Freeman
The Doorbell Rang by Pat Hutchins
The First Snowfall by Anne and Harlow Rockwell
Flossie and the Fox by Patricia McKissack
Flying by Donald Crews
Frog on His Own by Mercer Mayer
Goldilocks and the Three Bears by Jan Brett
Green Eggs and Ham by Dr. Seuss
"The Green Grass Grew All Around" (many versions)
Hello Kangaroo by Nan Bodsworth
Henny Penny by Paul Galdone (illustrator)
I Don't Want to Go to School by Christine Harris
If You Give a Mouse a Cookie by Laura Joffe Numeroff
If You Give a Pig a Pancake by Laura Joffe Numeroff
Imogene's Antlers by David Small
Island of the Skog by Steven Kellogg
It's Pumpkin Time by Zoe Hall
Jamberry by Bruce Degen
The Judge by Margot and Harve Zemach
Just Like You and Me by David Miller
Koala Lou by Mem Fox
Leo the Late Bloomer by Robert Kraus
A Letter to Amy by Ezra Jack Keats
"The Little Red Hen" (many versions)
Look Book by Tana Hoban

Make Way for Ducklings by Robert McCloskey
The Mitten by Jan Brett
Mouse Paint by E.S. Walsh
The Napping House by Audrey and Don Wood
Over in the Meadow by Ezra Jack Keats
Owl Moon by Jane Yolen
Pancakes for Breakfast by Tomie DePaola
Picasso the Green Tree Frog by Amanda Graham
Rosie's Walk by Pat Hutchins
Silly Sally by Audrey Wood
The Snowy Day by Ezra Jack Keats
Swimmy by Leo Lionni
There Was an Old Lady by Simms Taback
"The Three Billy Goats Gruff"
Titch by Pat Hutchins
Tough Boris by Mem Fox
The Very Busy Spider by Eric Carle
The Very Hungry Caterpillar by Eric Carle
Wacky Wednesday by Theo Le Sieg
Whistle for Willie by Ezra Jack Keats
Zoom by Istvan Banyai

Brain Connections

- Books display ideas in complete sentences, assisting full thought development.

- Brain connections are strengthened through repetition of experiences. This is one reason children enjoy hearing the same story over and over again. Each time they hear the story they enhance their understanding of patterns in the story plot and patterns in the story language. This enhancement strengthens brain connections.

- Make repetition interesting, relevant, and challenging. Sing a song in a different way, read a book in a different location, or do an activity backward.

- Children love to hear a story over and over again. Rereading familiar stories reinforces how children learn. The repetition improves their vocabulary, sequencing, and memory skills. Research shows that children often ask as many and sometimes the same questions after a dozen readings as they do after the first reading. This is because they are learning language in increments—not all at once. Each reading brings a little more meaning to the story.

2

Comprehending Stories

Enacting, Dramatizing, and Recreating Stories

Enacting and Dramatizing Activities

Enacting and dramatizing stories require making application of what you have seen and heard. It means that children must put themselves in the place of the characters, then reword the dialogue to suit their memory of the original story, and use their own vocabulary. This process solidifies understanding.

1. Invite children to act out stories substituting their own words. The following stories are good for dramatizing and reenacting:
   Moira's Birthday by Robert Munsch
   "Three Billy Goats Gruff" (Traditional)
   "The Three Little Pigs" (Traditional)

2. Make paper plate masks for children to use as they reenact stories. Provide other simple props, too.

3. Read suggestions for other ways to tell stories on pages 66-70 and utilize some of them with reenactments and dramatizations.

Recreating Activities

Recreating stories allows children to expand on an author's concept by bringing their own imagination to the story. It is, again, a form of application that enhances comprehension while it develops creativity.

1. Tell children the story of "The Great Big Turnip" (traditional). Ask children to recreate the story from the turnip's point of view. Another idea is to ask children to rewrite the story using different characters.

2. Read *Mud Puddle* by Robert Munsch. Challenge children to rewrite or retell the story from the point of view of the mud puddle.

3. Read *Brown Bear, Brown Bear, What Do You See?* by Bill Martin, Jr. Invite the children to expand the story to include some new animals.

4. Read *If You Give a Mouse a Cookie* by Laura Joffe Numeroff. Invite children to expand the story to include new cause-effect relationships.

5. Read *Imogene's Antlers* by David Small. Challenge the children to continue the story by writing the sequel.

6. Rewrite the story of the "The Little Red Hen." Change the theme of the story from animals that won't help to animals that can't wait to help. What does this do to the story?

7. Rewrite "The Three Billy Goats Gruff." Change the troll into a helpful gatekeeper. How does the story change? Does the change improve the story or make it less interesting?

8. Rewrite *Are You My Mother?* by P.D. Eastman. Instead of the main character being a bird, make it a button. What happens to the story?

Brain Connections

● We remember 10% of what we read, 20% of what we hear, 50% of what we see, 70% of what we say, and 90% of what we say and do. Enacting, dramatizing, and recreating are key strategies for allowing children the opportunity to experience "saying and doing," or applying what they have learned.

● Enacting, dramatizing, and recreating stories engages emotions, which increase memory, and build problem-solving skills, which strengthens brain connections.

● Enacting, dramatizing, and recreating stories stimulates kinesthetic, spatial, and verbal linguistic intelligences.

Using Questions to Enhance Comprehension

Questioning children helps us know if children understand what they read. The answers children provide are an important gauge of comprehension. However, if teachers limit their questions to those that only get at rote memory and basic understanding, then children will be limited to lower levels of comprehension and meaning.

Asking questions is an art. A skillful teacher is able to help children expand their comprehension by posing questions that require children to use higher levels of thinking. With just a little exposure to some examples and a little practice, teachers can refocus their questions to ensure that children are challenged to think beyond the levels of rote recall and application. The following questions are examples of higher level thinking questions based on Bloom's taxonomy. These questions are based on "The Three Billy Goats Gruff."

Knowledge (accurate recall)

There are some things I would like to know about the three billy goats named Gruff.

1. Where were the goats going?
2. Who lived under the bridge?
3. Who crossed the bridge first?

CHAPTER 2

Comprehension (understanding of information)

I am confused about some of the things I heard about the three goats and the troll. Can you help me understand:

1. When did the troll come out from under the bridge? Did he come out any other time?
2. How many characters had big, gruff voices? Who were they?
3. Did the middle-size goat have a gruff voice?

Application (use of information)

Let's talk about other things you know about trolls and goats.

1. The troll wanted to scare the goats with his scary voice. Can you think of other ways the troll could have frightened the goats?
2. Have you ever been frightened like the goats were? What happened to frighten you?

Analysis (taking information apart)

The story has several parts. The first part told about the little goat. Let's talk about some of the other parts of the story.

1. Some parts of the story could not really happen. What parts are they?
2. Other parts of the story could happen. What parts could happen?
3. How was the part of the story about the little goat and the troll different from the part about the big goat and the troll?

Synthesis (putting information together in a new way)

Let's see how changing one part of the story might make the story different.

1. What if the troll said, "I am so happy to see you? You can cross my bridge whenever you want to"? How would the story be different?
2. How would the story be different if the big goat had gone first?

Evaluation (critical judgment)

I want to find out what you thought about the story.

1. If you could choose to be any character in the story, who would you be? Why?
2. The little goat and the middle-size goat didn't want to fight the troll. They both told the troll to wait for their brother. Do you think that was the right thing to do? Why?

Brain Connections

Questions verify that children understand what they are learning. Questions, when posed properly, also allow children the opportunity to organize the information being learned in a way that helps connect new information with information that has already been stored in the brain.

Soliciting Children's Questions

Questions should not just come from the teacher. It is important to encourage children to ask questions as well. Unasked questions block learning. Unsolicited questions keep the teacher from knowing vital information about what children are thinking. Make asking children for their questions a regular part of your routine. Provide ample time for children to form their question, and don't let them off the hook by moving on without a question or two. When children ask questions, we know they are thinking.

Strategies for Developing Higher Level Thinking

Using questions is only one way to increase higher level thinking skills. Literature is a great springboard for expanding children's thinking. The following is a list of skills and concepts that help children develop their higher-level thinking. With each skill or concept is an activity suggestion you can use to expand and extend thinking. Expanded thinking enhances comprehension.

Making Inferences

Inferring what hasn't been said is a difficult task for young children, but it adds greatly to comprehension and provides practice for noticing details.

1. Read *Who Is the Beast?* by Keith Baker. Ask children if they determine the beast's feelings by looking at his face and body.

2. Read *Rosie's Walk* by Pat Hutchins. Ask children if they can determine what is going to happen next by looking at the pictures.

Patterning/Sequencing

1. Read *Brown Bear, Brown Bear, What Do You See?* by Bill Martin, Jr. Ask children to identify the pattern in the story.

2. Read *The Very Hungry Caterpillar* by Eric Carle. Ask children to identify the sequence of the story. Is there more than one?

Drawing Conclusions

1. Read *The True Story of the Three Little Pigs* by Jon Scieszka. Ask children their opinion about who was telling the truth.

2. Read *Who's in the Shed?* by Brenda Parks. Can children guess who's in the shed by watching for clues while you read the story?

Comparing and Contrasting

1. Read two versions of *The Mitten*, one by Jan Brett and one by Alvin Tresselt. Invite children to compare the stories.

2. Read two stories with similar characters like "The Princess and the Pea" (traditional) and *The Paper Bag Princess* by Robert Munsch. Encourage children to compare the personality of the two princesses.

Analyzing

1. Read *Look Book* by Tana Hoban. Invite children to guess the whole by looking at the parts.

Establishing Cause and Effect

1. Read *Why Mosquitos Buzz in People's Ears* by Verna Aardema. Ask children to identify the chain of events, telling how each caused the next.

2. Read *If You Give a Mouse a Cookie* by Laura Joffe Numeroff. Encourage children to identify the cause and effect relationships.

Predicting

1. Read *Who Sank the Boat?* by Pamela Allen. Stop along the way in the story and ask children to predict what might happen next.

2. Read *David's Father* by Robert Munsch. Ask children to describe their image of David's grandmother based on what they know about David's father and the limited view they get of his Grandmother.

Brainstorming

1. Read *The Doorbell Rang* by Pat Hutchins. Let children think of a way to solve the problem each time before you turn the page and determine how the characters solve the problem.

2. Read *Thomas' Snowsuit* by Robert Munsch. See if the children can brainstorm a list of possible solutions that could have been used in the story.

Inventing

1. Read *It Looked Like Spilt Milk* by Charles Shaw. Take children outside to look at the clouds. What images do they see? Encourage them to rewrite or retell the story with their images.

Composing

1. Show the children *Pancakes for Breakfast* by Tomie DePaola. Invite children to dictate words to accompany the pictures.

2. Read *Imogene's Antlers* by David Small. Challenge children to finish the story.

Evaluating

1. Read or tell the story of "Goldilocks and the Three Bears" (traditional). Ask children their opinion as to whether is was okay or not okay for Goldilocks to go into the house when no one was home.

2. Read "The Little Red Hen" (traditional). Ask children how they feel about the Little Red Hen not sharing her bread. Was it okay?

Brain Connections

● We do not teach children to think. From birth they have all the necessary neural (brain) organization to begin thinking. We can, however, help children organize the content of their thinking to facilitate more complex reasoning.

● According to David Sousa, Bloom's Taxonomy offers a structure of organization that is compatible with the way the brain processes complex information. This section of the book utilizes Bloom's Taxonomy to support comprehension.

Developing Oral Language

Extending and Enriching Vocabulary

A Picture Elicits 1,000 Words

Photographs, posters, magazine, book illustrations, and children's own wonderful artwork can be used to enhance the development of oral language.

Photographs

Getting Started

Collect photographs from children and their families. Take photos yourself. Make copies of school pictures.

Idea Sparkers

1. Take pictures with a Polaroid camera during the day. Tape or glue the photos to a piece of poster board. Invite children to describe what is going on in each photo. Transcribe their description under each photo. Post the photos where parents will see them when they pick up their children. Or, use a regular camera, and go through the description/dictation after the film is developed.

2. Take photos of activities that occur over time and involve several steps. Let children use the photos to communicate with their parents about what they have been doing at school. Photos may be of several different

activities or of one project that has developed over time such as planting and caring for a vegetable garden. Post the photos with children's dictated descriptions at an open house or make a book with them and let children take turns borrowing the book to share with their families at home.

3. Let children bring in photos from birthday parties, family vacations, and other important events. Make a baggie book by stapling several ziplock bags together and then inserting photos for safekeeping. Encourage children to describe the events to their friends using the photos as a stimulus for language.

4. Bring your own photos. Let the children ask you questions about what they see in the photos.

5. Encourage children to bring pictures of their families and/or pets to school. Invite them to tell you about the people and animals in the pictures. Record their thoughts, and post both pictures and descriptions on the bulletin board.

Posters

Getting Started
Collect posters from any place you can. Ask for posters (after merchants are finished with them) you see in grocery stores, card shops, comics stores, and travel agencies.

Idea Sparkers
1. Use the posters to stimulate discussion and introduce new vocabulary words. Help children pay attention to detail. For example, say you display a poster of a girl eating an ice cream cone. When you ask the children to tell you what's going on in the picture, they will probably say, "The girl is eating an ice cream cone." To get them to expand on their sentence ask questions: What color is the ice cream? What flavor do you think it is? Does the girl seem to like the ice cream? Where do you think she got the ice cream? You should end up with a much more descriptive sentence. "The girl is enjoying a peppermint ice cream cone that she bought at the store."

2. Use the poster as a story starter. Let the children dictate a story about the poster.

3. Let children create their own posters. Choose subjects that they have some information about and challenge them to communicate what they know through creating a poster. Perhaps you want to create posters about

dental hygiene or fire safety. Help the children put their thoughts into a slogan and write it on their poster.

4. Challenge children to create posters advertising their favorite books. Talk to the librarian about displaying their posters in the library.

5. Make Alphabet Cards based on the names of the children in your classroom. Invite children to draw a self-portrait or use a snapshot from home to illustrate their poster. Encourage them to write a short autobiography to include with their picture. How many words can they use that begin with the same letter as their name?

6. Invite children to look at an existing advertising poster and dictate new text. Travel posters work well.

Children's Artwork

Getting Started
Assign children to draw something specific, or just spontaneously select artwork to use as a language enhancer.

Idea Sparkers
1. Encourage children to draw pictures that tell a story. They might draw pictures about their family or about their new pet. Transcribe their stories on the backs of their picture as they dictate to you.

2. Invite children to illustrate a popular story such as "The Little Red Hen." Write the appropriate text on the bottom of their drawings. Bind the pages together to make a class book.

3. Label children's artwork. Always ask their permission before you write on their drawings. Ask them to describe their work and label the items and the people they have drawn.

4. Make a scribble on a piece of drawing paper. Invite children to turn the scribble into a drawing. Invite them to create a story to go with the picture.

5. Use literature as a springboard for artwork. Read the book, *David's Father* by Robert Munsch. When you have finished, challenge children to draw a picture of David's grandmother based on the clues they heard about David's father. Or read *The Judge* by Margot and Harve Zemach. Stop before the end of the book and invite children to draw a picture of the "horrible thing" that is coming, based on the information the characters in the book have shared.

Wordless Books and Comics

Getting Started

Collect wordless books for your classroom. The library is full of them. Some publishers actually publish books that are intended to set children up as authors.

Idea Sparkers

1. Let children dictate text for wordless books. Here is a list of some tried-and-true favorites.

Wordless Books

Changes, Changes by Pat Hutchins
Do You Want to Be My Friend? by Eric Carle
Frog on His Own by Mercer Mayer
Good Dog, Carl by Alexandra Day
One Frog Too Many by Mercer Mayer
Pancakes for Breakfast by Tomie DePaola
Rosie's Walk by Pat Hutchins
The Snowman by Raymond Briggs

2. Use books such as *Imogene's Antlers* by David Small to inspire a sequel composed by the children.

3. Place sticky notes over the text of books and let children create a new story from the illustrations.

4. Use Wite-Out or Liquid Paper to cover over the dialogue on comic strips and invite children to use their imaginations to create new dialogue.

Rebus Pictures

Getting Started

Rebuses are pictorial representations of words and phrases. For young children, rebuses can communicate oral directions or instructions in a way that allows them to be able to "read" them by themselves.

Idea Sparkers

1. Read a rebus story such as *The Dress I'll Wear to the Party* by Shirley Neitzel.

2. Provide rebus directions for center activities, such as how to paint at the easel (Appendix page 378).

3. Use rebus directions for cooking recipes (Appendix page 380 has a fruit salad recipe).

4. Use sticky notes to illustrate words in the text of big books so that children can help you read the book.

5. Use rebus cards for movement activity directions (Appendix page 379).

6. Set up a rebus treasure hunt. Draw picture clues that direct the children toward the treasure.

7. Use the patterns on Appendix pages 367 and 368 to illustrate "Susie Moriar," or challenge the children to draw the illustrations. After the children have listened to the story, ask them if they are able to predict what the rebus picture is going to be before they see it. How?

> **Susie Moriar** (adapted by Pam Schiller)
> This is the story of Susie Moriar.
> It started one night as Susie sat by the _____. (fire)
> The fire was so hot,
> Susie jumped in a _____. (pot)
> The pot was so tall,
> Susie dropped in a _____. (ball)
> The ball was so red,
> She fell in a _____. (bed)
> The bed was so long,
> Susie sang a _____. (song)
> The song was so sweet,
> Susie ran down the _____. (street)
> The street was so big,
> Susie jumped on a _____. (pig)
> The pig jumped so high,
> He touched the _____. (sky)
> He touched the sky,
> And he couldn't touch higher
> But oh! What a ride
> Had Susie _____. (Moriar)

Sign Language

Getting Started

Just like pictures, sign language is a form of communication. It is another way we can express our thoughts and feelings. Learn a few signs and teach them to the children. You can pick up an American Sign Language book from the library or ask for help from someone who knows how to sign.

Idea Sparker

1. Teach children the signs for *hello, good-bye, yes,* and *no.* Use the signs daily. (See page 386 in the Appendix.)

2. Teach children the sign for *stop* and encourage them to use it with friends in the classroom who are bothering them.

3. Have someone who is skilled in sign language teach the class how to sign a song. Visit a school for the hearing impaired and let the children perform the song.

Making Words Meaningful

Show and Tell

Show and Tell encourages children to share information about familiar items. It is a great way to get children talking. You will want to monitor Show and Tell because too much of a good thing might get boring to the children. If everyone in the classroom brings something to share on Monday, Show and Tell will take half the morning. Here are a couple of ideas for monitoring Show and Tell.

● Open Show and Tell up every day of the week, but limit each child to bringing something only once each week. Keep clothespins with children's names written on them in a basket beside your circle area. After children share their Show and Tell item, have them attach their clothespin to the perimeter of the basket to indicate that they have had their turn for the week.

● Assign children a specific day for sharing so you can spread the activity across the week.

Oral Discussion

Oral discussion opportunities can take several forms. They provide a venue for children to relate meaningful events and experiences.

1. Discuss literature that you read aloud in the classroom. Talk about the outcome of the story. Evaluate the characters in the story. Talk about alternative endings.

2. Discuss situations that arise in the classroom. If you have a pet that dies, encourage children to express their feelings about losing the pet. They may even want to brainstorm a list of ways to say good-bye. If children are arguing over an activity or a toy, encourage them to talk out a solution.

3. Talk about events that occur in the news. Our daily lives are filled with exciting and tragic events. Talk about what children know about the weather, good deeds people have performed, and even politics when appropriate. In some classrooms this is called "News of the Day."

Dramatic Play

Dramatic play helps children make sense of stories they have heard. It enhances comprehension while allowing time for reflection.

Dramatic play allows you the opportunity to assess understanding. Watching children reenact the story helps you see what level of understanding they have regarding sequence of events and meaning of actions.

Children benefit from their interactions with other children. Sometimes one child has a better understanding of a story. As they play together, children are exposed to each other's interpretations and understanding.

1. Add props to the Dramatic Play Center. For example, after you read *I Wish That I Had Duck Feet* by Theo LeSieg, you can add flippers, a cat tail, a hose, and antlers for acting out the story.

2. Add flannel board props to the Language Center. For example, after you read *Moira's Birthday* by Robert Munsch, you can cut felt to represent cakes and pizzas and let the children recreate the story line.

3. After reading "The Three Little Pigs," you can add straw, sticks, and bricks to the Block Center.

4. Add cooking props such as rolling pins, play dough, aprons, bread tins, and so forth to the Home Center after you read "The Little Red Hen." Add farm props to the Block Center.

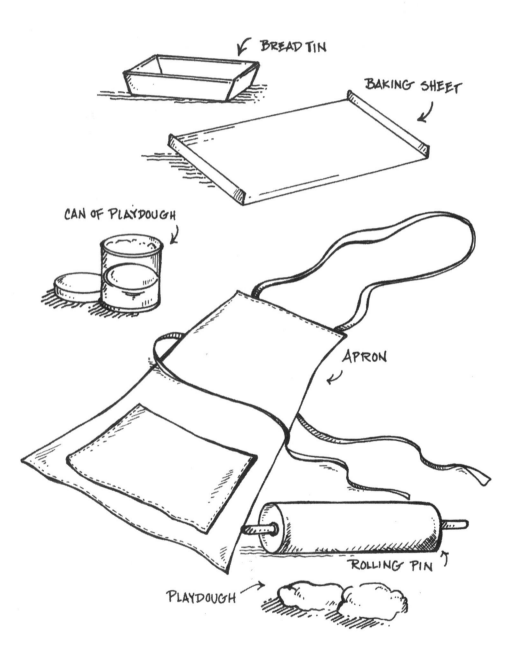

BREAD TIN

BAKING SHEET

CAN OF PLAYDOUGH

APRON

ROLLING PIN

PLAYDOUGH

Props for Dramatic Play

Costume Box

Dress-up clothes

Mirrors

Wigs (wash frequently)

Telephone

Paper

Empty food boxes and cans

Cookbooks

Notepads

Magic wands

Puppets

Prop Boxes (copy paper boxes are great storage boxes for props)

Office Supplies (paper, staplers, hole punches, pens, pencils, telephone, telephone book, notepads, binders, file folders, old typewriter)

Grocery Supplies (empty cans and boxes, cash register, play money, signs, bags, coupons)

Restaurant Supplies (menus, order pads, dishes, cookbooks, tablecloth, play money, cash register, signs with specials and operating hours)

Doctor's Office Supplies (magazines, books, telephone, telephone book, paper, pamphlets, file folders, play doctor's kit with medical supplies)

Post Office Supplies (stamps, rubber stamps and ink pad, envelopes, scales, zip code directory)

Pizza Parlor Supplies (pizza boxes, menu, order pads, play money, cash register, napkins, cups)

Ice Cream Shop Supplies (cones and cups, order pads, menus, play money, cash register)

Good Books for inspiring Dramatic Play

The Hat by Jan Brett

I Wish That I Had Duck Feet by Theo LeSieg

"Little Red Hen" (Traditional)

The Mitten by Jan Brett

Moira's Birthday by Robert Munsch

The Napping House by Don and Audrey Wood

The Teddy Bears' Picnic by Jimmy Kennedy

"The Three Bears" (Traditional)

"The Three Billy Goats Gruff' (Traditional)

"The Three Little Pigs" (Traditional)

Brain Connections

● Oral language is fundamental to reading. The more vocabulary the child hears from his or her family, teachers, and caregivers, the greater the life-long vocabulary. Without exposure to new words, a child will never develop the cells in the auditory cortex to discriminate well both between and among sounds.

Matching Words to Thoughts and Actions

A Dozen Ways to Tell a Story

Retelling, reenacting, and dramatizing a story are powerful ways for children to extend their oral language. They enable children to put the actions in their own words. Often children are able to advance their own vocabulary by using language from the original story. Here are a few suggestions for storytelling, retelling, reenacting, and dramatizing.

Puppets

Provide puppets for the children to reenact a familiar story or to create their own story. Here are some simple ideas for making puppets.

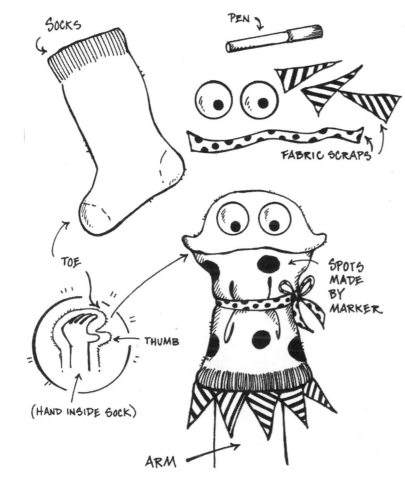

● Paper Plates: Use a marker to draw features on a paper plate or cut features out of construction paper and glue them onto the plate. Use wiggle eyes, yarn or ribbon for hair, and scraps of fabric to enhance the puppet. Glue or tape to a tongue depressor.

● Paper Bags: Create faces and glue them to the bottom of paper bags to make puppets. See Appendix pages 337-339 for patterns for The Old Lady Who Swallowed the Fly paper bag puppet.

● Socks: Use permanent markers, wiggle eyes, and fabric scraps to make sock puppets. The toe of the sock can be tucked to create a mouth.

● Coat Hangers and Hose: Bend a coat hanger to make a circle. Cover the circle with one leg of a pair of hose. Wrap leftover hose leg around the hanger handle and tape securely with duct tape to form a handle. Use felt to cut out features and glue the features to the hose with glue.

● Glove Puppet: Sew Velcro to the fingers (palm side) of a work glove. Create felt or poster-board puppet faces about the size of a poker chip or fifty-cent piece. Place the matching Velcro on the back of each face and adhere it to the glove. This type of puppet is great for fingerplays that count down from five such as "Five Little Snowmen," "Five Little Pumpkins," and "Five Little Valentines."

● Finger Puppets: See patterns on Appendix page 371 for finger puppets. Make up some puppets of your own. Use masking tape on the back of the finger holes before cutting them to reinforce the opening. Laminating the whole puppet will also preserve it.

● Finger Tip Puppets: Cut the fingers off a clean cotton glove and discard the rest of the glove or put it in the Dramatic Play Center for play. Use a permanent marker to create faces on the glove fingertips. Glue yarn on for hair. Small wiggle eyes add to the fun.

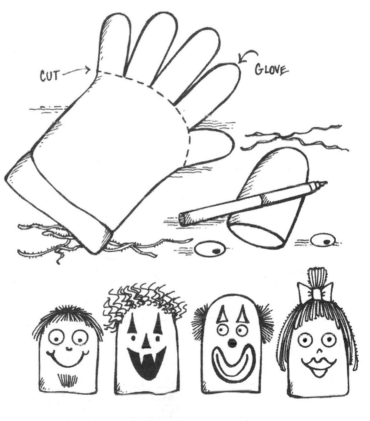

● Cup Animal Puppets: Make a hole large enough for a finger in the side of a paper cup. Lay the cup on its side with the hole in the bottom. The bottom of the cup is the puppet's nose. Use construction paper and markers to create facial features. Use yarn and fabric scraps to add other details.

● Stick Puppets: Use flannel board patterns or coloring book patterns to make stick puppets. Just color them, cut them out, laminate them, and attach them to a tongue depressor.

Reenactment

Let the children assume the roles of the various characters and retell the story. Two of the easiest stories for this retelling are "The Three Little Pigs" and "The Three Billy Goats Gruff."

Shadow Stories

Attach a sheet to the ceiling or suspend it across a rope. Place a light behind it. Let children stand between the light source and the sheet and act out the story. *Rosie's Walk* by Pat Hutchins works well as a Shadow Story. You will need a few basic props to make animal shadows distinguishable. You can also do "The Great Big Turnip" as a Shadow Story.

Flannel Board

Turn a favorite story into a flannel board story. Not only does it offer a different format, it provides a good activity for the Language Center after you have used it to tell the story.

Magnetic Stories

Similar to the flannel board story, but using another presentation concept, is the magnetic story. You start with patterns copied on drawing paper. Color them, cut them out, and laminate them. Trace the outline of the pattern onto magnetic backing. Cut out the backing piece and glue it to the back of the story piece and you will have magnetic characters. Use a cookie sheet or other metallic surface as a backdrop.

Storytelling Without Props of Any Kind

Tell a story with no props and no book—just tell it. You can also teach children that the hula is a form of story telling that is communicated through dance using the hands to communicate the story. If there is someone in your community that can do the hula, you might have them come in to demonstrate and perhaps teach the children a few movements.

Here are a few tips to remember when telling a story.
- Don't just summarize. Tell the story complete with adjectives and dialogue. It makes it much more interesting.
- Practice before you actually tell the story. Read the story several times to build familiarity.
- Don't memorize the story. If you forget a part, you'll lose your place.
- Don't try to be funny. Humor is often lost on children anyway.

Using Props

Tell a story using props. *I Wish That I Had Duck Feet* by Theo Le Sieg works well. You can collect swimming fins (for the duck feet), yarn (for the long, long tail), tree branches (for the antlers), and hose (for the elephant's trunk). "A Special Surprise" on page 104 is a good example of a prop story.

Walk-On Story

Do a walk-on story. Draw pictures and symbols of key elements and actions in the story on a piece of butcher paper and let children walk through the story. Below is an example using "The Three Bears."

Cut a piece of butcher paper 15' (5 m) long. Draw the following items on the paper in this sequence: set of footprints (trace shoes), a spiral arrow, footprints, grass, footprints, a door, footprints, a bowl, footprints, a chair, footprints, a bed, footprints, bear prints, footprints going off the end of the paper. You will want to have this laminated.

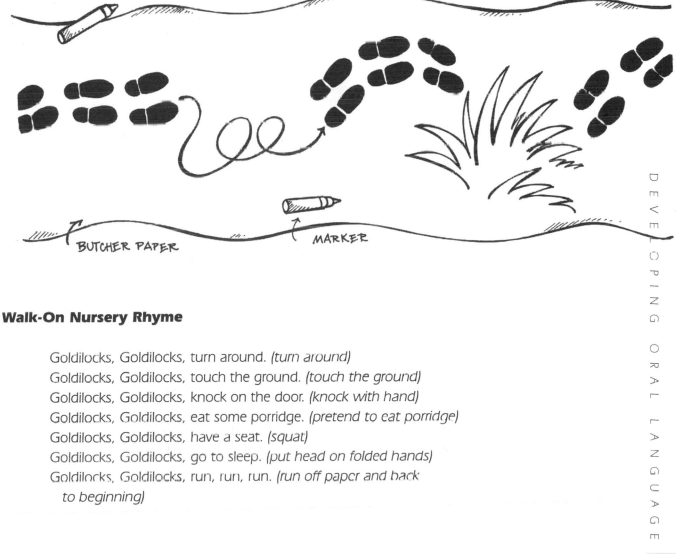

BUTCHER PAPER   MARKER

Walk-On Nursery Rhyme

Goldilocks, Goldilocks, turn around. *(turn around)*
Goldilocks, Goldilocks, touch the ground. *(touch the ground)*
Goldilocks, Goldilocks, knock on the door. *(knock with hand)*
Goldilocks, Goldilocks, eat some porridge. *(pretend to eat porridge)*
Goldilocks, Goldilocks, have a seat. *(squat)*
Goldilocks, Goldilocks, go to sleep. *(put head on folded hands)*
Goldilocks, Goldilocks, run, run, run. *(run off paper and back to beginning)*

Action Stories

Tell a story and have children act it out as you tell it. "We're Going on a Bear Hunt" (see page 112) is a good example of this type of story. Any story with lots of verbs works well as an action story. *The Very Hungry Caterpillar* by Eric Carle, *Five Little Monkeys Sitting in a Tree* by Eileen Christelow, and *Over in the Meadow* by Paul Galdone are good action stories. You can also make up your own stories about baking a cake, making a pizza, or walking through candy land.

Rebus

Turn a story or nursery rhyme into a rebus story. "Hey Diddle Diddle" from Mother Goose and "This Is the House that Jack Built" make good rebus stories.

Story Cards

Draw story pictures on cards and use them to tell the story. Pick a story that doesn't have too many actions such as *Brown Bear, Brown Bear* by Bill Martin, Jr. or "The Itsy Bitsy Spider" (see Appendix pages 319-321 for patterns to make this story).

Listening Tapes

Let children retell a story on a cassette tape and then put the tape in the Listening Center with the book. You can also let the children make their own illustrations of the story and put them together in book form to use with the tape instead of using the original book. "The Little Red Hen" makes a good Listening Tape. You can be the narrator and let children do the dialogue for the hen, the cat, the dog, and the pig.

It's Time to Celebrate

A good way to celebrate children's successful reenactments and dramatizations is to videotape their performance. Another way is to put on a performance for another class or for families. Find a way to say "Hooray for you!"

Following Directions

Children need to be able to follow directions as they move into more complex reading tasks. This section suggests some songs, games, and activities that provide practice in following directions. Remember perfect practice means you provide feedback and you also ask children to evaluate their own progress.

Songs

Songs are a great way to practice following directions. They are fun, and if you mess up it is only funny, not tragic. Here are a few songs that focus on following directions.

Hokey Pokey

You put your right hand in; (*children stand in circle and perform movements*)
You put your right hand out;
You put your right hand in;
And you shake it all about.
You do the Hokey Pokey, (*shake hands over head*)
And you turn yourself around. (*turn around*)
That's what it's all about. (*pat knees or clap three times*)

Continue, using other body parts.

Another great song to use is "One Finger, One Thumb, Keep Moving."

Games

Good, old-fashioned games are a good way to practice listening to and following directions. Most games are dependent on directions. Children are highly motivated to follow directions when playing games because you can't win if you don't. Below are a few game suggestions.

"Mother, May I?"

You play Mother. Stand about 20' (6 m) from the children, who stand in a line. Call out a child's name and directions for her to move. (e.g., "Take three bunny hops.") The child must first say, "Mother, May I?" before being granted permission to make the move. Once permission is granted, the child may move. The first child to reach you is the next mother.

Red Light, Green Light

In this game, the leader stands with her back facing the group. The group starts at a common start line about 20' (6 m) away from the leader. When the leader calls out "green light," the children may move any way they desire—run, hop, skip, or jump—toward the leader. When the leader calls out "red light," everyone must stop and be perfectly still when the leader turns around. If the leader sees someone moving, she can send that person back to the start line. The first child to reach the leader is the new leader.

Simon Says

In this game the leader is Simon. Simon calls out actions such as "pat your head" and "clap your hands." The rest of the group follow directions only when the leader adds "Simon Says" to the directions. If someone moves without first hearing "Simon Says," she is out of the game.

Freeze

One child is selected to be the Caller. The Caller calls out an action such as run, hop, spin, jump, or skip. All the children do as the Caller says. Then the Caller calls out, "Freeze." Everyone must be still. Anyone who moves is out of the game. Let children take turns being the Caller.

Activities

Using activities that include directions provides another chance to practice listening and following directions.

Treasure Hunt

Send the children on a treasure hunt with oral directions. Try a snack treasure hunt. Each item that they find can be part of their snack. After everything is found, put the ingredients together and have snack. Trail Mix (pretzels, raisins, miniature marshmallows, and cereal) works well.

Directions for Art Project

Record directions for an art activity and place them in the Art Center.

Action Activities

Do action activities that require listening and following directions. Here is a cute example.

Hey, My Name is Joe!

Hello! My name is Joe!
I have a wife, one kid, and I work in a button factory.
One day, my boss said, "Are you busy?"
I said, "No."
"Then turn a button with your right hand." (*make a turning gesture with right hand*)

Hello! My name is Joe!
I have a wife, two kids, and I work in a button factory.
One day, my boss said, "Are you busy?"
I said, "No."
"Then turn a button with your left hand." (*make a turning gesture with left hand as you continue with the right hand*)

Continue adding the number of children and adding right and left feet and head.

> Hello! My name is Joe!
> I have a wife, six kids, and I work in a button factory.
> One day, my boss said, "Are you busy?"
> I said, "Yes!"

Follow a Recipe

All recipes require following directions. Choose one of the recipes in the Appendix (pages 412-418) and invite children to prepare it.

Brain Connections

● This section is about applying what children know by allowing them to revisit the information in a different format. Retelling stories in different formats adds novelty to the experience. The brain pays closer attention to things that don't fit an established pattern, things that are new and different. Researchers say, "Unfamiliar activities are the brain's best friends."

● Retelling stories in different formats help children strengthen and expand existing patterns of understanding.

4

Understanding the Functions of Print

Adults often think of reading as a singular activity. You pick up a book and you read the words. But reading is so much more than this, and there are many other concepts children have to understand. Children have to understand spatial relationships (moving from left to right and top to bottom). They need to know what spaces mean. Why are some letters capitalized and others aren't? What are the funny marks that appear at the end of a sentence? What are the differences between letters, words, and sentences?

This section will provide activities to help children with directionality, conventions of print, and understanding of whole/part relationship.

Book Concepts

Knowledge that a book is for reading.

Functions and location of the front, back, top, and bottom of a book

How to turn pages properly.

Where to begin reading.

Functions of print and pictures and their relationship to each other.

Knowledge of the title, author, and illustrator.

Print Concepts

Words are read from left to right and top to bottom.

What are letters? Words?

There are spaces between words.

Function of capital letters and punctuation.

Oral language can be written down and then read.

Understanding Spatial Orientation

Activities

Left to Right/Top to Bottom

1. When you write children's names on their artwork or other paper, always start in the upper lefthand corner. This is helpful in two ways. First it gives you an opportunity to say, "I am writing your name on the top left corner of your paper." Second, it is a good modeling situation for children. When

they begin to write their own names in the large-size print they typically use, they will be less likely to run out of room to finish their name if they start on the left.

2. Move your finger under the words when you read to a few children. When you read a large book to several children, use a pencil or a dowel to show the direction in which you are reading the words. Tell children you are reading from the left to the right and from the top to the bottom. Children often enjoy knowing that in other countries people may read from right to left and from bottom to top.

3. Provide comic strips for children with the words covered. Let them create new dialogue. Point out the movement of action from box to box in the comic strips.

4. Make a left and right handprint. Give each child a piece of construction paper that has been folded in half. Invite children to place their right hand in a tray of paint and then press it on the right side of the construction paper to make a handprint. Do the same with the left hand. Lay the construction paper handprints above an open book. Show the children the directions the words go when you read them. Explain that the words go from the pinky on their left hand to the pinky on their right hand.

5. Show children how to fold a sheet of paper in three sections. Encourage them to draw a picture on the paper using the top, middle, and bottom sections, or to draw three pictures, one in the top, a second one in the middle and a third one in the bottom. Talk about the positions of their pictures.

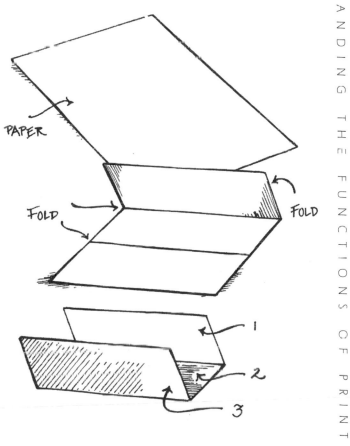

6. Do the "Hokey Pokey." Tie red ribbons around everyone's left hand. Instead of standing in a circle, stand in a line. Sing the "reading version" of "Hokey Pokey."

> When I read a book,
> I start from left to right. *(place left hand out front and shake, the right hand)*
> And I do the very same thing, *(repeat action)*
> When I want to write.
> I do the reader wiggle, *(put hand over*

head and shake, wiggle hips)
And I turn myself about. *(turn around)*
That's how I read and write. *(shake finger as if saying I told you so)*

When I read "The Three Bears," *(repeat actions)*
I move from left to right.
I go from word to word
And I know I've got it right.
I do the reader wiggle,
And I turn my self about.
That's how I read and write.

7. Play Pass the Beanbag in a line instead of in a circle. Tape the word *read* on the beanbag and have children chant "left to right" as they pass the beanbag to the beat of a drum. When the drum stops beating, the child with the beanbag must show her friends the direction the words go when you read them. Keep a book available. When the beanbag gets to the end of the line, the last child runs the bag back up to the start of the line and takes the first position in line.

8. Make a Pattern Grid. Cut an 8" (20 cm) square out of white felt or use white drawing paper. Divide it into sixteen 2" (5 cm) squares. Give children three items, such as red, blue, and yellow color tiles, to make a pattern with. Direct them to start at the left upper corner of the square. They will have to turn the corner in order to keep their pattern going. This is a great activity for teaching left to right and top to bottom.

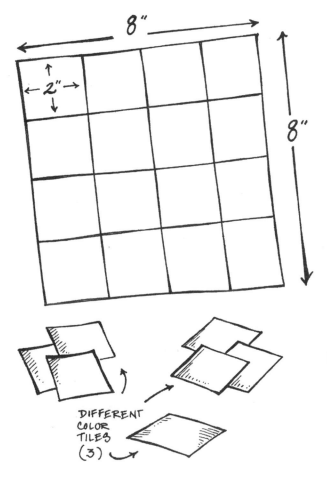

9. Encourage children to paint a picture at the easel, starting at the top instead of the way they normally start at the bottom. Watch their progress and talk with them while they paint about moving from top to bottom.

10. Invite children to build a tower out of at least six blocks. Challenge them to take a block from the top, then the middle, and finally the bottom of the tower without knocking the tower down.

11. Do this chant with the children. Say it several times increasing the speed as you complete a verse. After you have finished stretching talk about the directions. Which side of the room are the windows on? Which side of the room is the door on? What part of the room is the ceiling? What part of the room is the floor?

Stretching Chant

Stretch to the windows, (*suit actions to words*)
Stretch to the door,
Stretch up to the ceiling,
And bend to the floor.

Beginning, Middle, and End

Children need to be clear on these position words before they begin working on beginning and ending sounds.

1. When you read to children, talk about the beginning, middle, and end of the story. Who can remember the first thing that happened? What happened in the middle of the story? How did the story end?

2. Use the sequence cards in Appendix pages 381-385 to sequence the familiar stories of "The Three Bears" and "The Little Three Pigs."

3. Sing "I Know an Old Lady Who Swallowed a Fly." Use the pattern cards in Appendix pages 337 339 to sequence the things the old lady ate. What did the lady eat first? Which thing did she eat last?

4. Use the "Itsy Bitsy Spider" pattern cards (Appendix pages 319-321) to show what happened first, next, and last in the song.

5. Invite the children to make some peanut butter and jelly crackers. Talk about what you do first, next, and last. What is the position of the crackers, the peanut butter, and the jelly?

Books, Songs, and Stories About Spatial Concepts

Read stories and sing songs that center around spatial concepts. On the next page is an example of a good spatial story. There are also lists of books and songs that focus on spatial concepts in the boxes located on page 81.

Smart Cookie's Great Journey (Pam Schiller)

Directions: Gather a cookie jar, a cookie, a carpet square, and a box for a TV. Use these props and the kitchen set in your Dramatic Play Center to tell this story.

One day Smart Cookie pushed *up* the lid of the cookie jar and rolled *out* onto the *top* of the kitchen counter. She was bored. She looked *out across* the kitchen and wondered what the rest of the house looked like. She decided to find out.

She rolled *off* the counter and *down* to the floor. She rolled *under* the table and *around* the chair legs and right *out* of the kitchen and *into* the living room. "Wow!" she said. "This is great!" She wasn't bored anymore.

She saw the sofa and the television. She had heard of these things, but she had never seen them. She jumped *up* on the sofa. It was soft. She jumped *up* and *down* and *up* and *down* again. "Whee!" she squealed.

She heard a song and turned to look at the television. A big elephant was marching. He was *first* in a line of animals. A dog, a cat, and a monkey were *behind* him. A small mouse was the *last* one in the line. The elephant was *first*, the dog, cat, and monkey were in the *middle*, and the mouse was on the *end*.

"This is like magic," thought Smart Cookie. She rolled *off* the sofa and right *in front of* the TV. Then she rolled *behind* the TV. She couldn't figure out how the big animals got *inside* the little box.

"Oh, well," thought Smart Cookie, "it's time to be getting back home." She turned *around* and started *across* the living room. She rolled *over* the big blue carpet, *beside* the coffee table, and *through* the door *to* the kitchen.

She rolled *around* the legs of the chair and *under* the table. When she came to the kitchen counter, she looked *up* at the cookie jar. It looked really high. She jumped *up* on the *bottom* drawer, then to the *middle* drawer, next to the *top* drawer, and finally to the counter.

She turned to look at the large room again and thought, "I'm one Smart Cookie! I traveled a great distance today! And tomorrow is another day."

Books about Spatial Concepts

The Cat in the Hat by Dr. Seuss

Flower Garden by Eve Bunting

Green Eggs and Ham by Dr. Seuss

Inside, Outside, Upside Down by Jan and Stan Berenstain

Over, Under and Through and Other Spatial Concepts by Tana Hoban

Rosie's Walk by Pat Hutchins

Snail Trail by Ruth Brown

Wacky Wednesday by Theo LeSieg

We're Going on a Bear Hunt by Michael Rosen

Songs About Spatial Concepts

"A-Hunting We Will Go"

"The Bear Went Over the Mountain"

"Five Little Speckled Frogs"

"Go In and Out the Windows"

"The Grand Old Duke of York"

"The Green Grass Grew All Around"

"Hokey Pokey"

"On Top of Spaghetti"

"One Elephant"

"Over in the Meadow"

"This Old Man"

"Three Little Monkeys"

"Wheels on the Bus"

Brain Connections

● Using physical orientation will help children remember directions and positions better. The physical movement creates a more complex and wider sensory input to the brain than only cognitive activity. This makes the information easier to master and remember.

Recognizing Part/Whole Relationships

Activities

1. Invite children to make a name puzzle. Write their name on a strip of tag board approximately 4" x 8" (10 cm x 20 cm). Leave enough space between letters to cut them apart, puzzle style. Let children practice putting their names together. Can they put their friends' names together?

2. Sequence Cards help reinforce the concept of parts making up a whole. Use the sequence cards in the Appendix pages 381-385 to help children recognize this relationship.

3. Stop occasionally when you are reading to ask children what they think is going to happen next. Avoid stopping too often; you know how you feel when the commercials get too frequent. You don't want to interrupt the flow of the story.

4. When you finish reading a story, ask questions that help separate the parts from the whole. Which things in the story could really happen? Which things couldn't really happen?

5. Play a xylophone. Talk about the fact that it takes several notes to make a song. If you can play a simple song, do so. If you can't play an instrument, invite a family member or colleague to come play. Explain that musical notes are to a song what letters and words are to a book.

6. Provide lots of opportunities to work puzzles. They reinforce the concept of whole/part relationships.

7. Invite children to clap out the syllables of their names. Who claps once? How many children clap twice? Does anyone clap three times? Does

anyone clap four or more times? How many claps make up you full name? This activity makes a nice graphing activity. The following is a cute chant that can be used for clapping, snapping, and tapping syllables of names.

Hicky Picky Bumblebee (JoAnn Nally)
Hicky Picky Bumblebee
Won't you say your name to me? (*direct the question to a child by pointing to her*)
(Child says name—Carmela)
Carmela! (*repeat name*)
Let's clap it—Car-me-la (*clap each syllable*)
Let's snap it—Car-me-la (*snap each syllable*)
Let's tap it—Car-me-la (*tap foot to the syllables*)

Repeat the chant using another child's name.

Story Maps

Story maps help children understand the organization and structure of a story. In narrative text there is a setting, some characters, a sequence of events, and usually some type of problem the characters solve. There is a plot and a theme. Story maps help children see how these parts of a story make up the whole story. Children need many experiences with story maps. Here are a couple of different styles of maps you may want to use. You can also experiment and develop your own.

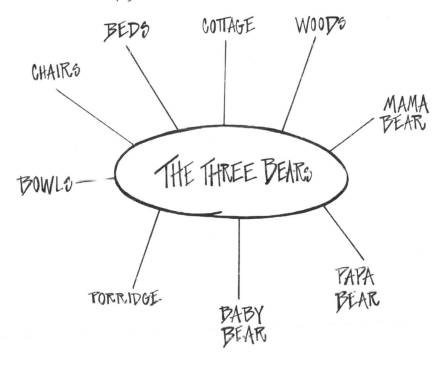

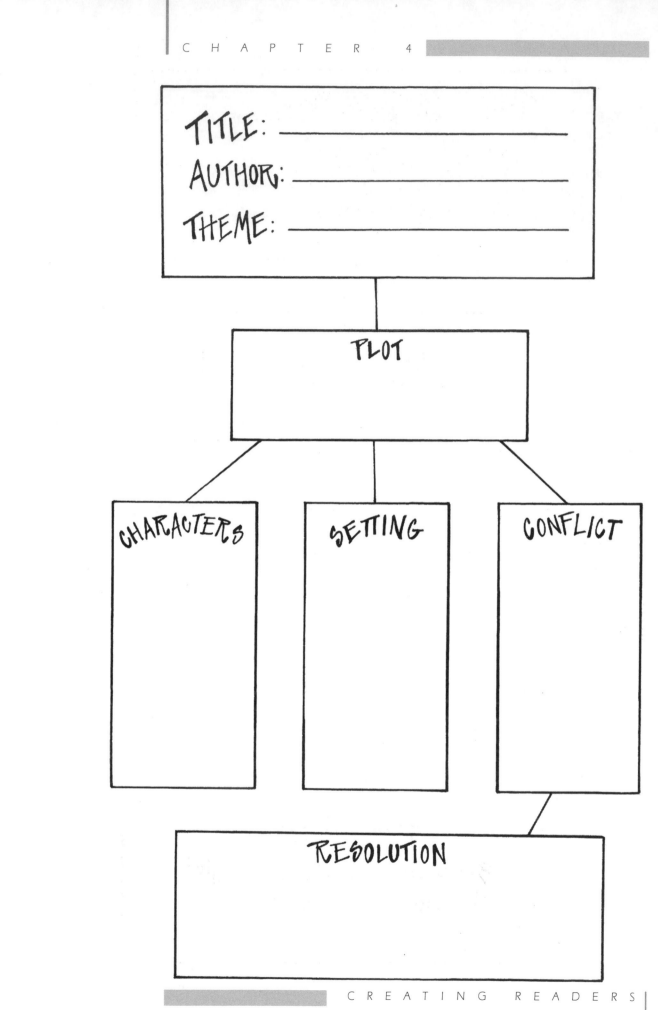

TITLE: _____

AUTHOR: _____

THEME: _____

PLOT

CHARACTERS

SETTING

CONFLICT

RESOLUTION

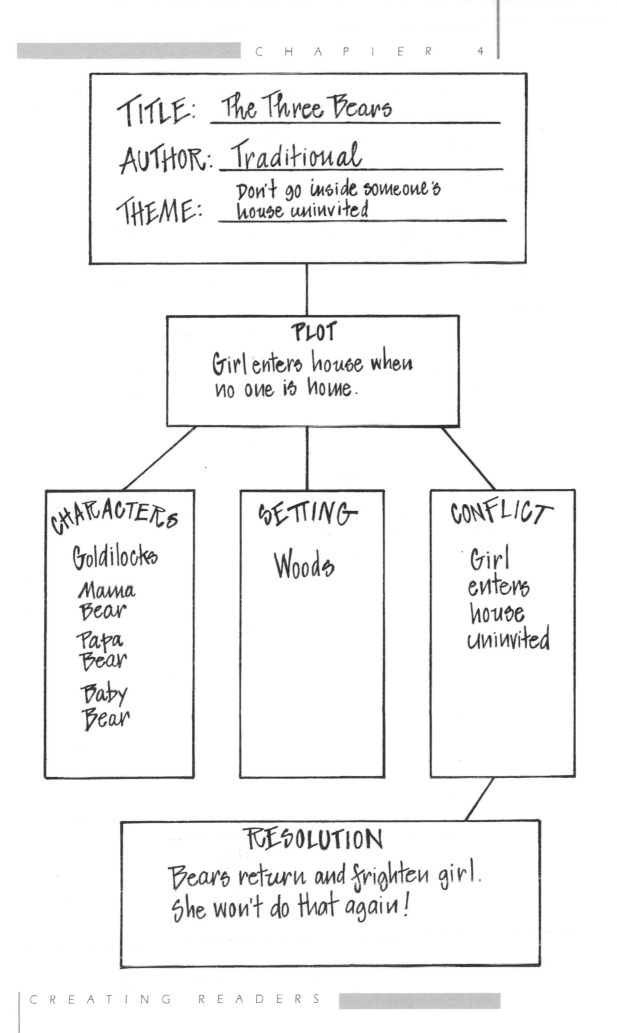

TITLE: The Three Bears

AUTHOR: Traditional

THEME: Don't go inside someone's house uninvited

PLOT
Girl enters house when no one is home.

CHARACTERS
Goldilocks
Mama Bear
Papa Bear
Baby Bear

SETTING
Woods

CONFLICT
Girl enters house uninvited

RESOLUTION
Bears return and frighten girl. She won't do that again!

Brain Connections

● Reading is a good example of a task that requires the integration of the left and right hemisphere during processing. The right hemisphere examines the whole of the concept (the gestalt) and the left hemisphere examines the details.

● Left/right hemisphere integration is more fluid when you take time throughout the day to do some cross-lateral movements. Researchers suggest doing cross-lateral movements about every 90 minutes.

Putting Thoughts on Paper

Children need many opportunities to write. Keep a Writing Center in your room, but be sure writing materials are part of every center. The box on page 87 provides a list of Writing Center supplies. You will want this center to have a good table surface for writing, lots of light, and inspirational posters and charts. An old typewriter is a nice addition and a computer, if you have access to one, is wonderful. This section will explore ways to get children writing.

Why Use Creative Writing?

1. Writing develops the concept that writing is talk written down.
2. Writing reinforces left to right and top to bottom concepts.
3. Writing encourages and enhances creative expression.
4. Writing expands vocabulary.
5. Writing reinforces and develops sequencing skills.
6. Writing allows for reflection on the past.
7. Writing provides an outlet for emotions.
8. Writing promotes the desire to understand letter sounds.
9. Writing empowers the writer to create his own ideas.
10. Writing creates great "first readers" for children.

Material for Writing Center

Pencils (several different types and sizes)

Colored pencils

Markers (several different widths)

Lined and unlined paper

Tracing paper

Index cards

Envelopes

Construction paper for card making

Chalkboard and chalk

Magic slate

Hole punch

Glue stick

Scissors

Stapler

Magnetic letters

Wallpaper scraps

Old magazines

Writing Activities

Dictionaries

Ask each child to bring a notebook to class. Let children cut words from old magazines and paste them on the cover of their notebooks. Write the letters of the alphabet inside, one at the top of each page in each child's notebook.

As children learn new words, encourage them to add the words to their dictionaries. As you introduce new words, have children write the words in the appropriate place in their dictionaries.

You may also want to encourage children to illustrate their dictionaries. This is a yearlong project that will evolve and grow more sophisticated over time.

Journal Writing

There are several wonderful learning experiences associated with journal writing. There are also several different types of journals you may want to explore with your children. Children can bring a notebook from home or you can create one at school by stapling several sheets of writing paper together. The box on page 89 provides several ideas for topics to write about. One great use of journals is the daily recording of what a child hopes to accomplish during the day. When the end of the day arrives, the child can look back and see how well he did in meeting those goals. The purpose of a journal is not to achieve perfection. It is a place to practice the concepts of left to right and top to bottom, to internalize the notion that writing is talk written down, to use sight words, and to develop understanding of letter/sound combinations.

Journals should begin early in the journey to literacy. In the beginning, children will only be able to draw pictures of their thoughts, and that is an important first step. It can be compared to the infant who babbles before actually pronouncing a word. From drawing, letters will begin to emerge, and eventually, letters will begin to connect into words. Don't worry about children's misspelling. Eventually you will want to help them make corrections (edit their work) but not until they are able to get some words right. As children practice writing, they will learn from their own mistakes. Writing is a process that will evolve over time.

Be sure to write in your journal each day. Modeling is an important part of journal writing just as it is an important part of reading.

Beginning Writing/Print Concepts

Scribbling

Drawing

Letter-like forms

Letters in sequence

Phonetic spelling

Conventional spelling

Suggestions for Journal Writing Topics

- My favorite person
- My favorite things
- Things I like about me
- I'm happy when...
- My favorite story
- My best friend
- Friends are...
- My family
- My pet
- My wish list
- I'm good at
- I got in trouble one time when...
- Sometimes I'm afraid...
- When I get big
- I want to learn to...
- My favorite food
- I feel big when...
- I taught...

Wordless Books

Wordless books are another nonthreatening way to get children writing. They allow children to retell familiar stories in their own words. They also encourage children to tell new stories based on pictures that provide characters, plots, themes, and settings. Provide wordless books for children to use as inspiration for their writing. Younger children will be able to dictate stories to you; older children will be able to write their own. See page 60 for a list of wordless books.

Group Writing Activities

Writing as a group is another good way to reinforce the concept that print is language written down.

1. When children return from a field trip, make summarizing the event a group activity. Let everyone contribute to the story. Post the finished story where family members and other children can read it.

2. Make lists when children are brainstorming about a certain event or topic.

3. As a group, write the words to favorite songs or poems on chart paper.

4. Summarize each day's activities with a list or story that is generated by the children.

5. Give children a story starter and let them complete the story as a group. For example, you might say, "Yesterday in the mall I saw a very large creature with green eyes. She…"

6. Write group thank-you notes to people who visit the classroom or donate materials to the classroom.

7. Invite another class in the same building, or around the world, to be a pen pal. Write group letters to your pen pals.

8. Each morning the group can write together the day and date, the weather conditions, and even a thought for the day.

9. Put two or three props in a Story Box and encourage children to make up a story using them. Record the story on chart paper. Invite volunteers to illustrate it.

Bookmaking

Encourage children to write their own books. Less experienced children may need to have you take dictation. Others may use invented spelling. Some children may want to use the computer or typewriter. Below are some clever ways to present their books.

● Book in a Can
Have children roll their story up and place it in a can. Decorate the can.

● Book in a Box
Provide a stationery box for children to keep their books in. Encourage them to decorate the outside of the box.

Baggie Book

Cut poster board to fit inside whatever size sandwich bag you are using. Let children write their stories on the poster board inserts and illustrate their pages as desired. Place their drawings in the bags and zip shut. Staple the bags together on the bottom (the bottom of the bag, if you were using the bag as intended). Cover staples with vinyl tape.

Accordion Books

Tape several pieces of poster board together to form a book. Let children write their stories and illustrate as desired.

Metal Ring Books

Provide pages of poster board or construction paper for children to write their stories and illustrate. Punch holes in the side of their pages and use metal rings to hold the books together.

Felt Books

Sew five felt squares together down the left side to make a book. Cut felt scraps into different shapes and objects. Children can use the shapes on each page to make a wordless book.

5 SQUARES OF FELT

SEW A SEAM

FELT SCRAPS

SUN
CLOUDS
TREES
HOUSE
MOON
STARS
CAT
SNAKE
DOG
GRASS
DUCK

Brain Connections

● Writing is stimulating for growing brains. However, research suggests that children are not ready to do their own writing until around the age of 5 or 6 when the visual motor area of the brain is better prepared to make the fine distinction between alphabet letters that look similar. Research also suggests that when children are ready to write, cursive is far easier for them to master than standard print.

● Letting children see you transcribe their thoughts onto paper helps them develop the concept of thoughts being able to take the form of print.

UNDERSTANDING THE FUNCTIONS OF PRINT

Acquiring Reading Skills

"Reading" Predictable Text

Predictable books are books with controlled or repeating vocabulary and language. There are many examples of predictable text in traditional literature, such as "The Three Little Pigs" and "The Gingerbread Man." Children love predictable text because they are able to chime in, and that makes them feel like they are reading.

Predictable text should be used with children when they are still in the "read-to" phases of the literacy journey. It is very important when they are starting to work on the mechanics of reading. Predictable text serves as a bridge between not being able to read and reading on your own. It is a strong motivator for young children. The praise and acknowledgment they receive when they pick up a predictable book and start to "read" it goes a long way toward keeping them going when the challenges of figuring out letter sounds begin to emerge. Children should, as soon as possible, hold a book in their hands—one that they can joyfully "read" from cover to cover.

There are several forms of predictable text, and children need experience with all of them. Each form provides more information about story structure. Below is a list and description of the types of predictable text along with some examples.

- Repetitive Predictable Text has a repetitive line that occurs in predictable places in the story. "The Three Little Pigs" is a good example of this kind of predictable text. The closer to each other the repetitive lines appear, the easier it is for children to read the book themselves. Repetitive Predictable Text is the easiest for children and will likely be the form in that first book they "read" cover to cover by themselves.

- Rhyming Predictable Text has a rhyme that appears normally at the end of the sentence. Just like Repetitive Predictable Text, it can occur frequently or less frequently. In the beginning, children need rhyme that occurs in every other sentence. Susie Moriar (see page 61) is a good example of this kind of predictable text. There is a list of other good rhyming books on page 40.

- Cumulative Predictable Text has a repetition built on the preceding event. "This is the House that Jack Built" is a good example of Cumulative Predictable Text.

- Interlocking Predictable Text has a predictability that follows an interlocking format like question and answer. *Brown Bear, Brown Bear, What Do You See?* is a good example of Interlocking Predictable Text.

- Familiar Cultural Predictable Text is predictable based on a sequence that is culturally understood such as numbers, days of the week, months of the year, seasons, and so forth. *Chicken Soup With Rice* and *The Very Hungry Caterpillar* are examples of Familiar Cultural Predictable Text. Children can use what they know about counting, days of the week, order of the months, and so forth to predict the sequence of the story.

Predictable text helps children understand story structure. They are able to figure out what's coming next, difficult vocabulary, and the plan behind the plot. Below is a list of books that are rich in predictable text.

Predictable Books

A House Is a House for Me by Mary Ann Hoberman
Barnyard Banter by Denise Fleming
Brown Bear, Brown Bear, What Do You See? by Bill Martin, Jr.
Caps for Sale by Esphyr Slobodkina
Chicken Soup With Rice by Maurice Sendak
The Deep by Tim Winton
Fortunately by Remy Charlip
"The Gingerbread Man" (Traditional)
Goodnight Moon by Margaret Wise Brown

Hattie and the Fox by Mem Fox
"Henny Penny" (Traditional)
If You Give a Mouse a Cookie by Laura Joffe Numeroff
In a Small, Small Pond by Denise Fleming
Jump, Frog, Jump! by Robert Kalan
"The Little Red Hen" (Traditional)
The Napping House by Don and Audrey Woods
Over in the Meadow by Ezra Jack Keats
Rosie's Walk by Pat Hutchins
Silly Sally by Audrey Wood
"The Three Bears" (Traditional)
"The Three Billy Goats Gruff" (Traditional)
"The Three Little Pigs" (Traditional)
"This Is the House that Jack Built" (Traditional)
Vegetable Garden by Douglas Florian
The Very Busy Spider by Eric Carle
The Very Hungry Caterpillar by Eric Carle
Why Mosquitos Buzz in People's Ears by Verna Aardema

Brain Connections

- Children who pretend to read at an early age are more likely to become successful readers later. Pretend reading allows children to reinforce the concept of words being talk written down. It also allows them to practice spatial orientation.

Recognizing Sight Words

Sight words are a tool we use to help us read more quickly. Having a repertoire of sight words is one of the core elements in learning to read successfully. For young children, they become motivators to keep trying to achieve the more difficult task of sounding out letters to read an unfamiliar word.

Sight Word Games

● Environmental Print
Make puzzles and concentration games from box fronts and can labels.

● Basketball
Use index cards to create a set of sight words that the children know. Give each child a large paper or plastic cup to use as a basketball goal. Turn the cards over in the middle of the table. Have each child draw a card. If she

recognizes the word on the card, it goes in her cup (goal) and she scores two points. If she doesn't recognize the word, it goes back on the bottom of the stack. The child with the most points wins.

Bingo

Play sight word bingo. Make up several grids using key sight words that the children are beginning to recognize.

Concentration

Play sight word concentration with the words children have mastered.

Charade Cards

On an index card write words that are in your children's word banks. Invite children, one at a time, to draw a card. Ask the child to read the word on the card silently, then act out the word on the card so that her classmates can guess the word.

Word Bank

Provide each child with several index cards. You can keep cards in a shoe-box or punch a hole in the top lefthand corner and hold the cards together with a ring clasp. Encourage children to keep a running tab of all the words they are able to recognize by sight.

Journal Entries

Have children write new sight words they learn in their journal each day.

Scrabble Letters

Give the children scrabble letters or magnetic letters to make words.

Sentence Makers

Provide sight words on index cards or have children use their own collection of sight words to make sentences.

Predictable Sentences

Make up predictable sentences out of sight words. Take a word away. Who can choose the right word to go back in the blank space?

String a Word

Write letters on large string beads and encourage children to string a word.

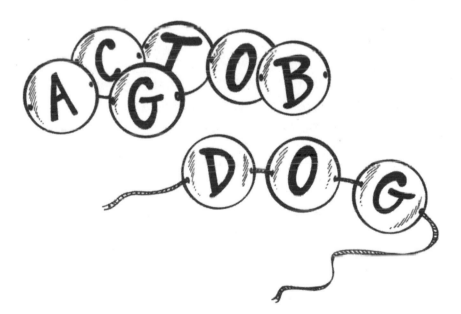

Alphabet Words

Have children match their word bank words to the letters of the alphabet they begin with. Talk about the sound of the beginning letter. This activity helps children begin to bridge between sight words and words that they will sound out.

Brain Connections

● Sight words enable the reader to use rote memory to unlock text. Rote recognition of words provides quick recall and, at the beginning stages of reading, provides the reader with a sense of accomplishment that, in turn, supports her struggle to discriminate the sounds of unfamiliar words.

Developing Phonological Awareness

Reading requires the use of many processes, including word configuration, context clue identification, sight word recognition, language pattern understanding, and phonetic analysis. Phonics is only one tool used for reading, but it is an important tool. Not every child will be ready to learn sound/symbol relationships at the same time. Before moving into the study of sound/symbol relationships, make certain children show signs of interest. The process of decoding is difficult enough when you want to tackle it. It is next to impossible when you aren't interested.

By the time you are ready to formally introduce phonemes (what letters stand for), children will already have had many opportunities to think about the sounds of a spoken word. Now is the time when all that practice with rhyming words and whole/part relationships, and all the other readiness activities will pay off. The following pages contain songs, poems, fingerplays, tongue twisters, stories, and activities for every letter of the alphabet. Take it slowly. Give children time to internalize the concepts, celebrate along the way, and enjoy this phase of the journey.

Phonological Awareness Activities

Songs

(Long A)

I'm an Acorn

I'm an acorn, small and round,
Lying on the cold, cold ground.
Everyone walks over me,
That is why I'm cracked you see.
I'm a nut (click, click).
In a rut (click, click).
I'm a nut (click, click).
In a rut (click, click).

Apples and Bananas

I like to eat eat eat apples
 and bananas.
I like to eat eat eat apples
 and bananas.

I like to ate ate ate aypuls and
 baynaynays.
I like to ate ate ate aypuls and
 baynaynays.

I like to eet eet eet eeples and
 beeneenees.
I like to eet eet eet eeples and
 beeneenees.

I like to ite ite ite ipples and bininis.
I like to ite ite ite ipples and bininis.

I like to ote ote ote opples and bononos.
I like to ote ote ote opples and bononos.

I like to ute ute ute upples and bununus.
I like to ute ute ute upples and bununus.

(Short A)

Annie May

Annie May, where are you going?
Up the stairs to take a bath.
Annie May, with legs like toothpicks,
And a neck like a giraffe.
Annie May stepped in the bathtub.
Annie May pulled out the plug.
Oh my goodness!
Oh my soul!
There goes Annie May down that hole.
Annie May?
Annie May?
Gurgle, gurgle, glug.

(See page 376 in the Appendix for an Annie May puzzle.)

Animal Fair

I went to the animal fair.
The birds and the bees were there.
The big baboon by the light of the moon
Was combing his auburn hair.
You should have seen the monk.
He sat on the elephant's trunk.
The elephant sneezed and fell to his knees,
And what became of the monk, the monk?
What became of the monk?

Poems

(Long A)

April Fool!

Little bears have three feet,
Little birds have four.
Little cats have two feet,
And boys and girls have more.

Do you believe my story?
Do you think it's wrong?
I tell it only once a year,
When April comes along!

Little Acorn (Pam Schiller)
Little acorn on the ground,
If you are lucky and you're not found,
If squirrel and children let you be,
Someday you'll grow to be a tree.

Children will play in your leafy shade.
Squirrels will hide in nests they've made.
Oh, so happy we will be,
We let you grow into a tree!

(Short A)

Johnny Appleseed
Oh, the earth is good to me,
And so I thank the earth,
For giving me the things I need—
The sun, the rain, and the apple seed.
The earth is good to me.

Antonio (Laura E. Richards)
Antonio, Antonio,
Was tired of living alonio.
He though he would woo
Miss Lissamy Lou,
Miss Lissamy Lucy Molonio.

Antonio, Antonio,
Rode off on his polo-ponio.
He found the fair maid
In a bowery shade,
A-sitting and knitting alonio.

Antionio, Antonio
Said, "If you will be my ownio,
I'll love you true,
And I'll buy for you,
An icery creamery conio!"

"Oh, nonio, Antonio!
You're far too bleak and bonio!
And all that I wish,
You singular fish,
Is that you will quickly begonio."

Antonio, Antonio,
He uttered a dismal moanio.
Then ran off and hid
(Or I'm told that he did)
In the Antarctical Zonio.

Tongue Twisters/Alliterative Sentences and Phrases

My dame hath a lame tame crane,
My dame hath a crane that is lame.

Say the sentences or phrase below three times quickly if you can.
*Amy aimed aimlessly.
*Aunt Annie answered Andy.

Fingerplays/Action Rhymes

(Long A)

April
Two little clouds one April day (*hold both hands in fists*)
Went sailing across the sky. (*move fist from left to right*)
They went so fast that they bumped their heads (*bump fists together*)
And both began to cry. (*point to eyes*)

The big round sun came out and said, (*make circle with arms*)
"Oh, never mind, my dears.
I'll send all my sunbeams down (*wiggle fingers downward like rain*)
To dry your fallen tears."

An Airplane
If I had an airplane, (*use hand as an airplane*)
Zum, zum, zum.
I'd fly to Mexico. (*fly hand through the air*)
Wave my hand and off I'd go. (*wave*)
If I had an airplane, (*use hand as an airplane*)
Zum, zum, zum.

(Short A)

Little Red Apple

A little red apple grew high in a tree.
I looked up at it.
It looked down at me.
Come down, please, I called—
And the little red apple fell right on my head.

My Apple

Look at my apple, it is nice and round. (*cup hands*)
It fell from a tree, down to the ground. (*move fingers in a downward motion*)
Come, let me share my apple, please do! (*beckoning motion*)
My mother can cut it half in two— (*slicing motion*)
One half for me and one half for you. (*hold out two hands, sharing halves*)

Little Arabella Miller

Little Arabella Miller
Had a fuzzy caterpillar. (*tickle palm with two fingers*)
First it crawled up on her mother, (*walk fingers up left arm*)
Then upon her baby brother. (*walk fingers up right arm*)
They said, "Arabella Miller! (*walk fingers up over head*)
Put away your caterpillar!" (*hide hands behind back*)

Little Arabella Miller (*repeat action to last line*)
Had a fuzzy caterpillar.
First it crawled upon her brother,
Then upon her dear grandmother.
Gran said, "Arabella Miller, (*give fingers a kiss*)
How I love your caterpillar."

Story: A Special Surprise (Chalk and Prop Story)

Directions: You will need chalk and a chalkboard or a pen and a flip chart, a bag of apples, and a knife.

A Special Surprise

Once there was a little old lady, named Annie, who lived in the mountains in a little house right here. (Draw the stem and the top right part of the apple.) [illustration] One day Annie decided to go down the mountain to town, so she left her house and started down the road like this. (Draw one half of the left side of an apple.)

On the way she met Abraham, and he asked, "Where are you going on such a fine day?" "I'm going down to town," replied Annie. "What are you going to get?" asked Abraham. "You'll just have to wait and see," said Annie.

On she walked (draw more of the left side of the apple) until she met Ashley and the other boys and girls. They all asked her, "Where are you going on such a fine day?" "I'm going down to town," she replied. "What are you going to get?" they asked. "You'll just have to wait and see," Annie told them.

Annie finally reached town (continue drawing the left side of the apple; stop at the center of the bottom of the apple). She went in the store and she came out with a big bag. (Hold up the paper bag.)

She started back up the mountain like this. (Begin drawing the right side of apple from the bottom to the midpoint.) All the boys and girls came running up to her. "What did you get? What's in your bag?" they all begged. "I've got some stars," Annie answered. "Walk home with me, and I'll give you each one."

So the little old lady and all the boys and girls continued up the mountain like this. (Complete the drawing of the apple.) They finally reached Annie's house. Annie sat down and opened her bag. She pulled out an apple. (Take an apple from the bag.)

"But where are the stars?" asked the children.

Then Annie smiled and took out her knife. She cut the apple in half, and showed the children a beautiful star inside the apple. (Cut an apple in half horizontally and show the children the star.) Then she cut all the apples in half and gave all the children a star of their very own.

Small Group Enrichment

1. A Special Surprise
Give the children apples to cut open. Can they find the star? (Supervise closely.)

2. Acorn Art (long A)
Invite children to count acorns into numbered tubs. If real acorns are unavailable, draw some acorns.

3. April Showers (long A)
Let children draw pictures of April showers. Provide drawing paper and white crayons. Encourage the children to make raindrops on the paper. Provide blue watercolor paint to wash over their raindrops. Because April showers often bring May flowers, the children may want to add some construction paper flowers to their drawing.

4. Aces Concentration (long A)
Use two decks of cards. Remove the aces. Lay the aces from both decks face down. Invite the children to play concentration.

5. Aviators (long A)
Provide props and let children roleplay being an aviator.

6. Aiming (long A)
Provide beanbags and a service bell. Challenge children to stand several feet away from the service bell, take aim, and fire the beanbag to ring the bell.

7. Apricot Jam (long or short A, depending on where you live)
Provide apricot jam and crackers for snack.

8. Annie Mae Assembly (short A)
Give children the Annie Mae Puzzle Doll (Appendix page 376) and have them assemble her.

9. Applesauce (short A)

Peel one apple for every three children. Grate the apples. Season to taste with cinnamon and sugar. Serve and enjoy!

10. Active Ants (short A)

Make an ant farm. Dig up an ant bed. Be sure to get the queen. Place the contents in a large glass jar. Punch holes in the top. Feed your ants grains of sugar and pieces of fruit or cookies. Watch them tunnel and burrow. Please return the ants to nature after a few days of observation.

GRATER

APPLES

11. Ants on an Apple (short A)

Give the children apple wedges. Invite them to spread peanut butter on the apple and place raisins on top to represent ants.

12. Acrobats (short A)

Teach the children a few acrobatic tricks such as a front roll over, a cartwheel, and a headstand.

13. Actors and Actresses (short A)

Help the children put on a play. "The Three Billy Goats Gruff" works well. Be sure children know they are actors and actresses.

Word List

Long A	Short A
a	A
able	accent
ace	acrobats
acorn	act
age	actor
agent	actress
aim	alligator
amen	ambulance
angel	ant
apricot	antelope
aviator	apple
	as
	asteroid
	astronaut
	aunt

Book List

A Letter to Amy by Ezra Jack Keats

Abiyoyo by Pete Seeger

Abuela by Arthur Dorros

Alexander and the Terrible, Horrible, No Good, Very Bad Day by Judith Viorst

Alexander Who Used to Be Rich Last Sunday by Judith Viorst

Amos & Boris by William Steig

Andy and the Lion by Juan Daugherty

Animals Should Definitely Not Wear Clothing by Judi Barrett

Aster Aardvark's Alphabet Adventures by Steven Kellogg

ACQUIRING READING SKILLS

Songs

Baby Bumblebee

I caught myself a baby bumblebee.
Won't my mommy be so proud of me?
I caught myself a baby bumblebee.
Ouch! It stung me.
I'm talking to my baby bumblebee.
Won't my mommy be so proud of me?
I'm talking to my baby bumblebee.
"Oh," he said "I'm sorry."
I'm letting go my baby bumblebee.
Won't my mommy be so proud of me?
I'm letting go my baby bumblebee.
Look he's happy to be free!

John Brown's Baby (Tune: Battle Hymn of the Republic)

John Brown's baby (*rock baby*) had a cold (*place finger beneath nose as if sneezing*) upon his chest (*slap chest*).
John Brown's baby (*rock baby*) had a cold (*place finger under nose*) upon his chest (*slap chest*).
John Brown's baby (*rock baby*) had a cold (*place finger under nose*) upon his chest (*slap chest*).
And they rubbed (*rub chest*) it with camphorated oil (*hold nose and make a face*).

Repeat the song, omitting the word *baby* and do motions only. Repeat again and omit *baby* and *cold*. Repeat again, omitting *baby, cold,* and *chest*. Continue repeating, omitting *rubbed* and finally *camphorated oil*.

Billy Boy

Oh where have you been, Billy Boy, Billy Boy?
Oh where have you been, charming Billy?
"I have gone to seek a wife, she's the joy of my life.
She's a young thing and cannot leave her mother."
Are her eyes blue and bright, Billy Boy, Billy Boy?
Are her eyes blue and bright, charming Billy?
"Yes, her eyes are blue and bright, but they're also minus sight.
She's a young thing and cannot leave her mother."

Bingo

There was a farmer had a dog,
And Bingo was his name-o.
B-I-N-G-O,
B-I-N-G-O,
B-I-N-G-O,
And Bingo was his name-o.

Repeat the song, clapping for the first letter (B). Continue repeating and inserting a clap for the next letter until all letters have been replaced with claps. Try singing this song with children's names.

B-B-B-Bubbles (Pam Schiller) (Tune: K-K-K-Katie)

B-B-B-Bubbles, beautiful bubbles
You're the only b-b-b-bubbles we adore.
B-B-B-Bubbles, beautiful bubbles
We love you more and more
And more and more and more.
B-B-B-Bubbles, beautiful bubbles
You're the only b-b-b-bubbles we adore.

Poems

My Big Balloon

I can make a big balloon,
Watch me while I blow.
Small at first, then bigger,
Watch it grow and grow.

Do you think it's big enough?
Maybe I should stop.
For if I blow much longer,
My balloon will surely pop!

Bubble Gum (Tiffany Markle)
Bubble gum, bubble gum, chew and blow.
Bubble gum, bubble gum, scrape your toe.
Bubble gum, bubble gum, tastes so sweet.
Get the bubble gum off your feet.

Little Boy Blue

Little Boy Blue come blow your horn.
The sheep are in the meadow, the cow's in the corn.
But where is the boy who looks after the sheep?
He's under a haystack, fast asleep.

Tongue Twisters/Alliterative Sentences and Phrases

Betty Botter's Butter
Betty Botter had some butter,
"But," she said, "this butter's bitter.
If I bake this bitter butter,
It would make my batter bitter.
But a bit of better butter—
That would make by batter better."

So she bought a bit of butter,
Better than her bitter butter.
And she baked it in her batter,
And the batter was not bitter.
So 'twas better Betty Botter
Bought a bit of better butter.

(You can shorten this by separating almost any two lines. This will make it easier for the children to remember.)

Say these sentences and phrases three times quickly.

- A box of biscuits, a batch of mixed biscuits.
- Betty better butter Brad's bread.
- Brad's big black brush broke.
- The blue bluebird blinks.
- Betty and Bob brought back blue balloons from the big bazaar.

Fingerplays/Action Rhymes

Here Is the Beehive

Here is the beehive, (*make a fist*)
But where are all the bees?
Hidden inside where no one can see.
Soon they'll come creeping out of their hive…
One, two, three, four, five. Buzz-z-z (*pop out fingers one by one and buzz them around*).

Five Little Babies

One little baby (*hold up one finger*)
Rocking in a tree. (*rocking motion with arms*)
Two little babies (*hold up two fingers*)
Splashing in the sea. (*make splashing motion*)
Three little babies (*hold up three fingers*)
Crawling on the floor. (*crawling motion with hands and arms*)
Four little babies (*hold up four fingers*)
Banging on the door. (*pounding motion with fist*)
Five little babies (*hold up five fingers*)
Playing hide and seek. (*cover eyes and then peek*)
Keep your eyes closed tight, now,
Until I say…PEEK!

Five Little Bells

Five little bells hanging in a row. (*hold up five fingers*)
The first bell said, "Ring me slow." (*wiggle thumb*)
The second bell said, "Ring me fast." (*wiggle index finger*)
The third bell said, "Ring me last." (*wiggle middle finger*)
The fourth bell said, "I won't ring." (*wiggle ring finger*)
The fifth bell said, "I'd rather sing." (*wiggle little finger*)

Bouncing Ball

I'm bouncing, bouncing everywhere. (*stand up and bounce*)
I bounce and bounce into the air.
I'm bouncing, bouncing like a ball.
I bounce and bounce until I fall. (*fall on floor*)

A Little Ball

A little ball, (*make a circle with your fingers*)
A bigger ball, (*make a circle with you hands*)
A great big ball I see. (*make a circle with your arms*)

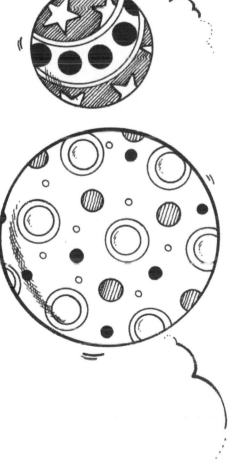

Are you ready to count them?
One, (make a circle with your fingers)
Two, (make a circle with you hands)
Three. (make a circle with your arms)

We're Going on a Bear Hunt (Action Story)
We're going on a bear hunt.
Want to come along? Well, come on then.
Let's go! (*stand and walk in place unless another motion is designated*)

Look! There's a river.
Can't go over it:
Can't go under it.
Can't go around it.
We'll have to go through it. (*pretend to swim; resume walking*)

Look! There's a tree.
Can't go under it.
Can't go through it.
We'll have to go over it. (*pretend to climb up and over the tree; resume walking*)

Look! There's a wheat field.
Can't go over it.
Can't go under it.
Can't go around it.
We'll have to go through it. (*make swishing sound and brush hands against each other; resume walking*)

Look! There's a cave.
Want to go inside?
Ooh, it's dark in here. (*look around, squinting*)
I see two eyes.
Wonder what it is. (*reach hands to touch*)
It's soft and furry.
It's big.
It's a bear! (*retrace steps, running in place through wheat field, over tree, across river and stop*)
Home safe! Whew!

Story: The Three Bears Rap (Musical Story)

Directions: Use a black sharpie pen to trace the patterns on Appendix pages 308-310 onto Pelon. Color them and cut them out. Use them with the flannel board to present the story.

The Three Bears Rap (see Appendix pages 308-310 for patterns)
Chh, chh-chh, chh, chh-chh, chh, chh-chh, chh
Out in the forest in a wee little cottage lived the three bears,
Chh, chh-chh, chh, chh-chh, chh, chh-chh,chh
One was the Mama bear and one was the Papa bear,
And one was the Wee bear.
Chh, chh-chh, chh, chh-chh, chh, chh-chh, chh
Out of the forest came a walkin', stalkin' pretty little Goldilocks,
And upon the door she was a knockin'. (*cluck, cluck, cluck*)
But, no one was there, uh-uh, no one was there.
So she walked right in had herself a bowl.
She didn't care, uh-uh, she didn't care.
Home, home, home came the three bears.
"Someone's been eatin' my porridge," said the Mama bear.
"Someone's been eatin' my porridge," said the Papa bear.
"Baa-baa baree bear," said the little Wee bear.
"Someone's broken my chair." ...Crash!
Just then Goldilocks woke up and broke up the party,
And she beat it out of there.
"Good-bye, good-bye, good-bye," said the Mama bear.
"Good-bye, good-bye, good-bye," said the Papa bear.
"Baa-baa baree bear," said the little Wee bear,
That's the story of the three little bears—Yeah!

Small Group Enrichment

1. The Three Bears
Do the Goldilocks Walk-On Nursery Rhyme (see page 69).

2. Bubble Blowing
Provide bubble soap mix (Appendix page 412) Encourage children to blow bubbles.

3. Back-to-Back Lifts
Show the children how to sit on the floor back to back and lean against each other to stand up.

ACQUIRING READING SKILLS

4. Blue Buttons in a Blue Bowl

Provide blue buttons for the children to toss or shoot into a blue bowl.

5. Ball in a Box

Challenge children to bounce a ball into a box.

6. Baby Bath Time

Provide a baby doll, a tub, and bathing and dressing supplies. Encourage children to bathe the baby.

7. Bowling

Use some empty potato chip cans to create bowling pins. Use a Nerf ball to knock them down.

8. Balance on the Balance Beam

Walk the balance beam with a blue beanbag on your head.

9. Bake Biscuits

Bake some biscuits in a toaster oven. Serve with blueberry jelly.

10. Batty Bugs

Create some batty bugs by using crates from egg cartons as a base and adding pipe cleaner legs. Paint with tempera and add some bug eyes.

FLAT BISCUIT (THAT'S BEEN ROLLED OUT)

CINNAMON and SUGAR

RAISINS

BABY BEDROLL

ROLL UP

11. Baby Bedrolls

Make Baby Bedrolls for a snack.
Ingredients
    Canned biscuits (one for each child)
    Raisins
    Cinnamon and sugar mixed together
Roll biscuit to make flat. Place a few raisins on each biscuit. Sprinkle with cinnamon and sugar mixture. Bake at 400° until brown. Cool and enjoy.

12. Everybody's Birthday

Have a birthday party and celebrate everyone's birthday.

13. Beautiful Blue Butterfly Blotto

Give children a piece of drawing paper. Show them how to fold the paper in half, crease it, and then unfold it. Place two tablespoons of liquid temper paint (use two shades of blue) on one side of the paper. Fold paper on original crease, press, and rub. Open to reveal a beautiful blue butterfly.

14. Bingo
Play a game of Bingo. Use "B" words instead of numbers.

15. Build a Big Building
Provide blocks and challenge the children to build a big building.

16. Bead in a Bucket
Play drop the bead in the bucket. Place felt or foam in the bottom of the bucket to reduce the noise.

17. Beginning Sound "B" Concentration
Use the patterns on the Appendix page 388 to make a concentration game of objects that begin with "B."

Word List

bad	best	bug
bag	big	bulk
bake	bike	bull
ball	bird	bum
bar	bite	bump
barn	boar	bunch
bath	boat	burn
beach	boil	bus
bean	bone	buzz
bed	boss	by
bee	bow	
beef	bowl	
beet	box	
bell	boy	

Book List

Bedtime for Frances by Russell Hoban

Ben's Trumpet by Rachel Isadora

Berenstain's B Book by Stan and Jan Berenstain

The Biggest Bear by Lynd Ward

Blueberries for Sal by Robert McCloskey

Bread and Jam for Frances by Russell Hoban

Bread Bread Bread by Ann Morris

Brown Bear, Brown Bear, What Do You See? by Bill Martin, Jr.

We're Going on a Bear Hunt by Michael Rosen

Songs

Color Song (Tune: I've Been Working on the Railroad)
Red is the color for an apple to eat.
Red is the color of cherries, too.
Red is the color for strawberries.
I like red, don't you?

Blue is the color for the big blue sky.
Blue is the color for baby things, too.
Blue is the color of my sister's eyes.
I like blue, don't you?

Yellow is the color for the great big sun.
Yellow is the color for lemonade, too.
Yellow is the color of a baby chick,
I like yellow, don't you?

Green is the color for the leaves on the trees.
Green is the color for green peas, too.
Green is the color of a watermelon.
I like green, don't you?

Orange is the color for oranges.
Orange is the color for carrots, too.
Orange is the color of a jack-o-lantern.
I like orange, don't you?

Purple is the color for a bunch of grapes.
Purple is the color for grape juice, too.
Purple is the color for a violet.
I like purple, don't you?

Crocodile Song
She sailed away on a sunny summer day on the back of a crocodile.
"You see," said she, "he's as tame as tame can be; I'll ride him down
 the Nile."
The croc winked his eye as she bade them all good-bye, wearing a
 happy smile.
At the end of the ride the lady was inside and the smile was on the
 crocodile!

Fuzzy Caterpillar

A fuzzy caterpillar went out for a walk.
His back went up and down.
He crawled and he crawled, 'til he crawled all over town.
He wasn't disappointed not a bit to be a worm.
Not a tear was in his eye.
Because he knew that he would become
A very, very, pretty butterfly.

Little Canoe

Just a boy and a girl in a little canoe. (*make canoe with hand*)
With the moon shining all around. (*make a circular motion with hand*)
They rowed those paddles so (*row*)
You couldn't even hear a sound. (*hand to ear*)
And they talked and they talked
'til the moon grew dim. (*touch fingers to thumb-yacking*)
He said, "You better kiss me
Or get out and swim." (*thumb over shoulder like "get out"*)
So what you gonna do in a little canoe (*hands out and open*)
With the moon shining all around, (*circular motion*)
Boats floating all around, (*make boat with hands, move like floating*)
Girls swimming all around. (*swimming motion.*)

Clean Up

Clean up! Clean up!
Everybody everywhere.
Clean up! Clean up!
Everybody do your share!

Clean up! Clean up!
Everybody everywhere.
Clean up! Clean up!
Everybody do your share!

Poems

Counting Rhyme

One, two, three, four, five,
I caught a fish alive.
Six, seven, eight, nine, ten,
I let it go again

Cows Chow (Tiffany Markle)
Carla's cow Carley
Can surely ear barley.
But Calvin's cow Chas
Prefers to eat grass.

Candy Caramels (Tiffany Markle)
Candy caramels oh so gooey.
Candy caramels oh so chewy.
Candy caramels oh so yummy.
Candy caramels in my tummy.

Crocodile

If you should meet a crocodile
Don't take a stick and poke him;
Ignore the welcome of his smile,
Be careful not to stroke him,
For as he sleeps upon the Nile
He gets thinner and thinner
And whene'er you meet a crocodile,
He's looking for his dinner.

Caterpillar (Christina Rossetti)
Brown and furry
Caterpillar in a hurry,
Take your walk
To the shady leaf, or stalk,
Or what not,
Which may be the chosen spot
No toad spy you,
Hovering bird of prey pass by you;
Spin and die,
To live again a butterfly.

The Tickle Rhyme
"Who's that tickling my back?" said the wall.
"Me," said a small caterpillar. "I'm learning to crawl."

Tongue Twisters/Alliterative Sentences and Phrases

Say the sentences or phrases below three times quickly.

- Cowardly cows cowered.
- Cassie carefully cracked candy canes.

Fingerplays/Action Rhymes

We Can

We can jump, jump, jump. (*suit actions to words*)
We can hop, hop, hop.
We can clap, clap, clap.
We can stop, stop, stop.

We can nod our heads for yes.
We can shake our heads for no.
We can bend our knees a tiny bit,
And sit down slow.

Ten Little Candles

Ten little candles standing on a cake. (*hold up the number of fingers that represent the number of candles mentioned*)
"Whh! Whh!" Now there are eight. (*blow twice with each verse and bend down two fingers each time*)

Eight little candles in candle sticks.
"Whh! Whh!" Now there are six.

Six little candles, not one more.
"Whh! Whh!" Now there are four.
Four little candles, yellow and blue.
"Whh! Whh!" Now there are two.

Two little candles, one plus one.
"Whh! Whh!" Now there are none.

ACQUIRING READING SKILLS

Story: Smart Cookie's Clever Idea (Flannel Board Story)

Directions: Use a black sharpie pen to trace the patterns on Appendix pages 311-312 onto Pelon. Color them with crayons and cut them out. Use them with the flannel board to present the story.

Smart Cookie's Clever Idea (Pam Schiller)
Smart Cookie was helping her mother bake cookies one day. It was her job to take the cookies off the cookie sheet when they came out of the oven and arrange them on the cookie platter. She really liked her job because every once in a while a cookie would break and that would make a good excuse for Smart Cookie to eat it. After all, broken cookies don't look pretty on the cookie platter.

Smart Cookie was putting all the Ginger Snaps on one platter and the Sugar Cookies on another, just like her mother had told her. She was really proud of the nice even rows she was making. She was paying close attention to her work. She wanted her mother to be proud of her.

Suddenly Smart Cookie thought about her math lesson at school that morning. It was about making patterns. Maybe with that idea, she could make her platters look even better.

Smart Cookie rearranged the cookies. She made a row of Sugar Cookie, Ginger Snap, Sugar Cookie, Ginger Snap, and so on across the platter. This was so much more interesting. She couldn't wait to show her mother.

Smart Cookie finished arranging the cookies on the platter, and then she took it to show her mother. Her mother grinned from ear to ear. She was so proud. The tray looked beautiful. She hugged Smart Cookie and said, "You are one Smart Cookie!"

Small Group Enrichment

1. Smart Cookie's Clever Idea
Make some felt cookies in different shapes. Invite children to make cookie patterns on the felt board.

2. Make No-Bake Cookies
Ingredients
   ½ cup (80 g) raisins
   ½ cup (75 g) chopped dates

2 tablespoons (60 g) of honey
3 graham crackers

Pour raisins, dates, and honey into mixing bowl. Put the graham cracker in a ziplock sandwich bag and crush them with a rolling pin. Add to honey and fruit mixture. Mix until the ingredients are able to form balls. Roll into balls. Let dry and serve.

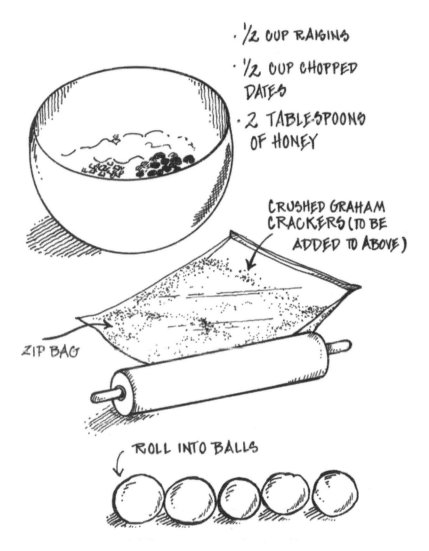

· ½ CUP RAISINS

· ½ CUP CHOPPED DATES

· 2 TABLESPOONS OF HONEY

CRUSHED GRAHAM CRACKERS (TO BE ADDED TO ABOVE)

ZIP BAG

ROLL INTO BALLS

3. Curly Curls

Give the children ribbon and show them how to curl it with a ruler or with a pair of children's scissors. Challenge them to find a way to use their curly curls—perhaps on a puppet's head or as a pig's tail.

ACQUIRING READING SKILLS

4. Counting Candles

Provide a felt cake and candles to use on the flannel board. Encourage children to count candles as they put them on the cake.

5. Copycats

Play a game of Copycats. Divide the children into pairs and invite them to stand facing their partners. Invite one of each pair to perform a series of movements for the other to mimic. Try the game again with partners back to back. Have one of the pair create a movement then describe it to the partner. Is the game more difficult now?

6. Cookie Cutter Creations

Provide cookie cutters and play dough to make some fancy cookies. Add confetti, beads, and buttons to decorate the cookies.

7. Crazy Car

Provide a tray of tempera paint, butcher paper, and some small cars. Invite children to run the cars through the paint and then across the paper to make crazy tracks.

8. Combs

Make Sand Combs by cutting interesting patterns such as "Vs" and scallops in one side of 4" X 6" pieces of cardboard. Use the combs like rakes in the sand.

9. Color Combinations

Provide several different colors of tempera paints and let the children experiment with different combinations to make new colors.

10. Comic Conversation

Use Wite-Out or Liquid Paper to cover the dialogue in comic strips. Challenge children to dictate new dialogue.

11. Caves

Provide dark blankets and encourage the children to drape them over tables and chairs to build caves.

12. Creep and Crawl

Use masking tape to make a crooked line across the floor. Have children crawl the length of the line.

13. Classify Colored Candy

Provide several different colors of wrapped hard candy. Let the children classify by color.

14. Beginning Sound "C" Word Concentration

Use the patterns on Appendix page 389 to make a Concentration Game of objects that begin with "C."

Word List

cab	cash	cool
cage	cat	cord
call	cave	corn
came	coal	cost
camp	cave	cot
can	coast	cough
cane	coat	count
cap	coin	cow
cape	cold	cub
car	colt	curl
card	comb	cut
cart	come	
case	cone	

Book List

Caps for Sale by Esphyr Slobodkina

The Carrot Seed by Ruth Krauss

A Chair for My Mother by Vera B. Williams

Chicka Chicka Boom Boom by Bill Martin, Jr., and John Archambault

Cloudy With a Chance of Meatballs by Judi Barrett

Color by Ruth Heller

Corduroy by Don Freeman

Cornelius by Leo Lionni

Curious George by H.A. Rey

The Cut-Ups Cut Loose by James Marshall

ACQUIRING READING SKILLS

Songs

Doodlely-Do

Please sing to me, that sweet melody called the
Doodlely-Do, Doodlely-Do.
I like the rest, but the part I like best goes
Doodlely-Do, Doodlely-Do.

It's the simplest thing there isn't much to it.
All you gotta do is Doodlely-Do it.
I like it so, wherever I go,
It's the Doodlely-Doodlely-Do.

Come on and Waddlely-Atcha, Waddlely-Atcha,
Waddlely-O, Waddlely-O,
Waddlely-Atcha, Waddlely-Atcha,
Waddlely-O, Waddlely-O.

It's the simplest thing there isn't much to it.
All you gotta do is Doodlely-Do it.
I like it so, wherever I go,
It's the Doodlely-Doodlely-Do.
Toot, Toot!

Movements for each stanza: Clap thighs twice. Clap hands twice. Cross arms in front of you four times (left on top twice, then right on top twice). Touch nose then right shoulder with left hand. Touch nose then left shoulder with right hand. Move fingers in "talking" motion just above shoulders, then above head. Repeat throughout the song.

Daisy (Bicycle Built for Two)

Daisy, Daisy, give me your answer true.
I'm half crazy all for the love of you.
It won't be a stylish marriage;
I can't afford a carriage.
But you'll look sweet
Upon the seat
Of a bicycle built for two.

Farmer in the Dell

The farmer in the dell,
The farmer in the dell,
Heigh-ho the derry-o,

The farmer in the dell.
The farmer takes a wife…
The wife takes a child…
The child takes a nurse…
The nurse takes a cat…
The cat takes a mouse…
The mouse takes the cheese…
The cheese stands alone…

Substitute characters whose names begin with "D" such as doctor, driver, doll, duck, and so forth.

Five Little Ducks

Five little ducks went out one day,
Over the hills and far away.
Papa duck called with a "Quack, quack, quack."
Four little ducks came swimming back.

Repeat, losing one more duck each time until you are left with one duck.
Have momma duck call and end with "five little ducks came swimming back."

Poems

Deedle, Deedle, Dumpling

Deedle, deedle, dumpling, my son John
Went to bed with his breeches on.
One shoe off and one shoe on,
Deedle, deedle, dumpling, my son John.

Mr. Dragon

Mr. Dragon's tail's a waggin'
All he says is "Boo!"
Mr. Dragon, don't go braggin'
I'm not scared of you!

The Dinosaur (Carl S. Junge)

A beast of yore,
Doesn't live here
Any more.

Downy Duck

One day I saw a downy duck
With feathers on his back.
I said, "Good morning, downy duck."
And he said "Quack, quack, quack."

Dame Duck's Lecture

Close by the margin of the brook,
The old duck made her nest,
Of straw and leaves and withered grass,
And down from her own breast.

And there she sat for four long weeks,
Through rainy days and fine.
Until the ducklings all came out,
Four, five, six, seven, eight, nine.

One peeped out from beneath her wing,
One scrambled on her back.
"That's very rude," said old Dame Duck,
"Get off—quack, quack, quack."

"Too close," said Dame Duck,
Shoving out the eggshells with her bill.
Besides, it never suits young ducks
To keep them sitting still.

So, rising form her nest, she said,
"Now, children, look at me.
A well-bred duck should waddle
From side to side—d'ye see?"

"Yes," said the little ones, and then
She went on to explain:
"A well-bred duck turns in its toes,
And do try again."

"Yes," said the ducklings, waddling on.
"That's better," said the mother,
"But well-bred ducks walk in a row
Straight, one behind the other."

"Yes," said the little ducks again
All waddling in a row.
"Now to the pond," said old Dame Duck.
Splash, splash, and in they go.

What Flower Is It?

Daffy-down-dilly
Has come to town,
In a yellow petticoat
And a green gown.

What flower is it?
Can you guess?
If you said, "Daffodil,"
The answer is yes!

Tongue Twisters/Alliterative Sentences and Phrases

Doctor

If one doctor doctors another doctor,
does the doctor who doctors the doctor
doctor the doctor the way
the doctor he is doctoring doctors?
Or does he doctor the doctor
the way the doctor who doctors doctors doctors?

Say the sentence below three times quickly if you can.

● Divers dive dangerously downward.

Fingerplays/Action Rhymes

My Doll

This is how my doll walks, (*walk around with stiff arms and legs*)
This is how it walks, you see?
This is how my doll talks, (*bend at waist*)
This is how it talks, you see?

Dance, Thumbkin, Dance

Dance, Thumbkin, dance: (*dance thumb around, moving and bending*)
Dance, ye merrymen, everyone. (*dance all fingers*)
For Thumbkin, he can dance alone,
Thumbkin he can dance alone.
Dance, Foreman, dance: (*dance index finger around, moving and bending*)
Dance, ye merrymen, everyone. (*dance all fingers*)
For Foreman, he can dance alone,
Foreman, he can dance alone.
Dance, Longman, dance: (*dance middle finger around, moving and bending*)
Dance, ye merrymen, everyone. (*dance all fingers*)
For Longman, he can dance alone,
Longman, he can dance alone.
Dance, Ringman, dance: (*dance ring finger around, moving and bending*)
Dance, ye merrymen, everyone. (*dance all fingers*)
For Ringman, he cannot dance alone,
Ringman, he cannot dance alone.
Dance, Littleman, dance: (*dance little finger around, moving and bending*)
Dance, ye merrymen, everyone. (*dance all fingers*)
For Littleman, he can dance alone,
Littleman, he can dance alone.

It's a Very Simple Dance to Do

Come on and do a dance with me.
It's just a little step or two.
I'll teach you how.
We'll start right now.

It's a very simple dance to do.
First you clap your hands, (*clap three times*)
Then stomp your feet. (*stomp three times*)

It's a very simple dance to do.
Wait I forgot to tell you.
There's another little step or two.
Turn around, (*turn around*)
And touch your toes. (*touch your toes*)
It's a very simple dance to do.

Clap your hands. (*clap three times*)
Stomp your feet. (*stomp three times*)
Turn around, (*turn around*)
And touch your toes. (*touch your toes*)
It's a very simple dance to do.

Wait I forgot to tell you.
There's another little step or two.
Pull your ears, (*pull your ears*)
And flap your arms. (*flap your arms*)
It's a very simple dance to do.

Clap your hands.
Stomp your feet.
Turn around,
And touch your toes.
Pull your ears,
And flap your arms.
It's a very simple dance to do.

Wait I forgot to tell you.
There's another step and then we're through.
Stretch up high. (*stretch up high*)
All fall down. (*fall down*)
It's a very simple dance to do.

Clap your hands.
Stomp your feet.
Turn around,
And touch your toes.
Pull your ears,
And flap your arms.
Now stretch up high.
All fall down.
It's a very simple dance to do.

(Repeat last chorus)

Story: The Duel (Listening Story)

Directions: This is a story for listening. It needs no pictures or props, just an imagination.

The Duel

The gingham dog and the calico cat
Side by side on the table sat.
Twas half-past twelve, and (what do you think!)
Nor one nor t'other had slept a wink!
The old Dutch clock and the Chinese plate,
Appeared to know as sure as fate,
There was going to be a terrible spat.
*(I wasn't there; I simply state
What was told to me by the Chinese plate!)*

The gingham dog went, "Bow-wow-wow!"
And the calico cat replied, "Mee-ow!"
The air was littered, an hour or so,
With bits of gingham and calico,
While the old Dutch clock in the chimney-place
Up with its hands before its face,
For it always dreaded a family row!
*(Now mind: I'm only telling you
What the old Dutch clock declares is true!)*

The Chinese plate looked very blue,
And wailed, "Oh dear! What shall we do?"
But the gingham dog and the calico cat
Wallowed this way and tumbled that,
Employing every tooth and claw
In the awfullest way you ever saw—
And, oh! How the gingham and calico flew!
*(Don't fancy I exaggerate—
I got my news from the Chinese plate!)*

Next morning, where the two had sat,
They found no trace of dog or cat.
And some folks think unto this day
That burglars stole the pair away!
But the truth about the cat and pup
Is this: They ate each other up!

Now what do you really think of that!
*(The old Dutch clock it told me so,
And that is how I came to know.)*

Small Group Enrichment

1. The Duel
Provide gingham and calico fabric or wallpaper samples. Provide a dog and cat pattern and encourage children to draw or trace the patterns, then cut out calico cats and gingham dogs. They may want to dictate a new ending to the story to go with their creations.

2. Donuts
Give each child a biscuit from a can of biscuits. Let them make a hole in the center of the biscuit using the lid from a pop bottle. Drop the donuts into a deep fryer set at 375°. Cook for two minutes. Remove from grease and cool. Let children sprinkle with powdered sugar or cinnamon and sugar. Cool; eat and enjoy.

3. Dime in a Dish
Provide several dimes and a dish to toss them into. Challenge children to stand back several feet and attempt to toss the dimes into the bowl.

4. Down, Down, Down
Make a ramp and provide cars to run down it.

5. Dirt Dump
Provide dump trucks for outdoor play. Encourage children to fill and empty the dump truck.

6. Dog and Bone

Use the Dog and Bone patterns (Appendix page 372) to make several sets of dogs and bones. Put numerals on the dog's collar and corresponding dots on the bones. Let children match the numerals to the dots.

7. Dots

Make up some dot patterns and give them to the children to connect.

8. Duck Dip

Place several rubber ducks in the water table. Give children a net (a fish net works well) and invite them to dip in to catch the ducks. Put a piece of tape with the letter "D" written on it on the bottom of one of the ducks. Who can catch the "D" duck?

9. Ding-Dong

Give children a service bell and a beanbag. Have them stand several feet away from the service bell and attempt to toss the beanbag on it to make it go ding-dong.

10. Dot and Dashes

Teach children how to write their names in Morse code.

11. Dish Designs

Give each child a paper plate and crayons. Challenge them to create a design for their dish.

12. Dippety Do Dots

Put Dippety Do or another hair gel in an empty, clear plastic half-liter soda bottle. Put some colored confetti dots in the bottle. Secure the lid with glue. Invite children to turn the bottle over and over to watch the dots move.

13. Dirt Doodles

Wet a pan of dirt. Provide a stick and invite children to create doodles in the dirt.

14. Beginning Sound "D" Concentration

Use the patterns on Appendix page 390 to make a concentration game with objects that begin with "D."

Word List

dab	dirt
damp	dish
dash	dive
date	do
dawn	dock
day	doe
deaf	dog
deal	doll
deck	dome
deep	done
deer	door
den	dose
dent	down
desk	doze
dew	duck
die	due
dig	dug
dike	dull
dim	dump
dime	dunk
dine	dusk
ding	dust
dip	dye

Book List

Dandelion by Don Freeman
The Day Jimmy's Boa Ate the Wash by Trinka Noble
Dear Zoo by Rod Cambell
Dinosaurs by Byron Barton
Doctor De Soto by William Steig
Five Little Ducks by Raffi
Make Way for Ducklings by Robert McCloskey

ACQUIRING READING SKILLS

E

Songs

(Long E)

Eensy Weensy Spider

The eensy weensy spider went up the waterspout. (*crawl fingers up arm*)

Down came the rain and washed the spider out. (*move hands across front of body*)

Out came the sun and dried up all the rain. (*Hold hands spread above head*)

The eensy weensy spider went up the spout again. (*crawl fingers up arm*)

Apples and Bananas

I like to eat eat eat apples and bananas.
I like to eat eat eat apples and bananas.

I like to ate ate ate aypuls and baynaynays.
I like to ate ate ate aypuls and baynaynays.

I like to eet eet eet eeples and beeneenees.
I like to eet eet eet eeples and beeneenees.

I like to ite ite ite ipples and bininis.
I like to ite ite ite ipples and
    bininis.

I like to ote ote ote opples
    and bononos.
I like to ote ote
    ote opples
    and bononos.

I like to ute ute ute
    upples and
    bununus.
I like to ute ute ute
    upples and
    bununus.

(Short E)

One Elephant

One elephant went out to play, (*one child walks in a circle with arm swinging in front like a trunk*)
Out on a spider's web one day.
He had such enormous fun,
He called for another elephant to come. (*Child points to a friend to join him. Sticks hand between legs to join hands with the second child. Repeat process.*)

Do Your Ears Hang Low?

Do your ears hang low? (*point to ears*)
Do they wobble to and fro? (*move hands side to side*)
Can you tie them in a knot? (*make tying motion*)
Can you tie them in a bow? (*pretend to tie a bow*)
Can you throw them over your shoulder (*toss hands over shoulder*)
Like a Continental soldier? (*salute*)
Do your ears hang low? (*point to ears*)

Poems

(Long E)

Eeny, Meeny, Miny, Mo

Eeny, meeny, miny, mo,
Catch an elephant by his toe.
If he hollers let him go,
Eeny, meeny, miny, mo.

(Short E)

Way Down South

Way down south where bananas grow,
A grasshopper stepped on an elephant's toe.
The elephant said, with tears in his eyes,
"Pick on somebody your own size."

The Elf and the Dormouse (Oliver Herford)

Under a toadstool
Crept a wee Elf,
Out of the rain
To shelter himself.

E

Under the toadstool
Sound asleep,
Sat a big Dormouse
All in a heap.

Trembled the wee Elf,
Frightened, and yet
Fearing to fly away
Lest he get wet.

To the next shelter—
Maybe a mile!
Sudden the wee Elf
Smiled a wee smile,

Tugged at the toadstool
Toppled in two.
Holding it over him
Gaily he flew.

Soon he was safe home
Dry as could be.
Soon woke the Dormouse—
"Good gracious me!

Where is my toadstool?"
Loud he lamented.
—And that's how umbrellas
First were invented.

Tongue Twisters/Alliterative Sentences and Phrases

Say the sentences and phrases below three times quickly if you can.

- Ebert eats Easter Eggs.
- Fred fed Ted bread and Ted fed Fred bread.

Fingerplays/Action Rhymes

(Long E)

Little Easter Rabbit

Little Easter Rabbit goes hip, hop, hip. (*hop hand*)
See how his ears go flip, flop, flip. (*hold hands by ears and flop them*)
See how his eyes go blink, blink, blink. (*blink eyes*)
See how his nose goes twink, twink, twink. (*wiggle nose*)
Pet his white coat, so soft and furry, (*stroke arm*)
Hip, hop, hip—he's off in a hurry. (*hop hand away*)

(Short E)

Five Little Elves

Said this little elf,
"I'm tired as can be."
Said this little elf,
"My eyes can hardly see."
Said this little elf,
"I'd like to go to bed."
Said this little elf,
"Come climb the stairs with me."
One, two, three, four, five, they tiptoed,
Just as quiet as quiet could be.

Good Day, Everybody

Good day, everybody, (*wave and nod at friends*)
Good day, everybody,
Good day, good day, good day!

Smile, everybody, (*smile at friends*)
Smile everybody,
Let's chase the blues away.

Shake hands, everybody, (*shake hands with friends*)
Shake hands, everybody,
How are you today?

Story: The Little Engine That Could (Puppet Story)

Directions: Check out the book *The Little Engine That Could* by Watty Piper from the library. Use the patterns on Appendix pages 313-314 to make puppets to accompany the story.

Small Group Enrichment

1. The Little Engine That Could
Encourage children to think of something that used to be difficult for them and that they kept trying and finally mastered. Sing "Eensy Weensy Spider." Compare the theme of the story with the theme of the song.

2. Easter Bonnets (long E)
Make paper plate hats and decorate them exquisitely.

3. Each is Equal (long E)
Assign helpers to pour juice and serve cookies for snack. Have them make sure that each serving is equal.

4. Easel Event (long E)
Try metallic or fluorescent colors at the easel today to make it an event.

5. Easy Eats (long E)
Provide a lunch or a snack that is all finger food.

6. Emergency (long E)
Talk to the children about emergencies. Teach them to dial 911.

7. Elastic Exercises (long or short E, depending on where you live)
Cut a 3' (1 m) length of 1" (2 cm) elastic for each child. Sew the ends together to make a circle. Invite children to stand on their elastic bands and stretch them over their heads. Have them form shapes with the elastic. Create other exercises for bending and stretching.

ACQUIRING READING SKILLS

8. Environmental Eggs (short E)

Make some natural (environmentally safe) dyes and dye some eggs. It doesn't have to be Easter. It will probably be more fun if it's not. Tea and coffee make great golden yellow colors. Blueberry juice makes purple. Cherry juice makes pink. The water you cook broccoli in makes a nice green color. Children can dye their eggs "eggzactly" like they want.

9. Egg Match (short E)

Put matching stickers on both halves of plastic eggs. Take the eggs apart and let the children put the pairs back together.

10. One Elephant (short E)

Invite children to sing "One Elephant" and play the accompanying game. One child begins as the first elephant. When she "calls for another elephant to come," she selects a friend to join in. The first child places one arm in front to represent a trunk and the other arm between the legs to grab the friend's hand.

11. Feed the Elephant (short E)

Paint two paper plates and an empty toilet paper tube gray. Cut one of the plates in half to make elephant ears. Glue the ears on the other paper plate. Glue the toilet paper tube in the middle of the plate to make a trunk. Provide peanuts in a shell and let children feed the elephant. Later the peanuts can be shelled and eaten for a snack.

Note: As with any food, be aware of food allergies. In addition, peanuts can be a choking hazard, especially with young children.

12. Echoes (short E)

Sing an echo song.

Word List

Long E	Short E
eagle	eggs
easel	elbow
Easter	elephant
easy	elf
eat	elves
ear	ember
eaves	end
eel	every
eject	

ACQUIRING READING SKILLS

Book List

A Chance for Esperanza by Pam Schiller and Alma Flor Ada

The Egg by Galimard Jeunesse and Pascale de Bourgoing

Eli by Bill Peet

Emma's Pet by David McPhail

The Enormous Crocodile by Roald Dahl

Exactly the Opposite by Tana Hoban

Green Eggs and Ham by Dr. Seuss

The Little Engine That Could by Watty Piper

ACQUIRING READING SKILLS

Songs

Fido

I have a dog.
His name is Fido.
He is nothing but a pup.
He can stand up on his hind legs
If you hold his front legs up.

Five Little Speckled Frogs (Five children sit in a row and the other children sit in a circle around them. All children act out the words to the song.)

Five Little Speckled Frogs, (*hold up five fingers*)
Sitting on a speckled log,
Eating some most delicious bug. (*pretend to eat bugs*)
Yum! Yum!
One jumped into the pool, (*one child from center jumps back into the circle*)
Where it was nice and cool. (*cross arms over chest and shiver*)
Now there are four little speckled frogs,
Burr-ump!

Repeat, counting down until there are no little speckled frogs.

Fiddle-I-Fee

I had a cat, and the cat pleased me.
Fed my cat under yonder tree,
Cat went fiddle-i-fee.

I had a hen, and the hen pleased me.
Fed my hen under yonder tree,
Hen went chimmey chuck, chimmey chuck,
Cat went fiddle-i-fee.

I had a dog, and the dog pleased me.
Fed my dog under yonder tree,
Dog went bow-wow, bow-wow,
Hen went chimmey chuck, chimmey chuck,
Cat went fiddle-I-fee.

Poems

Say Diddle, Diddle (Pam Schiller)
Say Diddle, Diddle,
I wish I could fiddle.
But I'm just too little
To play on the fiddle.

Make New Friends

Make new friends but keep the old,
One is silver and the other gold.

Tongue Twisters/Alliterative Sentences and Phrases

A Flea and a Fly

A flea and a fly flew up in a flue.
Said the flea, "Let us fly!"
Said the fly, "Let us flee!"
So they flew through a flaw in the flue.

Say the sentences and phrases below three times quickly if you can.
- Friendly Frank flips fine flapjacks.
- Freshly fried fresh flesh.
- Flee from fog to fight flu fast!
- Fat frogs flying past fast.

Fingerplays/Action Rhymes

The Chinese Fan

My ship sailed from China with a cargo of tea,
All laden with presents for you and for me.
They brought me a fan,
Just imagine my bliss,
When I fan myself daily, like this, like this,
Like this, like this.

Repeat the rhyme four times. Alter the way you fan yourself on the "like this" part of the rhyme as follows: first time fan four times with your right hand, second time fan four times with both hands, third time fan four times with both hands while sweeping your right foot up and over your left foot, fourth time fan four times with both hands while sweeping your left foot up and over your right foot, fifth time fan four times and alternate sweeping the right foot over the left and the left over the right.

Fee, Fie, Fo, Fum

Fee, fie, fo, fum,
See my finger, (*hold up pointer finger*)
See my thumb. (*hold up thumb*)

Fee, fie, fo, fum,
Finger's gone, (*bend down finger*)
So is thumb! (*bend down thumb*)

Ten Little Fingers

I have ten little fingers, (*hold up ten fingers*)
And they all belong to me. (*point to self*)
I can make them do things, (*wiggle fingers*)
Do you want to see? (*tilt head*)

I can make them point. (*point*)
I can make them hold. (*hold fingertips together*)
I can make them dance, (*dance fingers on arm*)
And then make them fold. (*fold hands in lap*)

Floppy

Flop your arms, flop your feet, (*suit actions to words*)
Let your hands go free.
Be the floppiest rag doll
You'll ever see.

F

Find a Foot (*suit action to words*)
Find a foot and hop, hop, hop,
When you're tired, stop, stop, stop.
Turn around and count to ten,
Find a foot and hop again.

Story: Frosty the Snowman (Flannel Board Story)

Directions: Use a black sharpie pen to trace the patterns on Appendix pages 315 and 316 onto Pelon. Color them with crayons and cut them out. Use them with a flannel board to present the story.

Frosty the Snowman

Frosty the Snowman was a jolly happy soul,
With a corncob pipe and a button nose and two eyes made out of coal.
Frosty the Snowman is a fairy tale they say:
He was made of snow but the children know how he came to life one day.
There must have been some magic in that old silk hat they found.
For when they placed it on his head, he began to dance around.
Oh, Frosty the Snowman was alive as he could be,
And the children say he could laugh and play just the same as you and me.

Frosty the Snowman knew the sun was hot that day,
So he said, "Let's run and we'll have some fun now before I melt away."
Down to the village with a broomstick in his hand,
Running here and there all around the square, sayin', "Catch me if you can."
He led them down the streets of town right to the traffic cop.
And he only paused a moment when he heard him holler, "Stop!"
For Frosty the Snowman had to hurry on his way.
So he waved goodbye, sayin', "Don't you cry; I'll be back again someday."

Thumpety, thump thump, thumpety thump thump,
Look at Frosty go;
Thumpety thump thump, thumpety thump thump,
Over the hill of snow.

Small Group Enrichment

1. Frosty the Snowman

Provide white felt and let children design a snowman. Provide colored pieces of felt for the children to make features, clothing, and accessories. Invite children to display their creations on the flannel board.

2. Fee Fi Fo Fum Hide and Seek.

Play a game of hide and seek. As IT begins her search, have her say "Fee Fi Fo Fum, ready or not here I come."

3. Floaters and Droppers

Give children several items they can use to experiment with gravity. You want some items that are lightweight and that will float to the ground when dropped and you want some heavier items that will drop quickly.

4. Fingerpaint Fun.

Mix up some fingerpaint (Appendix page 413) and let children paint on fabric wallpaper samples.

5. Play Fact or Fantasy

Make statements and let children vote as to whether each is fact (true) or fantasy (not true). For example, dogs wag their tails when they are happy; cows have three ears.

6. Fantastic Fudge

Ingredients

> 1 pound (450 g) powdered sugar
> ½ cup (60 g) powdered milk
> ⅓ cup (55 g) cocoa powder
> dash of salt
> ⅓ cup (80 ml) water
> ½ cup (120 ml) butter (melted)

Mix all the ingredients in a large bowl. Pour mixture into a shallow pan. Refrigerate until stiff.

7. Footprint Painting

Spread a 12' (4 m) sheet of butcher paper on the floor. Provide a shallow tray of paint at one end and a tub of soapy water and a towel at the other end. Invite children to remove their shoes and socks, step in the paint, and then walk the length of the paper to make a trail of footprints. Use the soapy water to clean feet.

8. Feathered Friend Feeder

Make a bird feeder. Attach a string to the top of a pinecone. Spread a thin layer of peanut butter on the pinecone and then roll it in birdseed. Hang close to the windows so children can watch their feathered friends feed.

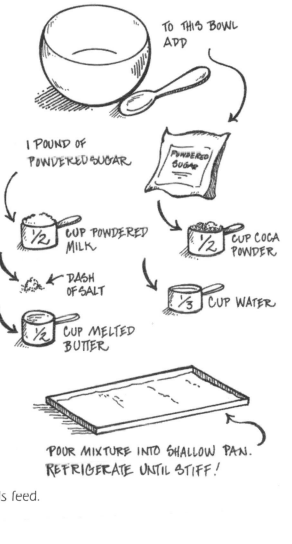

TO THIS BOWL ADD

I POUND OF POWDERED SUGAR

½ CUP POWDERED MILK

½ CUP COCA POWDER

DASH OF SALT

⅓ CUP WATER

½ CUP MELTED BUTTER

POUR MIXTURE INTO SHALLOW PAN. REFRIGERATE UNTIL STIFF!

9. Folding Fans

Give children a sheet of paper each. Invite them to draw a design. Teach them how to fold their paper into a fan. Play some classical music and invite each child to create a fan dance.

10. Fetch a Fish

Make a fishing game. Cut several fish from construction paper and place a paper clip on each mouth. Attach a piece of yarn with a round magnet on one end to a round coat-hanger insert to make a fishing pole. Encourage children to catch a fish.

11. Follow the Feet

Make a trail of footprints from the door where children enter in the morning to the circle area of the classroom or to an exciting activity you have planned. Encourage children to follow the footprints.

12. Feather Paint

Provide tempera paints and feathers. Encourage children to paint with the feather brushes.

13. Frisbee Fun

Provide a Frisbee for outdoor play.

14. Farm Fences

Set up a farm in the block center. Invite children to make fences for the animals by gluing craft sticks together.

15. Folksongs

Teach the children a folksong such as "If I Had a Hammer," "Michael, Row Your Boat Ashore," or "Puff the Magic Dragon."

16. First

Provide sequence cards and, as children decide on their order, talk about what comes first.

17. Beginning Sound "F" Concentration

Use the patterns on the Appendix page 391 to make a concentration game of objects that begin with "F."

Word List

fad	fish
fade	fist
fail	five
faint	foam
fair	foe
fake	fold
fall	folk
false	food
fan	fool
far	foot
farm	for
fast	force
feed	form
feel	fort
fence	four
fight	fowl
film	fox
fine	fun
fire	fur
first	fuss

Book List

Bedtime for Frances by Russell Hoban
Feathers for Lunch by Lois Elhert
Ferdinand the Bull by Munro Leaf
Fish Eyes by Lois Elhert
Fish Is Fish by Leo Lionni
Fredrick by Leo Lionni
Freight Train by Donald Crews

ACQUIRING READING SKILLS

Songs

The Green Grass Grew All Around

There was a tree, (there was a tree)
All in the wood. (wood)
The prettiest little tree, (tree)
That you ever did see. (see)
The tree in a hole and the hole in the ground,
And the green grass grew all around, all around,
And the green grass grew all around.

And on that tree.
There was a limb.
The prettiest limb…

That you ever did see.
The limb on the tree,
And the tree in a hole,
And the green grass grew all around, all around,
And the green grass grew all around.

And on that limb…there was a branch…
And on that branch…there was a nest…
And in that nest…there was an egg…
And in that egg…there was an bird…
And on that bird… there was a wing…
And on that wing…there was a feather…
And on that feather…there was a bug…
And on that bug…there was a germ…

Goodnight
Goodnight, ladies. Goodnight, gentlemen.
Goodnight, everyone.
It's time to say good-bye.

Poems

Grasshopper Green
Grasshopper Green is a comical chap;
He lives on the best of fare.
Bright little trousers, jacket, and cap,
These are his summer wear.
Out in the meadow he loves to go,
Playing away in the sun.
It's hopperty, skipperty, high and low,
Summer's the time for fun.

Grasshopper Green has a quaint little house;
It's under the hedge so gay.
Grandmother Spider, as still as a mouse,
Watches him over the way.
Gladly he's calling the children, I know,
Out in the beautiful sun.
It's hopperty, skipperty, high and low,
Summer's the time for fun.

Generosity (Pam Schiller)
Generous people know how to care,
How to take turns and how to share.
Generous people know that it's quite true—
If you are kind to others, they'll be kind to you.

Tongue Twisters/Alliterative Sentences and Phrases

Three Gray Geese
Three gray geese on the green grass grazing. (Honk! Honk!)
Gray were the geese and green was the grazing. (Honk! Honk!)

Say the sentences and phrases below three times quickly if you can.
- Gabby girls get giddy gazing at goofy guys.
- Cows graze in groves on grass which grows in grooves in groves.

Fingerplays/Action Rhymes

Grandma's Glasses

These are Grandma's glasses. (*use thumbs and fingers to make circles over eyes*)
This is Grandma's hat. (*pat top of head*)
This is how she folds her hands, (*fold hands*)
And puts them in her lap. (*place hands in lap*)

Making a Garden

Dig, dig, dig, (*suit actions to words*)
Rake just so.
Plant the seeds,
Watch them grow.

Chop, chop, chop,
Pull up the weeds.
Sun and rain,
My garden needs.

Up, up, up,
Green stems climb.
Open wide,
It's blossom time!

Go Bananas!

Bananas unite! (*put hands together overhead*)
Bananas split! (*hands out to side*)

Go bananas! (*turn in circle, waving arms for next four lines*)
Go, go bananas!
Go bananas!
Go, go bananas!

Bananas to the left (*point left*)
Bananas to the right (*point right*)
Peel your banana and, mmmmmm, take a bite! (*peel and bite banana*)

Story: The Gingerbread Man (Flannel Board Story)

Directions: Use a black sharpie pen to trace the patterns on Appendix pages 317 and 318 onto Pelon. Color them with crayons and cut them out. Use them with the flannel board to present the story.

The Gingerbread Man

Once upon a time, a little old woman and a little old man lived in a little old house in a little old village.

One day the little old woman decided to make a gingerbread man. She cut him out of dough and put him in the oven to bake. After a while, the little old woman said to herself, "That gingerbread man must be ready by now." She went to the oven door and opened it. Up jumped the gingerbread man, and away he ran.

As he ran he shouted, "Run, run as fast as you can. You can't catch me. I'm the gingerbread man!"

The little old woman ran after the gingerbread man, but she couldn't catch him. He ran past the little old man who was working in the garden. "Stop, stop!" called the little old man.

But the gingerbread man just called back, "Run, run as fast as you can. You can't catch me. I'm the gingerbread man."

The little old man joined the little old woman and ran as fast as he could after the gingerbread man, but he couldn't catch him.

The gingerbread man ran past a dog. "Stop, stop!" said the dog.

But the gingerbread man just called back, "Run, run as fast as you can. You can't catch me. I'm the gingerbread man."

The dog joined the little old woman and the little old man and ran as fast as he could after the gingerbread man, but he couldn't catch him.

The gingerbread man ran past a cat. "Stop, stop!" said the cat.

But the gingerbread man just called back, "Run, run as fast as you can. You can't catch me. I'm the gingerbread man." The cat joined the little old woman

and the little old man and the dog, but she couldn't catch the gingerbread man.

Soon the gingerbread man came to a fox lying by the side of a river, and he shouted.

"Run, run, as fast as you can. You can't catch me. I'm the gingerbread man! I ran away from the little old woman, the little old man, the dog, and the cat, and I can run away from you, I can."

But the sly old fox just laughed and said, "If you don't get across this river quickly, you will surely get caught. If you hop on my tail I will carry you across."

The gingerbread man saw that he had no time to lose, so he quickly hopped onto the fox's tail.

"Oh!" said the fox. "The water is getting deeper. Climb on my back so you won't get wet."

And the gingerbread man did.

"Oh!" said the fox. "The water is getting deeper. Climb on my head so you won't get wet."

And the gingerbread man did.

"Oh!" said the fox. "The water is getting deeper. Climb on my nose so you won't get wet."

And the gingerbread man did.

Then the fox tossed the gingerbread man into his mouth. And that was the end of the gingerbread man!

Small Group Enrichment

1. The Gingerbread Man

Bake gingerbread men. Use the recipe on the back of a box of gingerbread mix to bake the cookies. Provide decorations for the children to use to dress their gingerbread men. Use a rebus chart of recipe directions and see if children can follow them.

2. Goop and Gak

Mix some Goop and some Gak (see recipes on Appendix pages 413-414). Let children try a little of each. How are they different? How are they alike?

3. Glue Drop Art

Mix several drops of food coloring in glue. Invite children to squeeze drops of glue onto their paper to make a design.

4. Gadget Painting

Provide a tray of tempera paints and some kitchen gadgets to make prints. Which gadget makes the most interesting print?

5. Green Eggs and Ham

Cook up some green eggs and ham.

6. Green Grass

Invite children to plant rye grass and watch it grow.

7. Gorgeous Glasses

Use the glasses pattern (Appendix page 373) to make a pair of glasses for each child. Provide confetti, glitter, and other sparkling materials to make their glasses gorgeous.

8. Gold Rush

Spray some rock salt gold and put it in the sand table. Give the children strainers and encourage them to pan for gold.

9. Grandparent Happy Gram

Invite children to make a happy card for their grandparents. If they don't have grandparents, encourage them to make a card for someone else's grandparent.

10. Goose, Goose, Gander

Play Goose, Goose, Gander just like you would Duck, Duck, Goose.

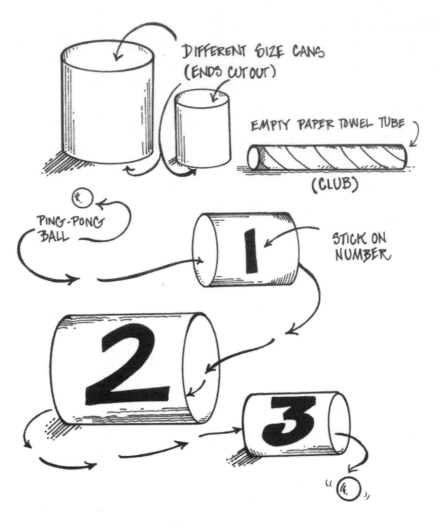

11. Goofy Golf

Cut out the ends of five coffee cans (a variety of sizes makes it more fun). Use stick-on numbers to number each can from 1-5. Provide an empty paper towel tube to use as a club and some Ping-Pong balls or tennis balls. Challenge the children to hit the balls through the cans in order. After the ball has made it through all the cans, play the game backward.

12. Goggles

Cut an egg carton into two-crate sections. Cut a hole in the bottom of each crate. Attach pipe cleaners for earpieces on each side. Let the children play with the goggles in the Dramatic Play Center.

13. Guitars

Stretch two or three rubber bands lengthwise around an empty tissue box. Attach an empty paper towel tube to one end of the box for a neck. Strum the rubber bands and sing a favorite tune.

14. Guessing Game

Glue animal pictures on index cards to create Guessing Game playing cards. Invite a child to draw a card and act out the movements and antics of the animal pictured. When someone guesses the correct animal, they can have the next turn.

15. Beginning Sound "G" Concentration Game

Use the patterns on Appendix page 312 to make a concentration game of objects that start with "G."

Word List

gain	goal
game	goat
gap	goes
gas	gold
gasp	golf
gate	gone
gave	good
gaze	goof
gear	goose
geese	gulp
get	gull
gift	gum
gill	gush
girl	gust
give	

Book List

Gilberto and the Wind by Marie Ets
Go Away, Big Green Monster! by Ed Emberley
Goggles by Ezra Jack Keats
The Golden Goose by Margaret Hillert
Good Night, Gorilla by Peggy Rathmann
Goodnight Moon by Margaret Wise Brown

ACQUIRING READING SKILLS

Songs

Hunk of Tin (Tune: I'm a Little Acorn Brown)
I'm a little hunk of tin,
Nobody knows what shape I'm in.
Got four wheels and a running board.
I'm a four door, I'm a Ford.
Honk, honk, rattle, rattle, rattle, crash, beep, beep.
Honk, honk, rattle, rattle, rattle, crash, beep, beep.
Honk, honk, rattle, rattle, rattle, crash, beep, beep.
Honk, honk, rattle, rattle, rattle, crash, beep, beep.

Johnny Works With One Hammer

Johnny works with one hammer, one hammer, one hammer. (hammer
  with right hand)
Johnny works with one hammer, then he works with two.

Johnny works with two hammers… (*continue hammering with right
  hand and add left*)
Johnny works with three hammers… (*add right foot moving up
  and down*)
Johnny works with four hammers… (*add left foot moving up
  and down*)
Johnny works with five hammers… (*add head moving up
  and down*)
Then he goes to bed. (*place head on hands*)

If You're Happy and You Know It
If you're happy and you know it—clap your hands.
If you're happy and you know it—clap your hands.
If you're happy and you know then your face will surely
show it.
If you're happy and you know it—clap your hands.

Continue to stomp your feet, shout "hooray," and any other
actions you desire.

Poems

The New Humpty Dumpty (Pam Schiller)
Humpty Dumpty sat on a hill,
Humpty Dumpty had a great spill.
That genuis, Jack Horner, pulled out his glue
And Humpty Dumpty's as good as new!

Holding Hands (Lenore M. Link)
Elephants walking
Along the trails

Are holding hands
By holding tails.

Trunks and tails
Arc handy things

When elephants walk
In circus rings.

Elephants work
And elephants play

And elephants walk
And feel so gay.

An when they walk
It never fails

They're holding hands
By holding tails.

The Horses of the Sea (Christina Rossetti)
The horses of the sea
Rear a foaming crest,
But the horses of the land
Serve us the best.

The horses of the land
Munch corn and clover,
While the foaming sea-horses
Toss over and over.

The Neck (Mrs. Orleans)
The neck of a calf
Is a half
Of a half
Of a half
Of a half
Of a half
Of a half
Of a half
Of a half
Of the size
Of the neck
Of a little
Giraffe.

Tongue Twisters/Alliterative Sentences and Phrases

Say the sentences and phrases below three times quickly if you can.

- Hillary heals horses.
- Hobbs heats hotcakes.

Fingerplays/Action Rhymes

I'm Hiding

I'm hiding, I'm hiding, (*place hands over face as if hiding*)
And no one knows where. (*shake head no*)
For all they can see are (*place fists over eyes as if looking through
   binoculars*)
My toes and my hair. (*point to toes and hair*)

Two Little Houses

Two little houses,
Closed up tight. (*close fists*)
Let's open the windows,
And let in some light. (*open fists*)

My Head

This is the circle that is my head. (*suit actions to words*)
This is my mouth with which words are said.
These are my eyes with which I see.
This is my nose that is part of me.
This is the hair that grows on my head,
And this is my hat I wear on my head.

My Little Horn

Watch me play my little horn,
I put my fingers so. (*place fist together to make a horn*)
Then I lift it to my mouth
And blow and blow and blow. (*blow into fists*)

Story: Perky Pumpkin's Open House. (Prop Story)

Directions: You will need a 12" x 18" (30 cm x 45 cm) piece of orange construction paper and a pair of scissors. Follow the directions in the story.

ORANGE PAPER

12" 18"

Perky Pumpkin's Open House

Once upon a time there was a little man named Perky. Perky liked pumpkins so much he even looked like a pumpkin. He was jolly and round. People called him Perky Pumpkin.

Perky's best friend was a cat named Kate. Everywhere that Perky went, Kate went too. They played together, they slept together, they went for walks together—they did everything together.

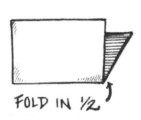

FOLD IN ½

Perky didn't live in a house. He lived in a field among the pumpkin vines. He had been thinking a lot about how nice it would be to have a nice, warm, snug house that he could call his very own. He mentioned it to Kate, and they decided to find a house together.

One crisp, fall morning they set out. In front of a school, they found a large piece of orange paper. "My favorite color," said Perky, "It's just what we need." Kate agreed.

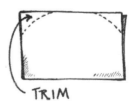

TRIM

With Kate's help, Perky tugged and pushed and pulled until he put the paper together like this (fold paper in half).

With a pair of scissors, Perky carefully and slowly rounded off the corners, so the paper looked like this.

"Meow," said Kate. "Let's set it up and take a look at our work." And for a time, they just smiled in admiration.

But then Perky remembered he would need a door. He cut out a tall one, like this "I think I'll add a window, too," he said. And he did, like this.

Perky was pleased with himself. But not Kate—she was curious to know where she came in. "Meow…Meow," she grumbled.

A DOOR

Perky laughed. He quickly added another door—a teeny, tiny one that was just the right size for a rather thin cat. "This will always be open so you can come in and out as you like," Perky said. Kate purred her thanks.

On Halloween night, Perky and Kate invited all their Mother Goose and story-book friends to an open-house party. And when they opened the house to their friends, everyone was surprised and delighted—including Perky and Kate. For this is what they saw.

A WINDOW

Just what Halloween needs—a nice round Jack-o-Lantern.

Small Group Enrichment

1. Perky Pumpkin's Open House
Give children a piece of orange construction paper and a pair of scissors. Can they make a house for Perky and Kate?

A TINY DOOR

2. Haystacks
Combine one small package of butterscotch chips and one small package of chocolate chips. Melt over low heat (you can use a warming tray, if available). Add one package of Chinese noodles. When cool enough to touch shape into haystacks. Let cool. Enjoy!

JACK-O-LANTERN

3. Helping Hands
Invite children to trace around their hands and then cut out the handprint. Encourage children to dictate an idea about what they can do to be helpful to their friends. Transcribe their thoughts onto their handprints.

4. Hula Hoop Hop
Arrange several Hula Hoops in a path on the floor. Challenge children to jump from the center of one to the center of another.

5. Hopscotch

Draw a hopscotch pattern with chalk or lay one out with masking tape. Provide a beanbag to use as a marker. Invite children to play a game of Hopscotch. Children toss the beanbag to a different box each turn and jump and hop through the pattern in numerical sequence.

6. Hearts' Habits

Brainstorm a list of nice things you can do to help others.

7. Hokey Pokey

Do the Hokey Pokey (page 71).

8. Humpty Dumpty

Read "Humpty Dumpty." Make up other rhymes about how Humpty might fall. For example: Humpty Dumpty sat on a stool. Humpty Dumpty fell in a pool.

BEANBAG

CHALK

9. Hats, Hats, Hats

Invite children to bring a hat to class and have a hat parade. You could also make hats. To make a newspaper hat, place two sheets of newspaper on the child's head. Wrap masking tape around the child's head to form the crown of the hat. Roll edges of the newspaper lightly toward the crown to form a brim. Offer colored tissue paper, feathers, lace, bows, and other items for children to decorate the hats.

10. Hula Hands

Teach the children to do a hula. Explain that the dance is a form of storytelling where the hands are used to communicate. If you know someone who hulas, invite him or her to teach the children a few of the storytelling hand movements.

11. Half of Half

Invite children to tear a piece of paper in half. Then tear the half piece of paper in half and so on until they have only a tiny piece of paper left. Put the paper in the collage box for later use.

ACQUIRING READING SKILLS

12. Heel to Toe

Challenge the children to walk heel to toe around the playground. How many steps does it take? How long does it take? Try walking around the perimeter with regular steps. How are you going to walk if you are in a hurry?

13. Hands High

Invite children to measure things in the room using their hands as a measuring tool. How many hands high is the table? How many hands high is the windowsill?

14. Hummers

Tape waxed paper around a comb to make a hummer. Change the paper and let each child have a turn to "hum the hummer."

15. Beginng Sound "H" Concentration

Use the patterns on Appendix page 393 to make a concentration game of objects that begin with "H."

Book List

Happy Birthday, Moon by Frank Asch
Harold and the Purple Crayon by Crockett Johnson
Harry the Dirty Dog by Gene Zion
Henny Penny by Paul Galdone (illustrator)
Here Are My Hands by Bill Martin, Jr.
Horton Hatches the Egg by Dr. Seuss
A House for Hermit Crab by Eric Carle
A House Is a House for Me by MaryAnn Hoberman
The Napping House by Don and Audrey Wood
The Very Hungry Caterpillar by Eric Carle

Word List

hair	hill
half	him
hall	hip
halt	hive
ham	hoe
hand	hog
hare	hold
has	home
hat	hood
hate	hoof
have	hook
hay	hop
he	hope
head	horn
hear	horse
heart	hose
heat	hot
heel	house
help	hum
her	hunt
here	hurt
high	hut

Songs

(Long I)

Apples and Bananas

I like to eat eat eat apples and bananas.
I like to eat eat eat apples and bananas.

I like to ate ate ate aypuls and baynaynays.
I like to ate ate ate aypuls and baynaynays.

I like eet eet eet eeples and beeneenees.
I like eet eet eet eeples and beeneenees.

I like to ite, ite, ite, ipples and bininis
I like to ite, ite, ite, ipples and bininis

I like to ote ote ote opples and
    bononos.
I like to ote ote ote opples
    and bononos.

I like to ute ute ute upples
    and bununus.
I like to ute ute ute upples and
    bununus.

(Short I)

Itsy Bitsy Spider

The itsy bitsy spider went up the
    waterspout.
Down came the rain and washed
    the spider out.
Up came the sun and dried up all the rain.
And the itsy bitsy spider went up the spout again.

Poems

(Long I)

Ice Cream
I scream.
You scream.
We all scream for ice cream.

An Icicle
An icicle
Lives in the winter,
Dies in the summer,
And grows with its roots upward!

(Short I)

Icky Bicky Soda Cracker
Icky bicky soda cracker
Icky bicky boo.
Icky, bicky, soda cracker
Up goes you!

Tongue Twisters/Alliterative Sentences and Phrases

Say the sentences and phrases below three times quickly if you can.

● Is he Izzy?
● Icy icicles.

Fingerplays/Action Rhymes

(Long I)

Five Ice Cream Cones (Pam Schiller)
Five ice cream cones from the ice cream store, (*suit actions to words*)
Mommy takes strawberry now there are four.
Daddy takes chocolate, which leaves only three.

Will there be any ice cream for me?
Sam says he'll have chocolate like dad.
Now there are only two cones to be had.
I have an idea; I'm not sure they'll agree.
I think I'll take both cones just for me.

(Short I)

If
If your fingers wiggle (*wiggle your fingers*)
Cross them one by one. (*clasp hands together*)
Until they hug each other (*fold fingers down*)
It really is quite fun.

Story: "Itsy Bitsy Spider" (Poster Story)

"Itsy Bitsy Spider" (see Appendix pages 319-321 for pattern cards)
The itsy bitsy spider went up the waterspout.
Down came the rain and washed the spider out.
Up came the sun and dried up all the rain.
And the itsy bitsy spider went up the spout again.

(New Verse) (Pam Schiller)
The little boy wants to throw a ball.
It's not easy to throw a ball.
But if he tries and tries some more,
In no time at all his ball will soar.

My grandma wants to learn to skate.
It's not easy to learn to skate.
But if she keeps right on trying,
In no time at all she'll be flying.

My baby sister wants to smile.
It's not easy to learn to smile.
But if she tries again and again,
In no time at all she'll learn to grin.

My dad is teaching our dog to fetch.
It's not easy teaching a dog to fetch.
But if my dad keeps right on believing,
In no time at all the dog'll be retrieving.

ACQUIRING READING SKILLS

I've been trying to tie my shoe.
It's not easy to tie a shoe.
I keep thinking of that famous spider,
And every day my laces get tighter.

So when you think you just can't do it,
Remember that you must just stick to it.
The lesson of the Itsy Bitsy Spider
Is to face each battle as a fighter.

Small Group Enrichment

1. Itsy Bitsy Spider

Encourage children to brainstorm a list of things they are having to practice. Let each child make an Itsy Bitsy Spider out of pipe cleaners to keep close by as a reminder to keep on trying.

2. Ice Painting (long I)

Fill an ice tray with water. Place a Popsicle stick in each crate. After ice is frozen, give a cube to each child to use as a brush. Provide a couple of salt-shakers filled with dry tempera. Show the children how to sprinkle on the dry tempera and then use their ice paintbrush to create a picture or design.

3. Ice Cream (long I)

Make homemade ice cream.
Ingredients

> ½ cup (120 ml) milk
> ¼ teaspoon (1 ml) vanilla
> 1 tablespoon (20 g) sugar

Place milk, sugar, and vanilla in a small plastic bag and seal. Fill a large plastic bag with ice and 3 tablespoons of rock salt. Shake. Make one recipe per child.

4. Islands (long I)

Provide some clay and let children construct islands in the water play table.

5. Island to Island (long I)

Cut large brown circles out of butcher paper and lay them in a trail on the floor. Challenge children to some "island hopping."

6. I.D. Cards (long I)

Photocopy a picture of each child. Have children glue their photo on an index card and then make a fingerprint on it. Next have them write their name on the card. Finally have them dictate or write a sentence about themselves on

the card. Think of ways the children can use their I.D. cards. Maybe they could use them to check out books or to identify their cubicles.

7. Inchworm Inch-Along (short I)
Place a piece of masking tape on the floor to identify a start line. Place a beanbag about 12' (4 m) from the start line. Let children have an inchworm race to see who can get to the beanbag first.

8. Inkblots for Imagination (short I)
Make inkblots on several sheets of paper. Let children have fun identifying what they think the inkblots look like.

9. Interview (short I)
Talk to the children about interviewing, asking questions to gain information. Let them practice asking questions. Invite a guest (a family member, director, or principal) to come in and talk about some experience and then let the children try out their interviewing skills.

10. Insect (short I)
Provide insects or pictures of insects for children to look at with a magnifying glass.

11. Instrumentals (short I)
Play some instrumental music for the children. Provide rhythm band instruments and challenge children to create an instrumental piece of their own.

12. Insect Inventions
Challenge children to think of inventions that insects could use, such as something to help ants carry their food home or something to help bees get the nectar from flowers.

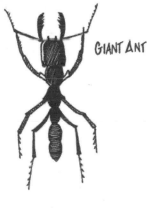

GIANT ANT

DRAGON FLY

BEETLE

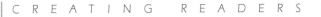

Word List

(Long i)	Short i
I	if
ice	igloo
ice cream	iguana
icon	illustrate
identification	in
identify	inch
iris	Indian
island	insect
isometric	invent
item	is
	it

Book List

I Know an Old Lady Who Swallowed a Fly by Nadine Westcott
If by Sarah Perry
If You Give a Mouse a Cookie by Laura Joffe Numeroff
Imogene's Antlers by David Small
Inch by Inch Leo Lionni
Ira Sleeps Over by Bernard Waber
Island Baby by Holly Keller
Island of the Skog by Steven Kellogg
The Island of the Skog by Steven Kellogg
"It Could Always Be Worse: A Yiddish Folktale" (Traditional)
It's Mine! by Leo Lionni
Itsy Bitsy Spider (Pam Schiller and Tracy Moncure, eds.)

Songs

Jim Along Josie

Hey, Jim along, Jim along Josie,
Hey, Jim along, Jim along Jo,
Hey, Jim along, Jim along Josie,
Hey, Jim along, Jim along Jo.

Jump, Jim along, Jim along Josie,
Jump, Jim along, Jim along Jo,
Jump, Jim along, Jim along Josie,
Jump, Jim along, Jim along Jo.

Add other verses—walk, hop, crawl, etc.

Jingle Bells

Jingle bells, jingle
  bells,
Jingle all the way.
Oh, what fun
It is to ride
In a one-horse
  open
  sleigh.

Dashing
  through
  the snow,
In a one-horse open
  sleigh.
O'er the fields we go,
Laughing all the way.
Bells on bobtails ring,
Making spirits bright.
What fun it is to laugh and sing
A sleighing song tonight.

Jingle bells, jingle bells,
Jingle all the way.
Oh, what fun
It is to ride
In a one-horse open sleigh.

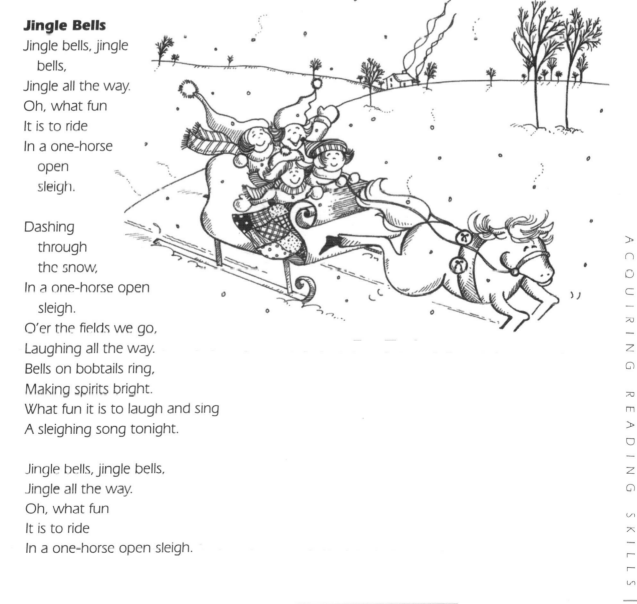

John Jacob Jingleheimer Schmidt

John Jacob Jingleheimer Schmidt,
His name is my name, too.
Whenever I go out,
The people always shout,
"There goes John Jacob Jingleheimer Schmidt!"
Da Da-Da Da-Da Da-Da Da!

Poems

Jelly

Jelly on my head,
Jelly on my toes,
Jelly on my coat,
Jelly on my nose.

Laughing and a-licking,
Having me a time.
Jelly on my belly,
But I like it fine.

Jack and Jill

Jack and Jill went up the hill
To fetch a pail of water.
Jack fell down
And broke his crown,
And Jill came tumbling after.

Tongue Twisters/Alliterative Sentences and Phrases

Say the sentences or phrases below three times quickly.

- Judges judge judiciously.
- John Jacob Jingleheimer.

Fingerplays/Action Rhymes

Two Little Blackbirds
Two little blackbirds (*hold up two fingers*)
Sitting on a hill.
One named Jack. (*put fingers to thumbs and perch right on shoulders*)
One named Jill. (*put fingers to thumbs and perch left on shoulders*)
Fly away, Jack. (*flap right hand and place behind your back*)
Fly away, Jill. (*flap left hand and place behind your back*)
Come back, Jack. (*bring right hand back to shoulder*)
Come back, Jill. (*bring left hand back to shoulder*)

Jack-in-the-Box
Jack-in-the-box (*tuck thumb into fist*)
Oh, so still.
Won't you come out? (*raise hand slightly*)
Yes, I will. (*pop thumb out of fist*)

Jack, Jack
Jack, Jack, down you go, (*crouch down low*)
Down in your box, down so low.
Jack, Jack, there goes the top. (*pop up*)
Quickly now, up you pop.

Hey! My Name Is Joe!
Hello! My name is Joe!
I have a wife, one kid, and I work in a button factory.
One day, my boss said, "Are you busy?"
I said, "No."
"Then turn a button with your right hand." (*make a turning gesture with right hand*)

Hello! My name is Joe!
I have a wife, two kids, and I work in a button factory.
One day, my boss said, "Are you busy?"
I said, "No."
"Then turn a button with your left hand." (*make a turning gesture with left hand as you continue with the right hand*)

(Continue adding number of children and adding right and left feet and head.)

ACQUIRING READING SKILLS

J

Hello! My name is Joe!
I have a wife, six kids, and I work in a button factory.
One day, my boss said, "Are you busy?"
I said, "Yes!"

Story: This Is the House That Jack Built (Flannel Board Story)

Directions: Use a black sharpie to trace the patterns on Appendix pages 322-324 onto Pelon. Color them and cut them out. Use them with the flannel board to present the story.

This Is the House that Jack Built

This is the House that Jack built.

This is the malt that lay in the house that Jack built.

This the rat that ate the malt
That lay in the house that Jack built.

This is the cat that killed the rat
That ate the malt
That lay in the house that Jack built.

This is the dog that worried the cat
That killed the rat
That ate the malt
That lay in the house that Jack built.

This is the cow with the crumpled horn
That tossed the dog
That worried the cat
That killed the rat
That ate the malt
That lay in the house that Jack built.

This is the maiden all forlorn
That milked the cow with the crumpled horn
That tossed the dog
That worried the cat
That killed the rat
That ate the malt
That lay in the house that Jack built.

This is the man all tattered and torn,
That kissed the maiden all forlorn
That milked the cow with the crumpled horn
That tossed the dog
That worried the cat
That killed the rat
That ate the malt
That lay in the house that Jack built.

This is the priest all shaven and shorn
That married the man all tattered and torn
That kissed the maiden all forlorn
That milked the cow with the crumpled horn
That tossed the dog
That worried the cat
That killed the rat
That ate the malt
That lay in the house that Jack built.

This is the cock that crowed in the morn
That woke the priest all shaven and shorn
That married the man all tattered and torn
That kissed the maiden all forlorn
That milked the cow with the crumpled horn
That tossed the dog
That worried the cat
That killed the rat
That ate the malt
That lay in the house that Jack built.

This is the farmer sowing the corn
That kept the cock who crowed in the morn
That woke the priest all shaven and shorn
That married the man all tattered and torn
That kissed the maiden all forlorn
That milked the cow with the crumpled horn
That tossed the dog
That worried the cat
That killed the rat
That ate the malt
That lay in the house that Jack built.

ACQUIRING READING SKILLS

Small Group Enrichment

1. This Is the House That Jack Built

Invite children to build graham cracker houses. Use powdered sugar icing to hold the crackers together. Provide sprinkles, cinnamon candies, marshmallows, and animal crackers for decorations.

2. Jumping Jacks

Start the day with some Jumping Jacks.

3. Jazzy Jewelry

Ask families to help you collect some old jewelry. Let children use the jewelry in the Dramatic Play Center.

4. Jiggety Jig

Teach the children an Irish jig.

5. Jogging

Take the children jogging. Be sure to warm up first.

6. Junk

Create a junk table. Collect old clocks, radios, appliances, and parts of appliances from families and let children explore the junk.

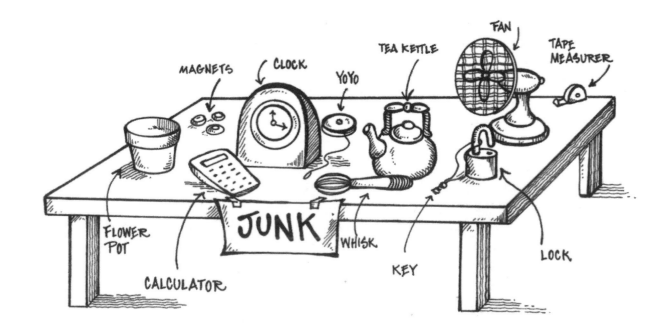

7. Juice and Jam

Invite children to serve themselves some juice and some bread and jam.

8. Jam Jar Jubilee

Fill four jars (jam jars work great) with water. Fill one ¼ full, the second one ½ full, the third one ¾ full and the fourth one full. Provide a stick and let children create a song using the various tones made by the different water levels of the jars.

9. Gelatin Jigglers

Mix gelatin using the amount of water requested. Chill and cut into cubes that can be eaten with the fingers.

10. Journals

If the children are not already using journals for the recording of daily activities, this is a good time to start (see page 88 for more information on journals).

11. Jazz

Play some jazz for children. Talk about the primary instruments used in jazz music. Play some blues music. Ask the children which they like best and why.

12. Jelly Jar Pets

Collect small animals you can keep in jelly jars for a day or two. Tadpoles can be kept until they turn to frogs. You will need to collect some of their habitat such as the water you find them in, some pebbles, and some algae. Be sure to punch some holes in the jar lid. Other animals such as lizards, grasshoppers, and crickets can be kept for a day. They need grass and pebbles as well. Let all jelly jar animals go after children have had a chance to observe them.

13. Jacks

Teach the children how to play Jacks. They will probably only be able to pick up one Jack at a time but with a little practice, who knows?

14. Beginning Sound "J" Concentration

Use the patterns on Appendix page 394 to make a concentration game of objects that begin with "J."

J

Word List

jab	jog
jacks	join
jade	joint
jail	joke
jam	jolt
jar	joy
jaw	jug
jay	juice
jeans	jump
jeep	June
jerk	junk
jet	jury
jig	just
job	justify

Book List

Bread and Jam for Frances by Russel Hoban
Jamberry By Bruce Degan
John Henry by Julius Lester
Johnny Appleseed by Steven Kellogg
The Jolly Postman by Janet and Allen Ahlberg
The Judge: An Untrue Tale by Harve Zemach
Julius by Angela Johnson
Jump Frog Jumpl by Robert Kalan

Songs

Kookaburra

Kookaburra sits in the old gum tree-ee,
Merry, merry king of the bush is hee-ee.
Laugh, kookaburra. Laugh, kookaburra,
Gay your life must be.

Kookaburra sits in the old gum tree-ee,
Eating all the gumdrops he can see-ee.
Stop, kookaburra. Stop, kookaburra,
Leave a few for me.

Katy

K-K-K-Katy, beautiful Katy,
You're the only g-g-g-girl that I adore.
And when the m-m-m-moon shines over the cowshed,
I'll be waiting at the k-k-k-kitchen door.

Poems

To Be a Kite (Pam Schiller)

I often wish I were a kite,
Flying high above
    the ground,
Sailing with the
    stars at night,
Cruising with
    clouds all day.

If only I were a
    kelly green kite,
I would feel like a
    king.
Everything
    would be just
    right,
If I could dance on a
    string.

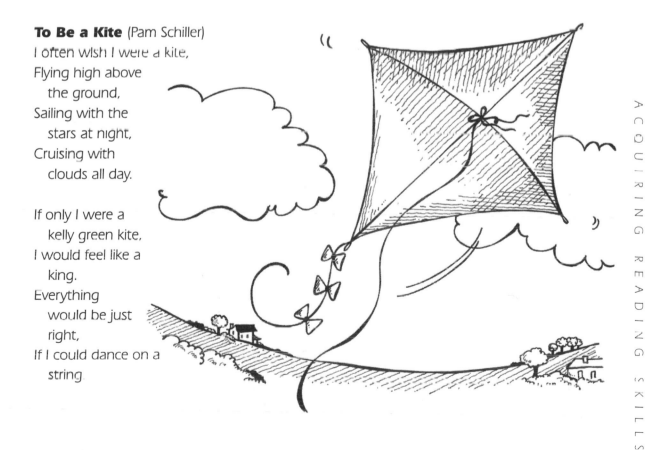

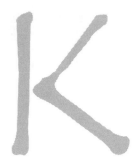

K Was a Kite (Edward Lear)
K was a kite,
Which flew out of sight,
Above houses so high,
Quite into the sky.
K
Fly away, kite!

Three Little Kittens
Three little kittens lost their mittens,
And they began to cry,
"Oh, mother dear, we very much fear
our mittens we have lost."

"What! lost your mittens, you naughty kittens!
Then you shall have no pie."
"Mee-ow, mee-ow, mee-ow, mee-ow."
"No, you shall have no pie."

The three little kittens they found their mittens,
And they began to cry,
"Oh, Mother dear, see here, see here!
Our mittens we have found."

"What! found your mittens! You good little kittens,
Now you shall have some pie."
"Purr, purr, purr, purr,
Purr, purr, purr."

Tongue Twisters/Alliterative Sentences and Phrases

Say the sentences and phrases below three times quickly if you can.

- Kit keeps kittens in the kitchen.
- Keith keeps keys.

Fingerplays/Action Rhymes

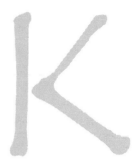

Kangaroo

Jump, jump, jump, (*jump right fist up and down*)
Goes the kangaroo.
I thought there was one, (*hold up one, then two fingers*)
But I see there are two.

The mother takes her baby (*place thumb inside palm of opposite
   hand*)
Along in a pouch,
Where he can nap
Like a baby on a couch. (*rest head on hands*)

Puppies and Kittens

One little, two little, three little kittens (*pop up three fingers*)
Were napping in the sun. (*rest head on hands*)
One little, two little, three little puppies (*pop up three fingers*)
Said, "Let's have some fun." (*make a sly smile*)

Up to the kittens the puppies went creeping (*walk fingers of right
   hand up left arm*)
As quiet as could be.
One little, two little, three little kittens (*wiggle fingers overhead*)
Went scampering up a tree!

The King of France (suit actions to words)

The King of France,
With forty-thousand men,
Marched up the hill
And then marched back again.

The King of France,
With forty-thousand men,
Gave salute
And then marched back again.

The King of France,
With forty-thousand men,
Banged their drums
And then marched back again.

A C Q U I R I N G   R E A D I N G   S K I L L S

The King of France,
With forty-thousand men,
Blew their horns
And then marched back again.

The King of France,
With forty-thousand men,
Waved their flags
And then marched back again.

The King of France,
With forty-thousand men,
All shook hands
And then marched back again.

Story: Katy No-Pockets (Prop Story)

Directions: Check out the book *Katy No-Pockets* by Emmy Payne from the library. Use the patterns on Appendix pages 325-331 to make your apron and little animal people.

Small Group Enrichment

1. Katy No-Pockets
Invite children to make up a story about what they would put in their apron if they had one like Katy's.

2. Kaleidoscopes
Provide kaleidoscopes for the children to explore.

3. Kazoos
Make simple kazoos. Let children decorate an empty toilet paper tube. Give each child a piece of waxed paper and a rubber band and help them secure the waxed paper with the rubber band to one end of the toilet paper tube. Show the children how to hum into the other end of the tube to make kazoo music.

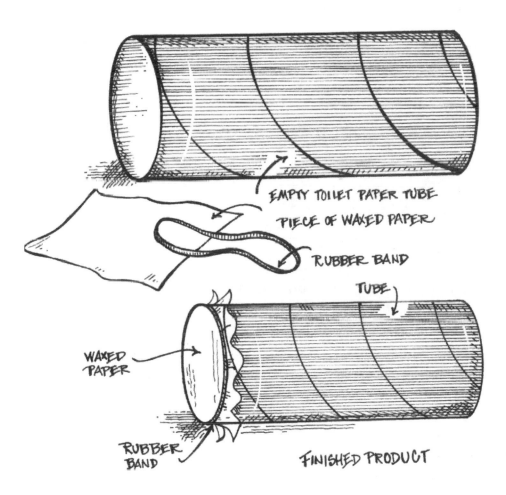

EMPTY TOILET PAPER TUBE

PIECE OF WAXED PAPER

RUBBER BAND

TUBE

WAXED PAPER

RUBBER BAND

FINISHED PRODUCT

4. Key Match

Trace several keys on a piece of black construction paper. Cut them out and glue them in a folder. Invite children to match keys to their shadows.

5. Kites

Fly a kite with the children.

6. King Concentration

Remove the kings from two decks of cards. Use the kings to play concentration.

7. Kitchen Band

Make a band from kitchen items such as pots, pans, spoons, and graters. Let the children play with some jamming music.

8. Random Acts of Kindness

Talk to the children about random acts of kindness. Integrate the concept into the classroom and watch for and acknowledge children who consciously try to perform acts of kindness.

9. Special Kisses
Teach the children how to give butterfly kisses and Eskimo kisses.

10. Kernel Transfer
Provide a margarine container with popcorn kernels in it, a pair of tweezers, and a second empty margarine tub. Invite children to transfer the kernels from one container to the other.

11. Kickball
Provide a ball and a laundry basket or box. Invite children to kick the ball into the basket.

12. Beginning Sound "K" Concentration
Use the patterns on Appendix page 395 and make a concentration game of objects that begin with "K."

Word List

kale	kill
keel	kilt
keen	kind
keep	king
keg	kiss
kelp	kit
kept	kitchen
key	kite
kid	kitten
kidding	koala

Book List

Curious George Flies a Kite by Margaret Rey
The Great Kapok Tree by Lynne Cherry
Katy No-Pockets by Emmy Payne
The Kissing Hand by Audrey Penn
Kitten Day by Jan Ormerod
Knots on a Counting Rope by Bill Martin, Jr.
Koala Lou by Mem Fox
Komodo! by Peter Sis

Songs

Lolly Loves Lollipops

One lollipop, two lollipops,
   three lollipops, pop!
Lolly loves lollipops, lollipops, lollipops.
Lolly loves lollipops,
   lollipops for
   Lolly!
One lollipop,
   two lollipops,
   three lollipops,
   pop!

Here We Go Looby Lou

Here we go Looby Lou,
Here we go Looby Light,
Here we go Looby Lou,
All on a Saturday night.

London Bridge

London Bridge is falling
   down,
Falling down, falling down.
London Bridge is falling down—
My fair lady!

Take the key and lock her up,
Lock her up, lock her up.
Take the key and lock her up—
My fair lady!

Poems

Fall Leaves

Leaves are drifting softly down,
They make a carpet on the ground.
Then, swish! The wind comes whistling by
And sends them dancing in the sky!

I Love You Little

I love you little,
I love you lots,
My love for you would fill ten pots,
Fifteen buckets,
Sixteen cans,
Three teacups,
And four dishpans.

Tongue Twisters/Alliterative Sentences and Phrases

Say the sentences and phrases below three times quickly if you can.

- Little lice like light.
- Lee let Lester leave.

Fingerplays/Action Rhymes

Falling Leaves

Little leaves are falling down, (*wiggle finger downward*)
Red and yellow, orange and brown. (*count on fingers*)
Whirling, twirling round and round, (*twirl fingers*)
Falling softly to the ground. (*wiggle finger downward to the ground*)

I Look in the Mirror

I look in the mirror (*hold hand up like a mirror*)
And what do I see?
I see a laughing face (*make a laughing face*)
Happy as can be.

I look in the mirror (*hold hand up like a mirror*)
And what do I see?
I see a laughing face (*laugh and point to self*)
Laughing at me.

Story: The Lion and the Mouse (A Listening Story)

Directions: You need no props for this story, just a listener with a good imagination.

A lion was awakened from sleep by a mouse running over his face. Rising up angrily, he caught the mouse by the tail and was about to kill her, when the mouse very pitifully said, "If you would only spare my life, I would surely repay your kindness some day." The lion roared with laughter. "How could a small little creature like you ever repay a mighty lion?" The lion roared another laugh and let the mouse go. He settled back down to finish his nap. As the little mouse ran away, she said, "Thank you, mighty lion. You won't be sorry."

It happened shortly thereafter that the mighty lion was trapped by hunters. The hunters caught him in a net made of ropes. The lion roared in anguish.

The little mouse was not far away. She recognized the lion's roar and came quickly to gnaw the ropes away and free the lion. The lion was very grateful and quite surprised to see the mouse—more surprised that such a small creature was able to save his life.

The mouse said, "You laughed at the idea that I might ever be able to help you or repay you. I hope you know now that even a small mouse can be a friend and a help to a mighty lion." The lion and the mouse were friends from that moment on.

Small Group Enrichment

1. The Lion and the Mouse
Ask children to think of other sets of friends where one of the friends is big and the other small. Read *Amos & Boris* by William Steig and compare the characters.

2. Looby Loo
Teach the children Looby Loo (page 183).

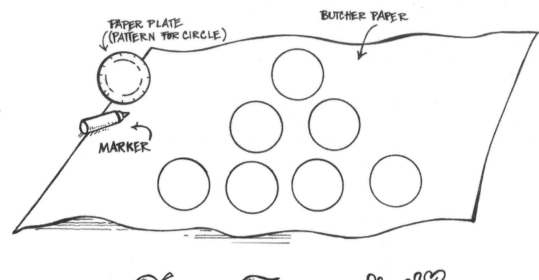

3. Leaf Sort

Give the children leaves to sort. Draw a sorting pattern on a piece of butcher paper. Use an 8" (20 cm) paper plate as a pattern. Draw one circle in the top center of the butcher paper. Draw two more circles side by side and a foot apart under the first circle. Under each of those, draw two more circles. Children pile the leaves in the first circle and then they create two categories, such as big and little, and sort the leaves into the next two circles. Then the children create new sorting categories for each new set of leaves, such as rough and smooth edges. Continue until the leaves are sorted into four categories in the bottom circles.

4. Lunch Outdoors

Serve lunch outdoors. Have a picnic.

5. Lily Pad Leap

Cut large lily pads out of green construction paper or bulletin board paper. Place them a couple of feet apart and encourage children to jump from pad to pad.

6. Library

Take a trip to the library. Let everyone check out a library book.

7. Leap Frog

Play Leap Frog.

8. Lemonade
Make lemonade and serve it to families when they pick up their children.

9. Lick a Lollipop
Give everyone a lollipop to lick. How many licks does it take to lick a lollipop until it's gone?

10. Log Rolls
Show the children how to do log rolls. Lie on the floor and roll with your body straight. Why is it impossible to roll in a straight line?

11. Hop the Line on Your Left Foot
Place a 10' (3 m) strip of masking tape on the floor and encourage children to hop the length of the line on their left foot.

12. Listening Walk
Take the children on a listening walk. Explain that in order to hear all of nature's sounds, you have to be very quiet.

13. Lullaby
Teach the children a lullaby, such as "Hush Little Baby" or "Rock-a-Bye, Baby." If there are younger children close by who might enjoy being sung to sleep, let the children try out their new lullaby.

14. Leaf Bracelets
Take the children out on a nature hike to look for leaves. Make the children leaf bracelets by turning strips of masking tape inside out and placing it around their wrists. Children can stick their leaves on their bracelets as they select the ones they like.

15. Beginning Sounds "L" Concentration
Use the patterns on Appendix page 396 to make a concentration game of objects that start with the letter "L."

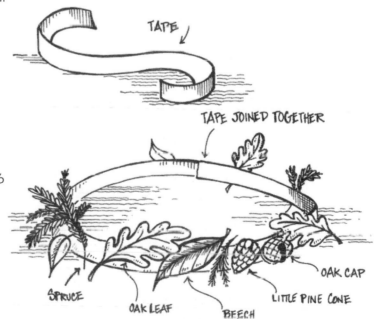

TAPE

TAPE JOINED TOGETHER

SPRUCE

OAK LEAF

BEECH

LITTLE PINE CONE

OAK CAP

Word List

lab	let
lace	lick
lack	life
lad	lift
lag	light
lake	like
lamp	limp
land	line
lane	link
lap	lion
late	lip
leaf	list
leak	lit
leap	live
least	loaf
leaves	log
left	long
leg	look
lend	love
less	luck
lest	lunch

Book List

Leo the Late Bloomer by Robert Kraus
Little Blue and Little Yellow by Leo Lionni
The Little Old Lady Who Was Not Afraid of Anything by Linda Williams
Lovable Lyle by Bernard Waber
Lunch by Denise Fleming
Lyle, Lyle, Crocodile by Bernard Waber

Songs

The Muffin Man

Oh, do you know the muffin man,
The muffin man, the muffin man?
Oh, do you know the muffin man
Who lives in Drury Lane?

Mulberry Bush

Here we go round the mulberry bush,
The mulberry bush, the mulberry bush.
Here we go round the mulberry bush,
So early in the morning.

This is the way we wash our clothes…
So early Monday morning.

This is the way we iron our clothes…
So early Tuesday morning.

This is the way we mend our clothes…
So early Wednesday morning.

This is the way we scrub the floor…
So early Thursday morning.

This is the way we sweep the house…
So early Friday morning.

This is the way we bake our bread…
So early Saturday morning.

This is the way we go to church…
So early Sunday morning.

Mister Moon

O, Mister Moon, Moon,
Bright and shiny Moon,
Won't you please
Shine down on me?

ACQUIRING READING SKILLS

O, Mister Moon, Moon,
Bright and shiny Moon,
Hiding behind that tree.

I'd like to linger,
But I've got to run.
Mama's callin'
"Baby, get your homework done!"

O, Mister Moon, Moon,
Bright and shiny Moon,
Won't you please
Shine down on,
Talk about your shine on,
Please shine down on me?

Merry Music Time (Tune: Mary Had a Little Lamb)
Play the band, it's music time,
Music time, music time.
Play the band, it's music time,
Merry music time.

Clang the cymbals, it's music time,
Music time, music time.
Clang the cymbals, it's music time
Merry music time.

Beat the drums, it's music time,
Music time, music time.
Beat the drums, it's music time
Merry music time.

(Continue adding instruments)

Mary Ann McCartney Went A-Fishing (Tune: Battle Hymn of
the Republic)
Mary Ann McCartney went a-fishin' for some clams,
Mary Ann McCartney went a-fishin' for some clams,
Mary Ann McCartney went a-fishin' for some clams,
But she didn't get a (clap, clap) clam!

All she got was influenza,
All she got was influenza,
All she got was influenza,
But she didn't get a (clap, clap) clam!

She dug up all the mud she found in San Francisco Bay,
She dug up all the mud she found in San Francisco Bay,
She dug up all the mud she found in San Francisco Bay,
But she didn't get a (clap, clap) clam!

All she got was influenza,
All she got was influenza,
All she got was influenza,
But she didn't get a (clap, clap) clam!

She kept on diggin' anyway but no luck did she have,
She kept on diggin' anyway but no luck did she have,
She kept on diggin' anyway but no luck did she have,
'Cause she didn't get a (clap, clap) clam!

All she got was influenza,
All she got was influenza,
All she got was influenza,
But she didn't get a (clap, clap) clam!

Poems

One Misty, Moisty Morning

One misty, moisty morning,
When cloudy was the weather,
I chanced to meet an old man
Clothed all in leather.
He began to compliment,
And I began to grin:
"How do you do?"
And "How do you do?"
And "How do you do?" again.

Mary Middling Had a Pig

Mary Middling had a pig
Not very little, not very big,
Not very pink, not very grey,
Not very dirty, not very clean,
Not very good, not very naughty,
Not very humble, not very haughty,
Not very thin, not very fat.
Now what world you give for a pig like that?

Little Miss Muffet

Little Miss Muffet sat on her tuffet,
Eating her curds and whey.
Along came a spider,
And sat down beside her,
And frightened Miss Muffet away.

(New verse) (Tamera Bryant)
Little Miss Muffet went back to her tuffet,
Looked the thing square in the eye.
"See here, you big spider,
Miss Muffet's a fighter.
And you're the one saying bye-bye."

Early Morning (Hilaire Belloc)

The moon on the one hand, the dawn on the other;
The moon is my sister, the dawn is my brother.
The moon on my left hand, the dawn on my right:
My brother, good morning: my sister, good night.

Mistress Mary

"Mistress Mary,
Quite contrary,
How does you garden grow?"

"With silver bell
And cockle shells,
And pretty maids, all in a row."

Tongue Twisters/Alliterative Sentences and Phrases

Say the sentences or phrases below three times quickly if you can.

- Moose noshing much mush.
- Mitch mixed Millie's meal.
- Madison's medicine makes her mad.

Fingerplays/Action Rhymes

I Measure Myself

I measure myself from my head to my toes. (*suit actions to words*)
I measure my arms starting here by my nose.
I measure my legs and I measure me all.
I measure to see if I'm growing tall.

How Many?

How many people live at your house?
One, my mother. (*count on fingers*)
Two, my father.
Three, my sister
Four, my brother.
There's one more.
Now let me see. (*touch head*)
Oh, yes, of course, (*nod head*)
It must be me! (*point to self*)

Repeat the rhyme letting each member of the group take turns counting his family member on his fingers.

Miss Mary Mack

Miss Mary Mack, Mack, Mack, (*make up a hand jive to go with the chant*)
All dressed in black, black, black,
With silver buttons, buttons, buttons,
All down her back, back, back.

She asked her mother, mother, mother,
For fifteen cents, cents, cents,
To see the elephant, elephant, elephant,
Jump the fence, fence, fence!

Story: This Old Man (Magnetic Story)

Directions: Color, cut out, and laminate the story patterns on Appendix pages 322 and 323. Trace the patterns on magnetic backing, cut out and glue to the back of the prepared story patterns. Tell the story on a cookie sheet or other magnetic surface.

This Old Man (Tamera Bryant and Tracy Moncure)
This Old Man, he played drums,
With his fingers and his thumbs.

Chorus
With a nick-nack paddy whack give a dog a bone
This Old Man is rockin' on.

This Old Man, he played flute,
Made it hum and made it toot.

Chorus

This Old Man, he played strings,
Twangs and twops and zips and zings.

Chorus

This Old Man, he played bass,
With a big grin on his face.

Chorus

This Old Man, he played gong,
At the end of every song.

Chorus

This Old Man, he could dance.
He could strut and he could prance.

Chorus

This Old Man was a band,
Very best band in the land.

Chorus

* Used with permission from SRA/McGraw-Hill

Small Group Enrichment

1. This Old Man
This song is recorded on *Here Is Thumbkin!* by Kimbo Recording Company.

Find a copy of this song or a recording of the original song and let children play rhythm band instruments with the music.

2. Mix a Milkshake
Invite children to put a scoop of ice cream, ½ cup (120 ml) of milk, and flavoring, if desired, in a jar. Shake and serve.

3. Micro Life
Give each child a 3' (1 m) strip of yarn and a magnifying glass. Take the children outside and let them select anyplace on the play ground to section off a circle of ground with their yarn. Encourage them to use their magnifying glasses to explore the small creatures in the circle they have made.

YARN CIRCLE

YARN CIRCLE

YARN CIRCLE

4. Mint Milk in a Mug
Use peppermint extract to flavor some milk and serve it in a mug.

5. Mud Pies
Provide props such as pie tins, spoons, twigs, acorns, and leaves for making mud pies. Challenge the children to a mud pie contest.

6. Marbles
Teach the children how to shoot marbles.

7. Marble Painting
Place a sheet of drawing paper in a shallow bowl or box lid. Place two or three marbles In some tempera paint and then on the paper in the box. Invite children to roll the marbles around to create a magnificent design.

8. Magnetic Maze
Use the maze path on Appendix page 377. Glue the maze to a piece of poster board. Place a round magnet on the start spot on the maze. Use another magnet under the poster board to move the magnet on the top along the maze.

9. Marching
Play some marching music and march.

10. Marker Magic
Use markers to color a coffee filter. Lay the filter on a piece of drawing paper and spray with water. Wait a few minutes and remove the filter to see that the design has transferred to the paper.

11. Monkey See, Monkey Do
Invite the children to pretend to be monkeys. One monkey is selected to be the "boss monkey." The monkeys must mimic the boss monkey's actions.

12. Mosaic
Discuss mosaic art. Cut several colors of construction paper into tiny odd shapes. Provide glue and drawing paper and invite children to create a mosaic.

13. The Mitten
Read different versions of *The Mitten* and compare the stories, illustrations, and characters.

14. Beginning Sound "M" Concentration

Use the patterns on Appendix page 397 to make a concentration game of objects that begin with "M."

Word List

mad	mice
made	mile
maid	milk
mail	mind
main	mine
make	miss
man	mix
march	moan
March	mole
mark	mom
Mars	moo
mash	mood
mask	moon
mat	mop
match	mouse
math	mouth
me	mow
meal	mud
mean	my
meet	

Book List

The Best Mouse Cookie by Laura Joffe Numeroff
If You Give a Mouse a Cookie by Laura Joffe Numeroff
The Milk Makers Gail Gibbons
The Mitten by Jan Brett
Morris' Disappearing Bag by Rosemary Wells
Mouse Paint by Ellen Stoll Walsh
Mud Puddle by Robert Munsch
Mushroom in the Rain adapted by Mirra Ginsburg
The Mystery of the Magic Green Ball by Steven Kellogg
The Mystery of the Missing Red Mitten by Steven Kellogg
Over in the Meadow by Ezra Jack Keats

Songs

No, No, Yes, Yes (Tune: Reveille)
No, no, no, no, no, no, no,
No, no, no, no, no, no, no,
No, no, no, no, no, no, no,
No, no, no, no, no, no, no,
No, no, no, no, no, no, no!

Yes, yes, yes, yes, yes, yes, yes,
Yes, yes, yes, yes, yes, yes, yes,
Yes, yes, yes, yes, yes, yes, yes,
Yes, yes, yes, yes, yes, yes, yes,
Yes, yes, yes, yes, yes, yes, yes!

Ninety-Nine Bottles of Pop
Ninety-nine bottles of pop on the wall,
Ninety-nine bottles of pop.
Take one down, pass it around,
Ninety-eight bottles of pop on the wall.

Continue counting down until children tire of the song.

I'm a Nut
I'm a little acorn, small and round
Lying on the cold, cold ground.
Everyone walks over me,
That's is why I'm cracked you see.
I'm a nut! (click, click)
I'm a nut! (click, click)
I'm a nut! (click, click)

**The Nickel and the
   Doughnut** (Tune: Turkey in the Straw)
I ran around the corner,
I ran around the block,
I ran right into the baker's shop.
I took me a doughnut right out of the grease,
And handed the lady a five-cent piece.
She looked at the nickel, she looked at me.
She said, "This nickel ain't no good to me.

There's a whole in the nickel and it goes right through."
Said I, "There's a whole in your doughnut, too.
Thanks for the doughnut! Good-bye!"

Poems

Never Say Never (Tiffany Markle)
Never say never, never again.
If you never say never,
Then surely you can.

Oodles of Noodles (Pam Schiller)
Noodles, noodles on my plate.
I want to eat them; I can't wait.
Noodles, noodles, nice and long.
I do not want to eat them wrong.

If I slurp them like a drink
What will all these people think?
Noodles, noodles still on my plate.
Boy it's getting really late.

Slurp, no more noodles on my plate!

My Noisy House (Tamera Bryant)
My house is always noisy,
Sound stirs all around.
We're hustling, bustling, bustling, on the move
We're making lots of sound.

Telephone rings,
Doorbell buzzes,
Someone's knocking,
Toilet flushes.

Television blares.
And the radio too,
Vacuum roars.
What can I do?

My house is always noisy
And busy as can be.
We're never ever quiet here,
We're loud and nois eeeeee!

Tongue Twisters/Alliterative Sentences and Phrases

Say the sentences and phrases below three times quickly if you can.

- Ned nabbed Nick's nickel.
- Nick nipped Ned's nose.
- Nancy naps at Nana's.

Fingerplays/Action Rhymes

Cozy Little Nest

If I were a bird, (*hook thumbs together and fly hands around*)
I'd sing a song,
And fly around
The whole day long.

And when it was dark,
I'd go to rest
Up in my cozy (*cup hands to form a nest*)
Little nest.

Nooty Na

Nooty na, nooty na,
Nooty na, na.

Thumbs up (*suit actions to words*)
Nooty na, nooty na,
Nooty na, na.

Elbows back
Nooty na, nooty na,
Nooty na, na.

A C Q U I R I N G   R E A D I N G   S K I L L S

Feet apart
Nooty na, nooty na,
Nooty na, na.

Knees together
Nooty na, nooty na,
Nooty na, na.

Bottoms up
Nooty na, nooty na,
Nooty na, na.

Tongue out
Nooty na, nooty na,
Nooty na, na.

Eyes shut
Nooty na, nooty na,
Nooty na, na.

Turn around
Nooty na, nooty na,
Nooty na, na.

Story: The Napping House (Flannel Board Story)

Directions: Check out the book *The Napping House* by Don and Audrey Woods from the library. Use a black sharpie pen to trace the patterns on Appendix pages 334-336 onto Pelon. Color them with crayons and cut them out. Use them with the flannel board to present the story.

Small Group Enrichment

1. The Napping House
Discuss the cause and effect aspect of the story. What caused all the commotion? Can anyone remember the sequence of who came to bed?

2. Newspaper Art
Provide newspaper to sponge paint on, make car tracks on, and paint at the easel. It makes an interesting background.

3. Newspaper Hats
Fold newspaper hats.

4. Nifty Nest

Give each child a medium-size paper sack. Show them how to roll the sack down from the top to the bottom to create a nest. Go on a nature walk and gather things to go in the nest.

5. Nut Sort

Provide a variety of nuts. Let children sort the nuts into a muffin tin using tongs.

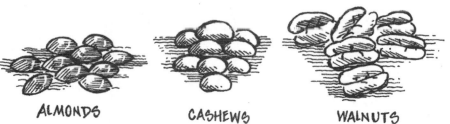

MUFFIN TIN

TONGS

— NUTS —

ALMONDS   CASHEWS   WALNUTS

6. Nighttime

Encourage children to brainstorm a list of nighttime activities. List their thoughts on chart paper.

7. Name Game

Challenge children to think of rhyming words for each other's names (nonsense words are OK). During the day try to use the children's names as rhyming riddles. For example: Will the girl whose name rhymes with ham pick up the blocks?

8. Next

Make up patterns. Ask the children to finish each pattern by identifying what comes next.

9. Nature Hike

Take children on a nature hike. Encourage children to collect nature treasures. Make a nature bracelet by turning a strip of masking tape inside out and placing it around each child's wrist. Children can stick their treasures on their bracelets.

10. Noisy/Not Noisy

Provide a variety of items such as pompoms, cotton balls, spools, chips, and so forth, to drop onto a cookie sheet. Which items make noise and which do not make noise?

A C Q U I R I N G   R E A D I N G   S K I L L S

11. Nickle Match
Encourage children to match five pennies to a nickel.

12. Name Puzzles
Write each child's name on a strip on tag board leaving room between each letter. Cut the letters apart to make a name puzzle. Let children put their names together.

13. Nose Nudging
Place two pieces of masking tape on the floor 12′ (4 m) apart for a start line and a finish line. Place two Nerf balls on the start line. Select two children to race each other. The children must move the ball from the start line to the finish line by nudging it with their nose.

14. Beginning Sound "N" Concentration
Use the patterns on Appendix page 398 to make a concentration game of objects that begin with "N."

Book List
Frozen Noses by Jan Carr
Nana Upstairs & Nana Downstairs by Tomie dePaola
The Napping House by Don and Audrey Wood
Noisy Nora by Rosemary Wells

Word List

nab	niche
nag	night
nail	nip
name	no
nap	nod
near	noise
neck	north
need	nose
nest	not
net	note
new	now
next	nub
nice	nurse
nick	nut

Songs

(Long O)

Apples and Bananas

I like to eat eat eat apples and bananas.
I like to eat eat eat apples and bananas.

I like to ate ate ate aypuls and baynaynays.
I like to ate ate ate aypuls and baynaynays.

I like eet eet eet eeples and beeneenees.
I like eet eet eet eeples and beeneenees.

I like to ite, ite, ite, ipples and
  binininis.
I like to ite, ite, ite, ipples
  and binininis.

I like to ote ote ote opples
  and bononos.
I like to ote ote ote opples and
  bononos.

I like to ute ute ute upples and
  bununus.
I like to ute ute ute upples and
  bununus.

Over in the Meadow

Over in the meadow, in the sand, in the sun,
Lived an old mother frog and her little froggie one.
"Croak!" said the mother; "I croak!" said the one,
So they croaked and they croaked in the sand, in the sun.

Over in the meadow, in the stream so blue,
Lived an old mother fish and her little fishies two.
"Swim!" said the mother; "We swim!" said the two,
So they swam and they swam in the stream so blue.

Over in the meadow, on a branch of the tree,
Lived an old mother bird and her little birdies three.

"Sing!" said the mother; "We sing!" said the three,
And they sang and they sang on a branch of the tree.

Over the River

Over the river and through the woods
To grandmother's house we go.
The horse knows the way to carry the sleigh
Through the white and drifted snow.
Over the river and through the woods
Oh, how the wind does blow.
It bites the nose and stings the toes
As over the ground we go.

Open, Shut Them

Open, shut them. Open, shut them. (*open and close hands*)
Give a little clap.
Open, shut them. Open shut them.
Put them in your lap.
Walk them, walk them. Walk them, walk them, (*creep fingers up chest
   to chin*)
Way up to your chin.
Open wide your little mouth, (*open mouth*)
But don't let them walk in.

My Bonnie Lies Over the Ocean

My Bonnie lies over the ocean,
My Bonnie lies over the sea,
My Bonnie lies over the ocean.
Oh, bring back my Bonnie to me.

Chorus
Bring back, bring back,
Oh, bring back my Bonnie to me, to me.
Bring back, bring back,
Oh, bring back my Bonnie to me.

O Me, O My

O me, o my,
We'll get there by and by!
If anybody here likes (*child's name*)
It's I, I, I, I, I!

O me, o my,
Our hearts are full of glee!
If anybody here likes (*child's name*)
It's me, me, me, me, me!

(Short O)

On Top of Spaghetti

On top of spaghetti, all covered with cheese,
I lost my poor meatball when somebody sneezed.
It rolled on the table,
And onto the floor,
And then my poor meat-
   ball,
It rolled out the door.

Sing a Song of
Opposites (Pam
   Schiller) (Tune: Sing a
   Song of Sixpence)
Sing a song of opposites.
How many can you
   find?
Let me say a few things
That I have in mind.

This is up and this is
   down. (*chant this part
   and point to appropri-
   ate items*)
This is square and this is
   round.
This is high and this is
   low.
This means "yes" and this means "no." (*shake head yes and no*)

Now that I have started
And shown you just a few.
Let's start all over
And see what you can do!

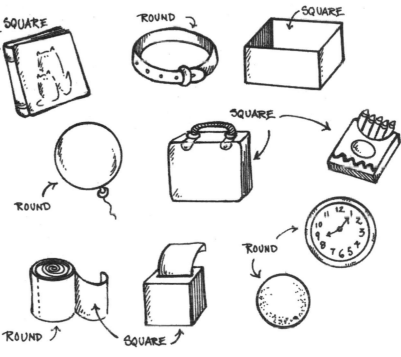

Poems

(Long O)

Old Mother Goose
Old Mother Goose
When she went to wander,
Would ride through the air
On a very fine gander.

The Sun Overhead
Over there the sun gets up
And marches all the day.
At noon it stands just overhead,
And at night it goes away.

(Short O)

The Octopus (Pam Schiller)
The octopus swims the ocean floor
With a soft body and arms galore.
She silently glides through coral reef
And settles gently to hide beneath.

What would you do with arms galore?
Could you navigate the ocean floor?
Would you tangle with the octopi
Who happen to pass as you swam by?

Oh I think it is a little odd
The submarine life of the octopod.

Little Owls
Little owls look bright
When you see their eyes at night.
But they're winking and blinking
In the daylight.

Tongue Twisters/Alliterative Sentences and Phrases

Moses

Moses supposes his toeses are roses,
But Moses supposes erroneously;
For nobody's toeses are posies of roses
As Moses supposes his toeses to be.

Say the sentences and phrases below three times quickly if you can.

- Toy boat. Toy boat. Toy boat.
- Owen owes Opie oats.
- Are our oars oak?
- The ochre ogre ogled the poker.
- Old oily Ollic oils old oily autos.

Fingerplays/Action Rhymes

(Long O)

Ocean Shell

I found a great big shell one day, upon the ocean floor. (*cup hands as if holding a shell.*)
I held it close up to my ear—I heard the ocean roar! (*raise hands to ear*)

I found a tiny little shell one day, upon the ocean sand. (*cup one hand as if holding a shell*)
The waves had worn it nice and smooth—It felt nice in my hand. (*rub other hand over cupped hand*)

Here Is an Oak Tree

Here is an oak tree straight and tall, (*place left hand under right elbow and extend right hand upward*)
And here are its branches wide. (*spread fingers of right hand*)
Here is a nest of twigs and moss, (*cup hands to make a nest*)
With three little birds inside. (*hold up three fingers*)

The breezes blow and the little leaves play, (*make tree again and sway arm*)
But the branches hold the nest (*make nest*)
As they swing and sway and bob and rock (*rock nest*)
So the little birds can rest. (*place hands on side of cheek*)

(Short O)

An Owl Sat Alone

An owl sat alone (*hold up one finger*)
On the branch of a tree.
He was as quiet (*put finger to lips*)
As he could be.
It was night
And his eyes were round like this. (*make circles over eyes with thumb and index finger*)
And when he looked around,
Not a thing did he miss. (*look from side to side*)

Opposites

Tall as a tree (*stretch up tall*)
Big as a house (*hold hands out to side*)
Thin as a pin (*hold arms tight to sides*)
Small as a mouse. (*squat down low*)

Story: I Know an Old Lady Who Swallowed a Fly (Puppet Story)

Directions: Make a photocopy of the Old Lady face pattern (Appendix page 337). Color it, cut it out, and laminate it. Glue the face on the bottom of a small paper bag with the chin pointed toward the open end of the bag. Cut a 2" (5 cm) slit in the fold that is under the fold of the bottom of the bag. This slit will become the mouth where you slip the various things the old lady eats down her throat. Cut a small square out of the front of the paper bag and tape a piece of clear acetate over it. This will allow children to see the items after they've been swallowed. Staple the bottom of the bag closed. Cut a 3" (7 cm) slit in the backside of the bag so you can retrieve the pieces to use again. Make a photocopy of the things the old lady eats. Color them, cut them out, and laminate them.

I Know an Old Lady Who Swallowed a Fly

I know an old lady who swallowed a fly.
I don't know why she swallowed the fly.
Perhaps she'll die.
I know an old lady who swallowed a spider
That wiggled and jiggled and tickled inside her.
She swallowed the spider to catch the fly.
But I don't know why she swallowed the fly.
Perhaps she'll die.

I know an old lady who swallowed a bird.
How absurd! She swallowed a bird.
She swallowed the bird to catch the spider
That wiggled and jiggled and tickled inside her.
She swallowed the spider to catch the fly.
But I don't know why she swallowed the fly.
Perhaps she'll die.

I know and old lady who swallowed a cat.
Think of that! She swallowed a cat.
She swallowed a cat to catch the bird.
She swallowed the bird to catch the spider
That wiggled and jiggled and tickled inside her.
She swallowed the spider to catch the fly.
I don't know why she swallowed the fly.
Perhaps she'll die.

I know an old lady who swallowed a dog.
What a hog! She swallowed a dog.
She swallowed the dog to catch the cat.
She swallowed the cat to catch the bird.
She swallowed the bird to catch the spider
That wiggled and jiggled and ticked inside her,
She swallowed the spider to catch the fly.
But I don't know why she swallowed the fly
Perhaps she'll die.

I know an old lady who swallowed a goat.
It stuck in her throat! She swallowed a goat.
She swallowed the goat to catch the dog.
She swallowed the dog to catch the cat.
She swallowed the cat to catch the bird.
She swallowed the bird to catch the spider

ACQUIRING READING SKILLS

That wiggled and jiggled and ticked inside her.
She swallowed the spider to catch the fly.
But I don't know why she swallowed the fly.
Perhaps she'll die.
I know an old lady who swallowed a horse.
She's dead, of course!

Read *There Was an Old Woman* by Steven Kellogg and compare the two stories.

Small Group Enrichment

1. There Was an Old Lady Who Swallowed a Fly

Use the story patterns to create sequence cards (Appendix pages 337-339). Invite children to sequence the items the old lady swallowed. Do they notice that the items increase in size?

2. Oatmeal

Invite the children to make oatmeal and eat it for a snack. Add different flavorings such as vanilla or cinnamon to the oatmeal. Offer raisins and berries for toppings.

3. Ocean in a Bottle

Mix one part clear vegetable oil and three parts denatured alcohol in a medium-size clear plastic bottle. Add blue food coloring. Glue the lid on securely. Let the children manipulate the bottle to make an ocean wave.

4. Ovals

Provide a variety of ovals in different sizes and colors. Ask children to sort the ovals by color or size.

5. Over and Under

Teach the children to weave crepe paper streamers in a chain-link fence or laundry basket.

6. Old

What is old? This is an interesting question to ask children.

7. Obstacle Course

Let the children help make an obstacle course.

8. Ordering

Discuss different ways to order the children in the classroom. Let the children think of ways they could be placed in order (alphabetically, tallest to shortest, who arrives at school first, by birthdays, and so forth).

9. Off or On

Place a piece of paper in the middle of the floor. Invite children to toss a bean-bag to land on the paper. Have them record with tally marks how many times they land on the paper and how many times they land off the paper.

10. Oil Designs

Place a few drops of oil-based paint in a tub of water. Swirl the water. Give children a piece of paper and show them how to lay the paper on the water and then lift it out to make a design.

11. Opposites

Brainstorm a list of opposites with the children. Write their ideas on a piece of chart paper. How many pairs of opposites are they able to think of?

12. Office

Provide office props such as paper, pens, envelopes, hole punch, stapler, and so forth for the Dramatic Play Center.

ACQUIRING READING SKILLS

Word List

Long O	Short O
oak	object
oar	observe
oat	occupy
oath	octopus
obey	odd
oboe	off
ocean	often
odor	opposite
old	ostrich
omen	
opal	
open	
over	
ozone	

Book List

Oceans by Seymour Simon
Old Henry by Joan W. Blos
Once Upon MacDonald's Farm by Stephen Gammell
Over in the Meadow by Ezra Jack Keats
Owen by Kevin Henkes
Owl Moon by Jane Yolen

Songs

Polly-Wolly-Doodle

Oh, I went down South for to see my Sal.
Sing "Polly-Wolly-Doodle" all the day.
My Sal, she is a spunky gal.
Sing "Polly-Wolly-Doodle" all the day.

Chorus
Fare thee well!
Fare thee well!
Fare thee well, my fairy fey.
For I'm off to Lousianna
For to see my Susy Anna,
Sing "Polly-Wolly-Doodle" all the day.

Oh, I came to a river and I couldn't get across.
Sing "Polly-Wolly-Doodle" all the day.
And I jumped upon a catfish and thought it was a horse.
Sing "Polly-Wolly-Doodle" all the day.

Chorus

Oh, a grasshopper sitting on a railroad track.
Sing "Polly-Wolly-Doodle" all the day.
A-picking his teeth with a carpet tack.
Sing "Polly-Wolly-Doodle" all the day.

Chorus

Oh, I went to bed but it wasn't any use.
Sing "Polly-Wolly-Doodle" all the day.
My feet stuck out for a chicken roost.
Sing "Polly Wolly Doodle" all the day.

Chorus

Pop! Goes the Weasel

All around the cobbler's bench,
The monkey chased the weasel.
The monkey thought 'twas all in fun—
Pop! Goes the weasel.

Johnny has the whooping cough,
Mary has the measles.
That's the way the money goes—
Pop! Goes the weasel.

A penny for a spool of thread,
A penny for a needle.
That's the way the money goes—
Pop! Goes the weasel.

All around the mulberry bush,
The monkey chased the weasel.
That's the way the money goes—
Pop! Goes the weasel.

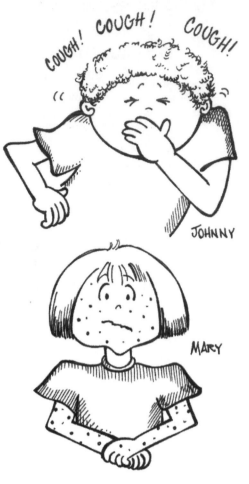

JOHNNY

MARY

Goober Peas

Sitting by the roadside,
On a summer's day,
Chatting with my messmates
Passing time away.
Lying in the shadows,
Underneath the trees,
Goodness, how delicious
Eating goober peas!

Chorus
Peas, peas, peas, peas!
Eating goober peas!
Goodness, how delicious,
Eating goober peas!

Poems

Please Pass the Peas (Pam Schiller)
Please pass the peas.
I just love peas.
Sweet peas, green peas, black-eyed peas,
Peas on a plate, peas on a platter,
Peas in a bowl—it just doesn't matter.
I love peas! Pass the peas, please.

I Eat My Peas With Honey

I eat my peas with honey,
I've done it all my life.
It makes the peas taste funny,
But it keeps them on my knife.

Picture People

I like to peek inside a book
Where all the picture people look.
I like to peek at them and see
If they are peeking back at me.

Higgelety, Pigglety, Pop! (Samuel Goodrich)

Higglety, Pigglety, Pop!
The dog has eaten the mop.
The pig's in a hurry,
The cat's in a flurry,
Higglety, pigglety, pop!

See a Penny

See a penny pick it up,
All the day have good luck.
See a penny let it lay,
Bad luck you'll have all the day.

Tongue Twisters/Alliterative Sentences and Phrases

Peter Piper Picked a Peck of Pickled Peppers

Peter Piper picked a peck of pickled peppers.
A peck of pickled peppers Peter Piper picked.
If Peter Piper picked a peck of pickled peppers,
Where's the peck of pickled peppers Peter Piper picked?

Or short version:

Peter Piper picked a peck of pickled peppers.
How many pecks of pickled peppers did Peter Piper pick?

Say the sentence below three times quickly if you can.

● Please pass the peas.

Fingerplays/Action Rhymes

Polly Pointer

Polly Pointer points up and Polly Pointer points down. (*point index finger up and down*)

Polly Pointer is pointing all around the town. (*point index finger all around*)

Prance her on your shoulders, prance her on your head. (*prance as directed*)

Prance her on you knees and put her into bed. (*prance on knees, then place finger inside palm*)

Five Little Pumpkins

Five Little Pumpkins sitting on a gate. (*hold up five fingers*)

First one said, "It's getting late." (*wiggle first finger*)

Second one said, "There's witches in the air." (*wiggle second finger*)

Third one said, "We don't care." (*wiggle third finger*)

Fourth one said, "Let's run, let's run." (*wiggle fourth finger*)

Fifth one said, "Oh, it's just Halloween fun." (*wiggle fifth finger*)

But whooo went the wind and out went the light (*hold hands on both sides of your mouth and blow*)

And five little pumpkins rolled out of sight. (*roll hand over hand*)

One Potato

One potato, two potato, (*make two fists—alternate taping on top of each other*)

Three potato, four,

Five potato, six potato,

Seven potato, more.

Eight potato, nine potato,

Where is ten?

Now we must count over again.

Pease Porridge Hot

Pease porridge hot, (*make up a partner clap*)

Pease porridge cold,

Pease porridge in the pot,

Nine days old.

Some like it hot.

Some like it cold.

Some like in the pot

Nine days old!

Story: The Princess and the Pea (Flannel Board Story)

Directions: Use a black sharpie pen to trace the patterns on Appendix pages 310 and 341 onto Pelon. Color them with crayons and cut them out. Use them with the flannel board to present the story.

The Princess and the Pea (adapted from the Hans Christian Andersen story) Once upon a time there was a prince who wanted to marry a princess. But the princess he married had to be a real princess in every way. The prince traveled all over the world, but nowhere could he find what he wanted. Everywhere he went there were women who claimed they were real princesses, but it was difficult to find one he believed was truly a princess in every way. There was always something about each one that was not as it should be. So he came home again and was sad, for marrying a real princess was very important to him.

One evening there was a terrible storm. There was thunder and lightning and the rain poured down in torrents. Suddenly a knocking was heard at the castle gate, and the old king went to open it.

There stood a princess in front of the gate. But good gracious! What a sight the rain and the wind had made of her good looks. The water ran down from her hair and clothes. It ran down into the heels of her shoes and out again at the toes. And yet she said that she was a princess nonetheless.

She was brought into the palace and given dry clothing to wear and food to eat. The prince was quite pleased when he saw how pretty she was. But how could he be sure she was indeed a real princess?

"Well, we'll soon find that out," thought the old queen when she heard what was happening. But she said nothing. Quietly she slipped into the guest room and took twenty mattresses and laid them on the pea, and then twenty feather comforters on top of the mattresses.

On this the princess had to lie all night. In the morning she was asked how she slept.

"Oh, very badly!" she said. "I scarcely closed my eyes all night. Heaven only knows what was in the bed, but I was lying on something so hard that I am black and blue all over my body."

ACQUIRING READING SKILLS

The old queen knew at once that the princess was a real princess because she had felt the pea right through the twenty mattresses and the twenty feather comforters. Nobody but a real princess could be as sensitive as that. So the prince took her for his wife, and the pea was put in the museum, where it may still be seen, if no one has stolen it.

Small Group Enrichment

1. The Princess and the Pea
This story presents a great opportunity to ask some critical thinking questions. Do you think anyone could feel a pea beneath twenty mattresses and twenty comforters? Why was it so important to the prince that he marry a princess? Are princesses any different from other women? Read *The Paper Bag Princess* by Robert Munch and make comparisons between the two princesses.

2. The Princess and the Pea Test
Provide pillows and a pea in the Dramatic Play Center. Encourage children to see if they can feel the pea beneath the pillows.

3. Pigs in a Blanket
Invite the children to make Pigs in a Blanket. Wrap a refrigerator biscuit around a precooked sausage and bake for 8 minutes at 400°. Ask the children why this tasty treat is called Pig in a Blanket.

4. Pick a Pair
Use the Rhyming Card patterns (Appendix page 410) to make a game of Rhyming Pairs. Glue the pictures onto yellow construction paper cut into pear shapes and let children pick a pair of rhyming words.

5. Plan a Picnic
Plan a picnic lunch. Let children decide what will be taken to eat and what will be taken to play with. Have your picnic at a local park or on the playground.

6. Pink Party
Have a Pink Party. Everyone wears pink. Serve pink punch (pink lemonade) and pink frosted cookies or strawberry ice cream.

7. Peg Patterns
Provide peg boards and pegs. Challenge the children to make a pattern with the pegs.

8. Pop Popcorn
Place butcher paper on the floor to cover an 8' x 8' (2 m x 2 m) space. Place

an old-fashioned popcorn popper in the middle of the paper and pop pop-corn without the lid on. Let children sit around the perimeter of the paper and watch. After popcorn has cooled, let the children eat it. (Supervise closely.)

9. Polishing Pennies
Provide a bowl of pennies, a toothbrush, and toothpaste. Invite children to polish the pennies with the toothpaste and toothbrush.

10. Pass the Penny
Pass a penny to music. When the music stops, whoever is holding the penny gets to keep it. Continue for several rounds. Who has the most pennies?

11. Push or Pull
Have children partially fill a box or basket with blocks. When they want to move the box, is it easier to push it or to pull it? Is it easier to move it alone or with a partner?

12. Pretzel Pass
Invite children to stand in a circle. Give each child a straw. Place a large pretzel on every other straw. Challenge children to pass the pretzels around the circle using only their straws.

13. Ping-Pong Ball Push
Place a piece of masking tape on the floor for a start line and about 12' (4 m) away a second piece of tape for a finish line. Place a couple of Ping-Pong balls on the start line. Provide several different instruments such as basters, fans, straws, and paper for children to use to "push" a ball to the finish line without touching it. Which instrument works best?

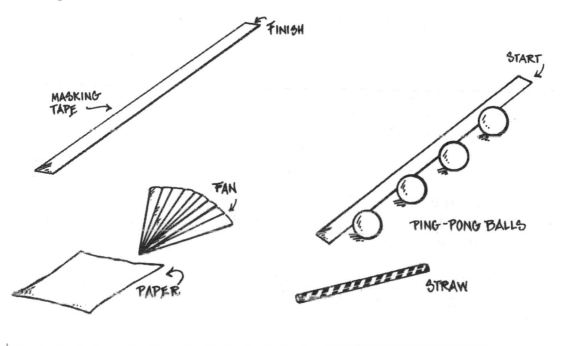

14. Perfect Puzzles.
Recycle greeting cards. Give each child a card and invite her to cut it into a puzzle.

15. Beginning Sound "P" Concentration
Use the patterns on Appendix page 399 to make a concentration game of objects that begin with "P."

Word List

pad	pig
page	pike
pain	pill
paint	pine
pal	pink
pan	pint
pants	pit
paper	pod
party	point
pass	poke
past	pole
pat	pond
patch	pork
paw	port
pay	post
pea	pull
peach	put
peak	puppy
peck	purse
peel	push
peg	put
pencil	putt
pie	

Book List

Pancakes! by Eric Carle
The Paper Bag Princess by Robert Munsch
Paul Bunyan by Steven Kellogg
Petunia by Roger Duvoisin
The Pokey Little Puppy by Janette Sebring Lowrey
Prehistoric Pinkerton by Steven Kellogg
"The Princess and the Pea" by Hans Christian Andersen
Pumpkin Pumpkin by Jeanne Titherington

Songs

Six White Ducks

Six white ducks that I once knew,
Fat ducks, skinny ducks, they were, too.
But the one little duck with the feather on his back,
He ruled the others with a quack, quack, quack!
Quack, quack, quack!
Quack, quack, quack!
He ruled the others with a quack, quack, quack!

The Quartermaster's Corp

Oh, it's beans, beans, beans
That turn us into fiends
In the corps, in the corps,
Oh, it's beans, beans, beans
That turn us into fiends
In the Quartermaster Corps.

Chorus
Mine eyes are dim.
I cannot see.
I have not brought my specs with me!
I have not brought my specs with me!

Oh, it's soup, soup, soup
That knocks you for a loop
In the corps, in the corps,
Oh, it's soup, soup, soup
That knocks you for a loop
In the Quartermaster Corps

Chorus

Oh, it's cheese, cheese, cheese
That brings you to your knees
In the corps, in the corps…

Chorus

Oh, it's cake, cake, cake
That makes your stomach ache
In the corps, in the corps…

Chorus

Oh, it's pie, pie, pie
That hits you in the eye
In the corps, in the corps…

Chorus

Oh, it's meat, meat, meat
That isn't fit to eat
In the corps, in the corps…

Chorus

Oh, it's peas, peas, peas
That make you want to sneeze
In the corps, in the corps…

Chorus

Oh, it's stew, stew, stew
That turns you black and blue
In the corps, in the corps…

Chorus

Oh, it's bread, bread, bread
Sits in your gut like lead
In the corps, in the corps…

Chorus

Oh, it's pears, pears, pears
That give you curly hairs
In the corps, in the corps…

Chorus

Poems

The Queen of Hearts
The Queen of Hearts,
She made some tarts,
All on a summer's day.
The Knave of Hearts,
He stole the tarts,
And took them clean away.

Tongue Twisters/Alliterative Sentences and Phrases

Say the sentences and phrases below three times quickly if you can.

- Quail quills, quail quills, quail quills.
- Quentin Quacker has a quart of quarters.

Fingerplays/Action Rhymes

Quiet Time
Let your hands go clap, clap, clap. (clap)
Let your feet go tap, tap, tap. (tap)
Fold your hands in your lap. (put hands in lap)
Don't go to sleep—It's not time to nap. (shake head no)
Do you know what time it is? (Answer: Quiet Time)

ACQUIRING READING SKILLS

Be Very Quiet

Shhh—be very quiet, (*suit actions to words*)
Shhh—be very still.
Fold your busy little hands,
Close your sleepy little eyes.
Shhh—be very quiet.

Story: The Quangle Wangle's Hat (Flannel Board Story)

Directions: Use a black sharpie pen to trace the patterns on Appendix pages 342-346 onto Pelon. Color them with crayons and cut them out. Use them with the flannel board to present the story.

The Quangle Wangle's Hat (Edward Lear)
On the top of the Crumpetty Tree
The Quangle sat.
But his face you could not see,
On account of his Beaver Hat.
For his Hat was a hundred and two feet wide,
With ribbons and bibbons on every side,
And bells and buttons and loops and lace,
So nobody ever could see the face
Of the Quangle Wangle Quee.

The Quangle Wangle said
To himself on the Crumpetty Tree,
"Jam and jelly and bread
Are the best food for me!
But the longer I live on this Crumpetty Tree,
The plainer than ever it seems to me
That very few people come this way,
And that life on the whole is far from gay!"

But there came to the Crumpetty Tree,
Mr. And Mrs. Canary.
And they said, "Did ever you see
Any spot so charmingly airy?
May we build a nest on your lovely Hat?
Mr. Quangle Wangle, grant us that!
O please let us come and build a nest

Of whatever material suits you best,
Mr. Quangle Wangle Quee!"

And beside, to the Crumpetty Tree
Came the Stork and the Duck and the Owl.
The snail and the Bumble-Bee,
The Frog and the Fimble Fowl.
(The Fimble Fowl, with a Corkscrew leg);
And all of them said, "We humbly beg,
We may build our home on your lovely Hat.
Mr. Quangle Wangle, grant us that!
Mr. Quangle Wangle Quee!"

And the Golden Grouse came there,
And the Pobble who has no toes,
And the small Olympian bear,
And the Dong with the luminous nose,
And the Blue Baboon, who played the flute,
And the Orient Calf from the Land of Tute,
And the Attery Squash, and the Bisky Bat,
All came and built on the lovely Hat
Of the Quangle Wangle Quee.

And the Quangle Wangle said
To himself on the Crumpetty Tree,
"When all these creatures move
What a wonderful noise there'll be!"
And at night by the light of the Mulberry moon
They danced to the Flute of the Blue Baboon,
On the broad green leaves of the Crumpetty Tree,
And all were as happy as happy could be
With the Quangle Wangle Quee.

Small Group Enrichment

1. Quangle Wangle Quee
Have children choose their favorite character from the story and draw a
picture of it.

2. Queenly Concentration
Remove the queens from two decks of cards. Use the eight queens to play
concentration.

3. Friendship Quilt

Encourage the children to draw a picture of an activity they enjoy doing with their best friend. When you have collected pictures from everyone, display them on the wall in a quilt design.

4. Quest for Quills

Go on a nature hike and look for bird feathers. If you find some, use them as quills. You can use food coloring for ink. Have a few feathers on hand just in case you don't find any on your hike. The children will be fascinated to see a feather used as a writing instrument.

5. Quacker Crackers

Provide cream cheese, graham crackers, and crushed pineapple. Show the children how to spread some cream cheese on their graham cracker and then top it with pineapple to make a Quacker Cracker. Can anyone guess why you call this snack a Quacker Cracker?

6. Quotable Quotes

Several times during the day, write statements you hear the children make on a chalk board or flip chart. Explain to the children that when their words are repeated they are being quoted and that their words are written with quotation marks around them.

7. The Quiet Game

Gather the children in a circle and explain that you are going to play the Quiet Game. Explain that everyone must stay totally quiet and still. The first person to talk or to laugh loses the game. Try playing this game in teams.

8. Yes/No Questions

Glue pictures of animals on 12"x 18" (30 cm x 45 cm) sheets of construction paper. Stack the pictures face down. Have one child draw the top picture and without looking at it, hold it out in front of him so that the other children can see it. Then have this child ask question of classmates to determine which animal is on the card. The one catch is that the children can only answer "yes" or "no."

9. A Quart of Quarters

Provide an empty quart container such as an empty milk carton. Give the children quarters to toss into the container.

10. Thirst Quencher

Explain to children how important it is for their body and their brain to have water. Explain that when they feel thirsty, it is a message from their brain that they need water. Start a Thirst Quencher Program. Encourage children to bring water bottles from home to keep in their lockers.

11. Quack Show
Make some duck puppets from paper plates or sacks and put on a duck puppet show.

12. Quarter Cover Up
Place a quarter in a tub of shallow water. Give children pennies to drop in the water one at a time to cover up the quarter. Why is it so hard?

13. Beginning Sound "Q" Concentration
Use the patterns on Appendix page 100 to make a concentration game of objects that begin with "Q."

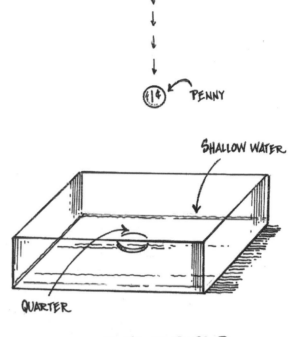

PENNY

SHALLOW WATER

QUARTER

PENNIES

Word List	
quack	quick
quarrel	quite
quarry	quiz
quart	quotable
quarter	quote
queen	
queer	
quench	
quencher	
query	
question	

Book List
It's Mine! by Leo Lionni
Quick as a Cricket by Audrey Wood
The Quilt by Ann Jonas
The Very Quiet Cricket by Eric Carle

Songs

Ring Around the Rosie

Ring around the rosie,
Pocket full of posy,
Ashes, ashes,
All fall down.

Row, Row, Row Your Boat

Row, row, row your boat
Gently down the stream.
Merrily, merrily, merrily, merrily,
Life is but a dream.

I've Been Working on the Railroad

I've been working on the railroad, all the livelong day.
I've been working on the railroad, just to pass the time away.
Don't you hear the whistle blowing?
Rise up so early in the morn!
Don't you hear the captain shouting,
Dinah, blow your horn?
Dinah, won't you blow?
Dinah won't you blow?
Oh, Dinah, won't you blow your horn, your horn?
Dinah, won't you blow? Dinah, won't you blow?
Oh, Dinah, won't you blow your horn?

Roll Over

There were five in the bed,
And the little one said,
"Roll over! Roll over!"
So they all rolled over
And one rolled out.

There were four in the bed…
Three in the bed…
Two in the bed…

There was one in the bed,
And the little one said,
"Alone at last!"

Raindrops

If all of the raindrops were lemon drops and gumdrops,
Oh, what a rain it would be.
I'd stand outside with my mouth open wide,
Ah, ah, ah, ah, ah, ah, ah,
I wouldn't care if I ever came inside.
If all of the raindrops were lemon drops and gumdrops,
Oh, what a rain it would be.

Poems

Round Is a Pancake (Joan Sullivan)

Round is a pancake,
Round is a plum,
Round is a doughnut,
Round is a drum.

Round is a puppy
Curled up on a rug.
Round are the spots
On a wee ladybug.

Look all around you,
On the ground, in the air.
You can find round things
Everywhere.

Ring-a-Ring (Kate Greenaway)
Ring-a-ring of little boys,
Ring-a-ring of girls.
All around—all around,
Twists and twirls.

You are merry children.
"Yes, we are."
Where do you come from?
"Not very far."

"We live in the mountains,
We live in the tree,
And I live in the river bed
And you won't catch me."

Falling Raindrops

I listen to the raindrops fall
On thirsty trees and flowers.
I hear the pitter-patter sound
And I'm thankful for the showers!

A Rainbow Gay

From big gray clouds
The raindrops fell,
Drip, drip, drip, one day.
Until the sunlight
Changed them all
Into a rainbow gay.

The Robin

When a robin cocks her head
Sideways in a flower bed,
She can hear the tiny sound
Of a worm beneath the ground.

Rain, Rain, Go Away

Rain, Rain, go away.
Little children want to play.

Rain, rain, come back soon. (Pam Schiller)
Little flowers want to bloom.

Rhinoceros Stew (Mildrid Luton)
If you want to make a rhinoceros stew
All in the world that you have to do
Is skin a rhinoceros—cut it in two
And stew it and stew it and stew it.

When it's stewed so long that you've quite forgot
What it is that's bubbling in the pot
Dish it up promptly—serve it hot—
And chew it and chew it and chew it
AND CHEW IT AND CHEW IT AND CHEW IT
And chew it and chew it and chew it
And chew it and chew it and chew it
And...

Tongue Twisters/Alliterative Sentences and Phrases

Say the sentences or phrases below three times quickly if you can.

- Red lorry, yellow lorry, red lorry, yellow lorry.
- Laura loves lasagna.

Fingerplays/Action Rhymes

Raindrops
This is the sun (*make sun by putting arms together in a circle*)
High in the sky.
Here comes a dark cloud (*sway arms from side to side*)
Sailing by.
These are the raindrops (*wiggle fingers downward*)
Pitter-pattering down.
They water the flowers (*cup hands as it holding a flower*)
That grow in the ground.

The Rabbit
Can you make a rabbit (*hold up index and middle finger of one hand*)
With two ears so very long?
And let him hop and hop about (*hop hand around*)
On legs so small and strong?

He nibbles, nibbles carrots (*nibble with thumb and index finger*)
For his dinner every day.
As soon as he has had enough, (*hide rabbit behind your back*)
He scampers far away.

Story: The Little Red Hen (Flannel Board Story)

Directions: Use a black sharpie pen to trace the patterns on Appendix pages 347 and 348 onto Pelon. Color them with crayons and cut them out. Use them with the flannel board to present the story.

The Little Red Hen

Once upon a time there was a Little Red Hen who shared her tiny cottage with a goose, a cat, and a dog. The goose was a gossip. She chatted with the neighbors all day long.

The cat was vain. She brushed her fur, straightened her whiskers, and polished her claws all day long. The dog was sleepy. He napped on the front porch all day long.

The Little Red Hen did all the work. She cooked, she cleaned, and she took out the trash. She mowed, she raked, and she did all the shopping.

One day on her way to market, the Little Red Hen found a few grains of wheat. She put them in her pocket. When she got home she asked her friends, "Who will plant these grains of wheat?"

"Not I," said the goose.
"Not I," said the cat.
"Not I," said the dog.
"Then I will plant it myself," said the Little Red Hen. And she did.

All summer long she cared for the wheat. She made sure that it got enough water.

And she hoed the weeds out carefully between each row.

And when the wheat was finally ready to harvest, the Little Red Hen asked her friends,

"Who will help me thresh this wheat?"

"Not I," said the goose.

"Not I," said the cat.

"Not I," said the dog.

"Then I will cut and thresh it myself," said the Little Red Hen. And she did. When the wheat had been cut and threshed, the Little Red Hen scooped the wheat into a wheelbarrow and said, "This wheat must be ground into flour. Who will help me take it to the mill?"

"Not I," said the goose.

"Not I," said the cat.

"Not I," said the dog.

"Then I will do it myself" said the Little Red Hen. And she did.

The miller ground the wheat into flour and put it into a bag for the Little Red Hen. Then, all by herself, she pushed the bag home in the wheelbarrow.

One cool morning a few weeks later the Little Red Hen got up early and said, "Today is a perfect day to bake some bread. Who will help me bake it?"

"Not I," said the goose.

"Not I," said the cat.

"Not I," said the dog.

"Then I will bake the bread myself," said the Little Red Hen. And she did.

She mixed the flour with milk and eggs and butter and salt. She kneaded the dough. She shaped the dough into a nice plump loaf. Then she put the loaf in the oven and watched it as it baked. The smell of the bread soon filled the air.

The goose stopped chatting, the cat stopped brushing, and the dog woke up. One by one they came into the kitchen.

When the Little Red Hen took the bread from the oven she said, "Who will help me eat this bread?"

"I will," said the goose.

"I will," said the cat.

"I will," said the dog.

"You will?" said the Little Red Hen. "Who planted the wheat and took care of it? Who cut the wheat and threshed it? Who took the wheat to the mill? Who baked the bread? I did it all by myself. Now I am going to eat it all by myself." And she did.

Small Group Enrichment

1. The Little Red Hen

Make a Little Red Hen Bake Shop in the Dramatic Play Center. Provide aprons, playdough, rolling pins, bread pans, and wooden spoons and spatulas. Encourage children to reenact the story.

2. Red Rubbings

Provide some cardboard cutouts of "R" items—round circles and rectangles—and a red crayon and paper for the children to use to make red rubbings of "R" things.

3. Rainy Day

Invite children to brainstorm a list of things they can do on a rainy day. Encourage them to draw a rainy day picture.

4. Relay Races

Play some relay races where children pass off an "R" item such as a race car or ring (plastic lid with center cut out) to the next runner.

5. Rising Raisins

Give children a clear plastic cup with a carbonated clear soda, such as 7-Up, and three or four raisins. Instruct them to drop the raisins in their drink. After a few seconds, the raisins will rise. (The air bubbles in the drink will surround the raisins and lift them to the surface.) As the bubbles pop, the raisins will sink again. Then the process will begin again.

6. Ramp Races

Make two ramps (inclined planes) and encourage children to race racing cars down them.

7. Raps and Rounds

Teach the children a rap. See page 113 for "The Three Bears Rap." Teach the children a song that can be sung in rounds like "Make New Friends" on page 142, "Hear the Lively Song" on page 24, or "Row, Row, Row Your Boat" on page 230.

8. Rollers

Provide several items for the children to experiment with to see which ones are "rollers" (will roll) and which aren't (won't roll).

9. Ring the Ringer

Place a service bell in the middle of a circle of children and invite them to take turns tossing a beanbag to ring the ringer.

BEANBAG

BELL

10. Rainbows

Provide prisms and let the children have fun making rainbows.

11. Rope Rhymes

Teach the children some jump rope rhymes such as "Mable, Mable" and "Cinderella."

> Mable, Mable,
> Set the table.
> Don't forget
> The Red Hot Pepper!
> 1, 2, 3, 4, 5…
>
> Cinderella dressed in yellow
> Went upstairs to kiss a fellow.
> How many kisses did she give?
> 1, 2, 3, 4, 5, 6, 7, 8, 9, 10…
> Then she went upstairs
> And kissed him again.

12. Run, Rabbit, Run

Choose four or five children to be foxes. The other children are rabbits. Designate an area at one end of the playground to be the brier patch where the rabbits are safe. Designate another area as a fox den. When the signal "Run, Rabbit, Run" is given, the rabbits must run all over the playground. The foxes try to catch the rabbits and take them to their den. The last four of five rabbits caught become the foxes in the next game.

13. Roundup

Choose four or five children to be cowboys. The other children are cattle. Designate a corral and several bases. When the signal is given, the cattle must run from one base to the another. If they are tagged by the cowboys, they must go to the corral and wait until the game is over. The last four or five children to be tagged become the cowboys for the next game.

14. Beginning Sound "R" Concentration

Use the patterns on Appendix page 401 to make a concentration game with objects that begin with "R."

Word List

race	raw	rise	rude
rack	ray	road	rug
rag	real	roast	rule
rail	red	rob	run
rain	rent	rock	rush
rake	rib	rod	rust
ram	rich	roll	rut
ramp	ride	roof	
ran	rig	room	
ranch	right	root	
range	rim	rope	
rank	ring	rose	
rap	rink	round	
rate	rip	row	
rave	ripe	rub	

Book List

A Bicycle for Rosaura by Daniel Barbot
"Little Red Riding Hood" (Traditional)
Read-Aloud Rhymes for the Very Young by Jack Prelutsky
The Relatives Came by Cynthia Rylant
The Reluctant Dragon by Kenneth Grahame
Rosie's Walk by Pat Hutchins
Roxaboxen by Alice McLerran
Rumpelstiltskin by Paul O. Zelinsky

Songs

You Are My Sunshine

You are my sunshine, my only sunshine.
You make me happy when skies are gray.
You'll never know, dear, how much I love you.
Please don't take my sunshine away.

A Sailor Went to Sea

A sailor went to sea, sea, sea,
To see what she could see, see, see.
But all that she could see, see, see,
Was the bottom of the deep blue sea, sea, sea.

A sailor went to chop, chop, chop…
A sailor went to sho-bop-sho-bop…

Gray Squirrel

Gray squirrel, gray squirrel,
Swish your bushy tail.
Gray squirrel, gray squirrel,
Swish your bushy tail.
Wrinkle up your funny nose,
Hold an acorn in your toes.
Gray squirrel, gray squirrel,
Swish your busy tail.

The Little Skunk's Hole (Tune: Turkey in the Straw)
Oh, I stuck my head
In the little skunk's hole,
And the little skunk said,
"Well, bless my soul!
Take it out! Take it out!
Take it out! Remove it!"

Oh, I didn't take it out,
And the little skunk said,
"If you don't take it out
You'll wish you had.
Take it out! Take it out!"
Pheew! I removed it!

I've Got Sixpence (Tune: Someone's in the Kitchen With Dinah)
I've got sixpence, jolly, jolly sixpence,
I've got sixpence to last me all my life.
I've got sixpence to spend and sixpence to lend
And sixpence to take home to my wife—poor wife!

No cares have I to grieve me.
No pretty little girls to deceive me.
I'm as happy as a lark, believe me,
As I go rolling, rolling home.

Sally the Camel
Sally the camel has five humps
Sally the camel has five humps
Sally the camel has five humps
So ride, Sally, ride,
Boom, boom, boom, boom.

Repeat, count down to no humps. End song with "Sally is a horse, of course!"

Poems

S

See-Saw

See-saw, see-saw,
Up and down we go.
See-saw, see-saw,
High and then down low.
See-saw, see-saw,
Fun as you can see.
See-saw, see-saw,
Play the game with me.
See-saw, see-saw,
See-saw, see.

Snow

It's snowing, it's snowing,
Snow is on the ground.
Silently, softly blowing
Like a blanket on the ground.

Our Seasons

Spring is showery, flowery, bowery
Summer: happy, choppy, poppy
Autumn: wheezy, sneezy, freezy
Winter: slippy, drippy, nippy.

The Swallow (Christina Rossetti)
Fly away, fly away over the sea,
Sun loving swallow, for summer is done;
Come again, come again, come back to me,
Bringing the summer, and bringing the sun.

The Swing (Robert Lewis Stevenson)
How do you like to go up in a swing,
Up in the air so blue?
Oh, I do think it the pleasantest thing
Ever a child can do!

Up in the air and over the wall,
'Till I can see so wide,
Rivers and trees and cattle and all
Over the countryside—

'Till I look down on the garden green,
Down on the roof so brown—
Up in the air I go flying again,
Up in the air and down!

A Riddle
I have something in my pocket.
It belongs across my face.
I keep it very close at hand
In a most convenient place.

I bet you couldn't guess it
If you guessed a long long while.
So I'll take it out and put it on.
It's a great big happy SMILE!

Who Ever Sausage a Thing?
One day a girl went walking
And went into a store.
She bought a pound of sausages
And laid them on the floor.

The girl began to whistle
A merry little tune,
And all the little sausages
Danced around the room!

The Snowman (Frances Frost)

We made a snowman in our yard,
Jolly, and round, and fat.
We gave him father's pipe to smoke
And father's battered hat.
We tied a red scarf around his neck,
And in his buttonhole
We stuck a holly spray.
He had black buttons made of coal.
He had black eyes, a turned up nose,
A wide and cheerful grin.
And there he stood in our front yard,
Inviting company in!

Tongue Twisters/Alliterative Sentences and Phrases

Silly Sally

Silly Sally swiftly shooed seven silly sheep.
The seven silly sheep Silly Sally shooed shilly-shallied south.
These sheep shouldn't sleep in a shack;
Sheep should sleep in a shed.

Say This

Say this sharply, say this sweetly,
Say this shortly, say this softly.
Say this sixteen times in succession.

She Sells Seashells

She sells seashells by the seashore,
By the seashore, she sells seashells.

Sawingest Saw

The sawingest saw I ever saw saw
Was the saw I saw in Arkansas.

Say the sentences and phrases below three times quickly if you can.

- Six sticky sucker sticks.
- Six sick slick slim sycamore saplings.
- Sam's shop stocks short spotted socks.

- Shy Shelly says she shall sew sheets.
- Sly Sam slurps Sally's soup.

Fingerplays/Action Rhymes

The Sun
A big size sun in a September sky (*make a big circle with arms*)
Winked at a cloud that was passing by. (*wink*)
The cloud laughed and called out the rain, (*wiggle fingers like falling rain*)
Then out came the shining sun again. (*make a big circle with arms*)

Five Little Snowmen
Five little snowmen happy and gay, (*hold up five fingers and move one for each snowman*)
The first one said, "What a nice day!"
The second one said, "We'll cry no tears."
The third one said, "We'll stay for years."
The fourth one said, "But what happens in May?"
The fifth one said, "Look, we're melting away!" (*hold hands out like saying all gone*)

Sometimes
Sometimes I am tall. (*stand tall*)
Sometimes I am small. (*crouch low*)
Sometimes I am very, very tall. (*stand on tiptoes*)
Sometimes I am very, very small. (*crouch and lower head*)
Sometimes tall. (*stand tall*)
Sometimes small. (*crouch down*)
Sometimes neither tall or small. (*stand normally*)

Story: Santa's Workshop (Flannel Board Story)

Directions: Use a black sharpie pen to trace the patterns on Appendix pages 349-352 onto Pelon. Color them with crayons and cut them out. Use them with the flannel board to present the story.

Santa's Workshop
In Santa's workshop far away,
Ten little elves work night and day.

This little elf makes candy canes;
This little elf builds choo-choo trains;
This little elf paints dolls for girls;
This little elf puts in their curls;
This little elf dips chocolate drops;
This little elf makes lollipops;
This little elf packs each jack-in-the-box;
This little elf sews dolly socks;
This little elf wraps books for boys;
This little elf checks off the toys
As Santa packs them in his sleigh
Ready for you on Christmas Day!

Small Group Enrichment

1. Santa's Workshop
Invite children to draw a picture of the elf they like best. Encourage them to draw or write a Christmas wish list.

2. Simon Says
Play Simon Says. See if children can think of directions that have a word in them that starts with "S." For example, children can be directed to sniff, slide, stand, skate, step, slip, stop, start, sleep, or sit. Some of these words are blends but the "S" sound is still prevalent. These activities are intended as phonemic awareness activities only.

3. I Spy.
Play I Spy. Select things that start with an "S."

4. Silly Socks
Have children bring a pair of old socks to school. Provide pompoms, glitter glue, lace, wiggle eyes, and other materials for decorating the sock. When everyone has a pair of Silly Socks, have a Sock Hop.

5. Smoothies
Place a scoop of orange sherbet and 1 cup (240 ml) of ginger ale in a blender and blend. Serve.

6. Stars and Suns
Cut a sun (circle) out of yellow poster board. Cut several stars from white poster board. Experiment with rolling both the sun and the stars. Which is the easiest to roll?

7. Sun Shadows

Invite children to look for shadows on the playground. Can they find shadows with a pattern? Can they use their own bodies to create shadows? Can they make up a shadow dance?

8. Scratch and Sniff Pictures

Mix flavored gelatin with ½ the amount of water called for. Use as paint. When it dries, scratch and sniff.

9. Soap Sculpting

Give children a bar of soap. Encourage them to sculpt the soap using a craft stick as a carver.

10. Seed Sorting

Give the children a muffin tin and some seeds to sort. You might try to gather flower and vegetable seeds that start with "S" such as sunflower seeds and squash seeds.

11. Sign Language

Teach the children a few signs using American Sign Language. Instructions for a few simple signs can be found in the Appendix page 386.

12. Make Stone Soup
Read *Stone Soup* by Marcia Brown. Have the children bring a vegetable from home and make stone soup. A crockpot will make the job easy. It will take a couple of hours to cook.

13. Sink and Float
Place a variety of items that begin with the letter "S" (stone, soap, sock, sack, seeds) in a tray. Provide a tub of water. Encourage children to experiment with the items to see if they sink or float.

14. Salt Paint
Mix some salt paint (see recipe in Appendix on page 413) and invite children to create a Salt Painting.

15. Beginning Sound "S" Concentration
Use the patterns on Appendix page 402 to make a concentration game of objects that begin with "S."

Word List

sack	serve	some
sad	set	son
safe	seven	song
sag	sew	soon
said	sick	sore
sail	side	sound
same	sign	soup
sand	silk	sow
sat	silly	sum
saw	sing	sun
say	sink	sunny
sea	sip	sunshine
see	sir	swim
seed	sit	
seek	size	
seen	so	
seesaw	soap	
sell	soar	
send	soft	
sent	soil	

Book List

The First Snowfall by Anne and Harlow Rockwell

Itsy Bitsy Spider by Iza Trapani

Sadie and the Snowman by Allen Morgan

Silly Sally by Audrey Wood

Sisters by David McPhail

The Snail's Spell by Joanne Ryder

The Snowy Day by Ezra Jack Keats

Stone Soup by Marcia Brown

Sun Song by Jean Marzollo

Swimmy by Leo Lionni

Sylvester and the Magic Pebble by William Steig

The Very Busy Spider by Eric Carle

Songs

Ten in a Bed

There were ten in a bed and the little one said,
"Roll over, roll over."
So they all rolled over and one fell out.

There were nine in a bed…

Continue counting down with each repetition until only one remains.

There was one in the bed and the little one said, "Goodnight."

Where Is Thumbkin?

Where is Thumbkin?
Where is Thumbkin?
Here I am, here I am.
How are you today, friend?
Very well, I thank you.
Run away, run away.

Where is Pointer?
Where is Pointer?
Here I am, here I am.
How are you today, friend?
Very well, I thank you,
Run away, run away.

Where is middle finger?
Where is ring finger?
Where is pinky?

Twinkle, Twinkle, Little Star

Twinkle, twinkle, little star,
How I wonder what you are!
Up above the world so high,
Like a diamond in the sky.

When the blazing sun is set,
And the grass with dew is wet,
Then you show your little light
Twinkle, twinkle, all the night.

Then the traveler in the dark
Thanks you for your tiny spark.
How could he see where to go
If you did not twinkle so?

In the dark-blue sky you keep,
And often through my curtains peep,
For you never shut an eye,
'Till the sun is in the sky.

As your bright and tiny spark
Lights the traveler in the dark,
Though I know not what you are,
Twinkle, twinkle, little star.

A Tisket, A Tasket

A tisket, a tasket,
A green and yellow basket.
I wrote a letter to my love
And on the way I lost it.

I lost it, I lost it,
And on the way I lost it.
A little boy, he picked it up,
And put it in his pocket.

His pocket, his pocket,
He put it in his picket.
A little boy, he picked it up,
And put it in his pocket.

Poems

Little Tommy Tucker

Little Tommy Tucker
Ate a lemon sucker.
It caused his lips to pucker.
Poor Tommy Tucker.

With a Tick and a Tock

With a tick and a tock, and a tick and a tock,
The clock goes 'round all day.
It tells us when to work
And when it's time to play.

Tick, Tock

Big clocks make a sound like
"TICK, TOCK, TICK, TOCK." (*say loudly with a low voice*)

Small clocks make a sound like
"Tick, tock, tick, tock." (*say softly with a high voice*)

And tiny clocks make a sound like
"Tick, tock, tick, tock." (*say quickly*)

Tiny Tim

I had a little turtle,
His name was Tiny Tim.
I put him in the bathtub,
To see if he could swim.

He drank up all the water.
He ate up all the soap.
Tiny Tim was choking
On the bubbles in his throat.

In came the doctor,
In came the nurse,
In came the lady
With the alligator purse.

They pumped out all the water.
They pumped out all the soap.
They popped the airy bubbles
As they floated from his throat.

Out went the doctor,
Out went the nurse,
Out went the lady
With the alligator purse.

Thanksgiving Song of a Little Mouse
For crumbs I find most every day,
And the cheese that sometimes comes my way,
For a good dark hole too small for a cat,
And for silent feet and a long tail
That helps me balance as I run,
And for all my gray fur, mousey-fun
I'm thankful!

Tongue Twisters/Alliterative Sentences and Phrases

A Tudor
A tudor who tooted a flute
Tried to tutor two tooters to toot.
Said the two to their tutor,
"Is it harder to toot
Or to tutor two tooters to toot?"

Say the sentences and phrases below three times quickly, if you can.

- The two-twenty-two train tore through the tunnel.
- Three twigs twined tightly.
- Tim, the thin twin tinsmith.
- Three free throws.
- Two toads, totally tired.

Fingerplays/Action Rhymes

Terry Thumb
Terry Thumb is up and Terry Thumb is down. (*move as directed*)
Terry Thumb is dancing all around the town.
Dance him on your shoulder, dance him on your head,
Dance him on your tummy, and tuck him into bed.

The Little Turtle (Vachel Lindsay)
There was a little turtle. (*make a fist*)
He lived in a box. (*draw a square in the air*)
He swam in a puddle. (*pretend to swim*)
He climbed on the rocks. (*pretend to climb*)

ACQUIRING READING SKILLS

He snapped at a mosquito. (*use your hand to make a snapping motion*)
He snapped at a flea. (*snapping motion*)
He snapped at a minnow. (*snapping motion*)
And he snapped at me. (*snapping motion*)
He caught the mosquito. (*clap hands*)
He caught the flea. (*clap hands*)
He caught the minnow. (*clap hands*)
But he didn't catch me. (*wave index finger as if saying no-no*)

Tying My Shoe (*suit actions to words*)
I know how to tie my shoe,
I make a loop and poke it through.
It's very hard to make it stay,
Because my thumb gets in the way.

My Turtle
This is my turtle. (*make a fist, leaving thumb outside.*)
He lives in a shell. (*hide thumb in fist.*)
He likes his home very well. (*nod your head.*)
He pokes his head out when he wants to eat, (*extend thumb.*)
And pulls it back when he wants to sleep. (*hide thumb in fist.*)

Tippy, Tippy, Tiptoe
Tippy, tippy, tiptoe, (*creep two fingers on floor*)
Here we go.
Tippy, tippy, tiptoe,
To and fro.
Tippy, tippy, tiptoe, (*creep fingers under leg*)
Through the house
Tippy, tippy, tiptoe,
Like a mouse.

Tippy, tippy, tiptoe, (*creep softly*)
Don't make noise.
Tippy, tippy, tiptoe,
Girls and boys.
Tippy, tippy, tiptoe, (*put fingers to eyes*)
Look at me.
Tippy, tippy, tiptoe, (*put fingers to lips*)
Quiet as can be.

Story: Turkey-Lurkey (Flannel Board Story)

Directions: Use a black sharpie pen to trace the patterns on Appendix pages 353 and 354 onto Pelon. Color them with crayons and cut them out. Use them with the flannel board to tell the story.

Turkey-Lurkey (Pam Schiller)

Turkey-Lurkey is one of the silliest turkeys you have ever seen. She has two very large turkey feet, a neck longer than a goose's neck, and an assortment of feathers that make her look like she belongs in a parade. Turkey-Lurkey has a mommy who thinks she is truly the most beautiful turkey in the world and a daddy who thinks she hung the moon.

Turkey-Lurkey also has more friends than anyone I know. Her friends like her not because she has big feet, or a long neck, or even because she has strange colored feathers. They like her because she has a big heart. She is always ready to help her friends.

The squirrels are thankful for her long neck because she can reach high up in the trees to pick an acorn that is growing on the end of a branch too fragile for the squirrels to climb on.

The rabbits like her because with her big feet she can run faster than they can hop. When the old barnyard dogs are chasing the rabbits, Turkey-Lurkey puts the rabbits on her back and carries them to safety.

All the animals enjoy Turkey-Lurkey's brightly colored feathers. They are so unusual. None of the animals have ever seen polka-dotted feathers. As a matter of fact, they have never seen striped feathers, hot pink feathers, or rainbow feathers. Just looking at Turkey- Lurkey's colorful feathers makes them feel happy.

There is a secret funny thing about Turkey-Lurkey that only her mommy and daddy, her animal friends, and now you know. That funny thing is that when Turkey-Lurkey is really happy, like when she is helping her friends, she gets a very silly, very funny grin on her turkey face.

Close your eyes for a minute, and I'll ask Turkey-Lurkey to show you her grin.

OK, now you can look. Here's Turkey-Lurkey!

Small Group Enrichment

1. Turkey-Lurkey
Invite children to draw a picture of Turkey-Lurkey.

2. I Can Tie
Encourage children to practice tying their shoes. If you have several children still learning to tie, ask an older class to come in to tutor.

3. Terrific Tie-Dyed Ts
Have children bring an old white T-shirt to school. Prepare a tub of dye. Give children rubber bands to section off portions of their shirt. Dip the shirts in the dye using tongs (to avoid getting dye on hands). Take the shirts out of the tub and place in the sun to dry.

4. Tip the Scales
Encourage the children to use the balance scales. Have them balance the scales first and then have them tip the scales.

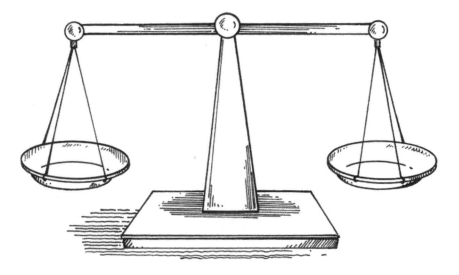

5. Turning Tops
Provide several tops for the children to explore.

6. Top Hat Tappers
Invite children to tape a washer to the bottom of their shoes and tap on a cement or hard floor surface. Provide top hats for the full effect.

7. Toothpick Structures
Provide toothpicks and marshmallows. Encourage the children to build a structure using the marshmallows to hold the toothpicks in place.

8. Twister

Play Twister.

9. Tiptoe on a Tightrope

Make a pretend tightrope with masking tape on the floor. Invite children to tiptoe across the tightrope.

10. The Twist

Put on the Chubby Checker song and do the "Twist."

11. Taste Test

Provide two types of juice and invite children to have a taste test. Let them taste both juices and then vote for their favorite.

12. Taking Turns

Play games that allow children to practice taking turns such as Tic-Tac-Toe and Pick-up Sticks.

13. Tabletop Painting

Provide finger paint and invite children to paint on the tabletop. When it's time for clean up, let them help wash the tabletop.

14. Tea Party

Serve cookies and juice like a formal tea in tea cups.

15. Tummy Ticklers

Instruct children to lie on the floor with their head on someone else's tummy (this should result in one long line of children). Have someone say something funny. When everyone is laughing the tummies move and that gets everyone more tickled. Enjoy!

16. Beginning Sound "T" Concentration

Use the patterns on Appendix page 403 to make a concentration game with objects that begin with "T."

Word List

tab	tease	toe
Tack	tee	toll
Tag	teen	ton
Tail	tell	tone
take	ten	tool
talk	tick	top
tall	tide	tore
tame	tie	toss
tan	till	touch
tape	time	tough
tar	tin	tow
tea	tip	town
teach	tire	toy
team	to	tub
tear	toad	tug

Book List

The Teddy Bears' Picnic by Jimmy Kennedy
Tikki Tikki Tembo by Arlene Mosel
Too Many Tamales by Gary Soto
The Train by David McPhail
Tuesday by David Wiesner

Songs

(Long U)

I Can Play the Ukulele (Tune: I've Been Working on the Railroad)
I can play the ukulele
All the livelong day.
I can play the ukulele
To pass the time away.

Can't you hear the strings a-strumming
From here to Cobbler's Run?
Can't you hear the people humming?
Please come and join the fun!

(Short U)

Apples and Bananas

I like to eat eat eat apples and bananas.
I like to eat eat eat apples and bananas.

I like to ate ate ate aypuls and
  baynaynays.
I like to ate ate ate aypuls and
  baynaynays.

I like eet eet eet eeples and
  beeneenees.
I like eet eet eet eeples and
  beeneenees.

I like to ite, ite, ite, ipples and
  binininis.
I like to ite, ite, ite, ipples and
  binininis.

I like to ote ote ote opples and bononos.
I like to ote ote ote opples and bononos.

I like to ute ute ute upples and bununus.
I like to ute ute ute upples and bununus.

ACQUIRING READING SKILLS

Calliope Song

Sound 1: Um pa pa, um pa pa…
Sound 2: Um tweedli-dee, um tweedli-dee…
Sound 3: Um shhh, um shhh, um shhh…

Divide children into four groups. Instruct group one to make sound 1. Group two to make sound 2. Group three to make sound 3. Group four will hum the circus song (the song you generally hear on a merry-go-round.

Under the Spreading Chestnut Tree

Under the spreading chestnut tree
There I held her on my knee.
We were happy, yesiree.
Under the spreading chestnut tree.

Poems

(Long U)

The Unicorn (Pam Schiller)
The one animal I just adore
Is one I've never seen before.

It looks a little like a horse
Except for its one long horn, of course.
It comes in only the color white.
I dream of seeing it day and night.
So if a unicorn you happen to see,
Whatever you do, please, please find me.

Our Mother Plays the Ukulele (Pam Schiller)
Our mother plays the ukulele.
She strums and hums and sings so gaily.
We clap our hands and tap our toes,
As easily from song to song she goes.

When our birthdays come each year,
The very first sound we expect to hear
Is "Happy Birthday" sung so gaily
On the strings of our mother's ukulele.

(Short U)

The Umbrella Brigade (Laura E. Richards)
But let it rain,
Tree toads and frogs,
Muskets and pitchforks,
Kitten and dogs!

Dash away! Splash away!
Who is afraid?
Here we go,
The Umbrella Brigade!

Tongue Twisters /Alliterative Sentences and Phrases

Say the sentences and phrases below three times quickly, if you can.

- Uniquely uniformed unicorns
- Under umbrellas
- Until umbrellas are up

Fingerplays/Action Rhymes

(Long U)

Uniquely Me (Pam Schiller)
My mom says I'm uniquely me. (*point to self*)
I look in the mirror 'cause I want to see. (*hold palm up like a mirror*)
Here are my eyes, nose, mouth, and hair, (*point to each body part*)
But nothing I see appears to be rare. (*shake head*)

I look around at all my friends. (*look at friends*)
And think about what makes them friends.
Then I know what I'm looking for. (*hold finger up like you just thought
   of something*)
Unique is what makes you who you are.
It's what you say and what you do (*turn right palm up, then left palm*)
That makes you so uniquely you! (*point to self*)

(Short U)

Five Umbrellas

Five umbrellas, not one more. (*hold up five fingers—put one down
  each time an umbrella is removed*)
Dad took one, then there were four.
Four umbrellas pretty as can be.
Sister took one, now there are three.
Three umbrellas, green, red, and blue.
Mom took one, then there were two.
Two umbrellas that's all I see.
Brother took one and left one for me.

Story: The First Umbrella (Stick Puppet Story)

Directions: Photocopy the patterns on Appendix pages 355 and 356. Color them, cut them out, and laminate them. Attach them to tongue depressors. When you tell the story, hold both pieces of the mushroom together until the elf departs with his half.

The Elf and the Dormouse (Oliver Herford)

Under a toadstool
Crept a wee Elf,
Out of the rain
To shelter himself.

Under the toadstool
Sound asleep,
Sat a big Dormouse
All in a heap.

Trembled the wee Elf,
Frightened, and yet
Fearing to fly away
Lest he get wet.

To the next shelter—
Maybe a mile!
Sudden the wee Elf
Smiled a wee smile,

Tugged at the toadstool
Toppled in two.
Holding it over him
Gaily he flew.

Soon he was safe home
Dry as could be.
Soon woke the Dormouse—
"Good gracious me!

Where is my toadstool?"
Loud he lamented.
—And that's how umbrellas
First were invented.

Small Group Enrichment

1. The First Umbrella

Ask children if they think the story is true. Go to the library or use the internet to research the real beginning of umbrellas.

2. Uniforms (long U)

Gather some uniforms and place them in the Dramatic Play Center.

3. Unicorns Ring Toss (long U)

Make a cone to represent a unicorn horn. Provide plastic rings (plastic lids with centers removed) and invite the children to toss the rings over the horn.

4. Ukulele Fun (Long U)

Invite a guest to come play a ukulele. Several church groups sponsor a Senior Citizen Ukulele Band. If you have access to a ukulele, let children explore playing it.

5. Where Is Uranus? (long U)

Bring in some pictures of the solar system and let the children see where the planet Uranus is located. Count its position from the sun.

6. What Makes Me Unique? (long U)

Challenge the children to think of something about themselves that is really unique. Maybe they own an iguana, perhaps they are a twin, or maybe they speak more than one language. Encourage them to draw a picture of what makes them unique.

7. Unicorn Hunt

Hide a unicorn or a picture of one and see who can find it. Read Shel Silverstein's "The Unicorn," from *Where the Sidewalk Ends.*

8. Underline the Words (Short U)

Write the story of "The Elf and the Dormouse" on chart paper. Invite the children to come forward and underline the words that start with the letter "U."

9. Ugly (Short U)

Let children brainstorm a list of storybook characters that were portrayed as ugly. For example, the duckling in "The Ugly Duckling," the troll in "The Three Billy Goat's Gruff," the stepsisters in *Cinderella,* and the witch in *Snow White.*

10. Under the Table (Short U)

Tape drawing paper to the underside of the table and let children lay on their back under the table and draw.

11. Unzip the Zippers (Short U)

Provide several items with zippers such as a pair of jeans, a jacket, a sleeping bag, a pair of boots, a jewelry box, and so forth. Invite the children to work the zippers.

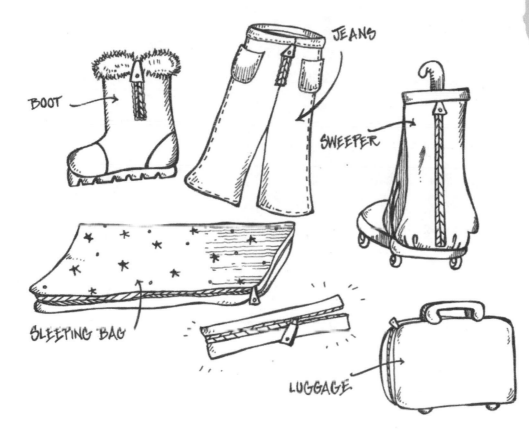

BOOT

JEANS

SWEEPER

SLEEPING BAG

LUGGAGE

12. Over and Under (Short U)

Teach the children to weave. Try letting them weave crepe paper strips into laundry baskets. Stress the over and under pattern.

A C Q U I R I N G   R E A D I N G   S K I L L S

Word List

(Long U)	Short U
ukulele	udder
unicorn	ugly
uniform	ulcer
union	ultimate
unique	umber
unit	umpire
unity	unable
universal	unaware
universe	unbalance
university	unbroken
Uranus	uncle
use	uncomfort-
utopia	able
	uncover
	under
	undercoat
	underline
	underneath
	underwear
	undress
	unearth
	unfold
	until
	up
	uphill
	us

Book List

"The Ugly Duckling" by Hans Christian Andersen (many versions available)
Umbrella by Taro Yashima
Up the Ladder, Down the Slide by Betsy Everitt

Songs

V

I Am the Happy Wanderer

I am a happy wanderer
Along the mountain track.
And as I go, I love to sing,
My knapsack on my back.

Chorus
Val-de-ri, Val-de-rah,
Val-de-ri, Val-de-rah—
Ha, ha, ha, ha, ha,
Val-de-ri, Val-de-rah,
My knapsack on my back.

I wave my hat to all I meet
And they wave back to me.
And blackbirds call so loud and sweet
From every greenwood tree.

Chorus
Val-de-ri, Val-de-rah,
Val-de-ri, Val-de-rah—
Ha, ha, ha, ha, ha,
Val-de-ri, Val-de-rah,
From every greenwood tree.

One Bottle o' Pop

One bottle o' pop,
Two bottle o' pop,
Three bottle o' pop,
Four bottle o' pop,
Five bottle o' pop,
Six bottle o' pop,
Seven bottle o'pop,
POP!

Don't chuck your muck,
In my dust bin,
My dust bin, my dust bin.
Don't chuck your muck
In my dust bin,
My dust bin's full!

V

Fish and chips and vinegar,
Vinegar, vinegar,
Fish and chips and vinegar,
Vinegar and Pop!

Poems

To My Valentine
If apples were
   pears,
And peaches
   were
   plums,
And the rose
   had a differ-
   ent name.
If tigers were
   bears,
And fingers were
   thumbs,
I'd love you just the same!

The Vulture (Hilaire Belloc)
The vulture eats between his meals,
And that's the reason why
He very, very rarely feels
As well as you and I.

His eye is dull, his head is bald,
His neck is growing thinner.
Oh! What a lesson for us all
To only eat at dinner.

Tongue Twisters/Alliterative Sentences and Phrases

Say the sentences and phrases below three times quickly, if you can.

● Valeria valued Victor's victory.

Fingerplays/Action Rhymes

Five Fancy Valentines
Five fancy valentines in the card store, (*hold five fingers up
   and put them down as valentines disappear*)
Austin bought one, then there were four.
Four fancy valentines, sweet as can be,
Sam bought one, then there were three.
Three fancy valentines waiting for you,
Madison bought one, now there are two.
Two fancy valentines, you better run,
Gabby's buying one, soon there'll be none.

Violets in My Garden
One purple violet in my garden grew,
Up popped another, and then there were two.
Two purple violets were all that I could see,
But Mommy found another, and that made three.
Three purple violets—if I could find one more,
I'd put them in a tiny vase—four violets by the door.

Story: Valencia Valentine (Flannel Board Story)

Directions: Use a black sharpie pen to trace the patterns on Appendix pages 357 and 358 onto Pelon. Color them with crayons and cut them out. Use them with the flannel board to present the story.

Valencia Valentine (Pam Schiller)
It was almost Valentine's Day. Valencia couldn't wait. She had been looking forward to finally being old enough to be a store valentine. Her brothers, Victor and Vance, had left home last year, and now it was her turn.

She wanted to look vibrant. She put on her Victorian lace trim. She thought it was her very best outfit. She found a good spot on the shelf at Valerie's Card shop. She put on her best smile and waited. The first day came and went and no one bought Valencia. She was very sad. She didn't want to sound vain but she really thought she looked better than any other card. Valencia decided to put on her black hat with the lace veil. That should do it.

The next day was the same. People came and went and never even picked her up. When the school van came loaded with children and no one even noticed her, she was devastated.

That night Valencia gathered a honeysuckle vine and wrapped it around her middle. Then she picked a vacant spot on the shelf where she would be right in view of the door. Surely this will work she thought.

But the next day was the same. When the store closed, Valencia started to cry. She was too sad to even think of another idea. Then suddenly she heard a voice beside her. It was Valentino, the Valentine Bear. He said he knew a secret that would be just the right thing to make Valencia the most special Valentine on the shelf. He whispered it into her ear. Do you know what it was?

It was a special verse. Valencia wrote it right across her face with a violet crayon. It said;

> "Roses are red.
> Violets are blue.
> Sugar is sweet,
> And so are you!"

And at last Valencia was victorious. She was the first valentine to be bought the next morning.

Small Group Enrichment

1. Valencia Valentine
Invite the children to make a valentine. Encourage them to give it to a friend even if it's not Valentine's Day.

2. Violet Pictures
Violet is a color children are not very familiar with. Mix up some violet paint for easel painting or collect some violet paper scraps for a collage.

3. Vases of Flower
Provide some flowers (real leftovers from the flower shop or plastic or cloth) and some vases and floral clay. Encourage the children to try some flower arranging.

4. Violins
Provide some violin music for children to listen to. If you know someone who plays the violin, ask her to come to class to demonstrate her talent.

5. Votes
Serve two different types of cookies at snack time. Encourage children to vote on their favorite.

6. Vines
Brainstorm a list of fruits, vegetables, and flowers that grow on vines.

7. Vegetables
Let children peel and cut some raw vegetables for a snack.

8. Mystery Voice
Record children's voices all saying the same thing on a cassette tape. Play the tape back and see if children can identify the speakers.

9. Version of Verse
Present some simple nursery rhymes and encourage children to rewrite them or add a verse to them. Share examples in this book. "Little Miss Muffett" with a new verse is on page 192 and "Humpty Dumpty" new version is on page 157.

10. Vanilla Paints
Put some vanilla extract in the tempera paint. Who recognizes the smell?

11. Vinegar and Soda
Place a small amount of baking soda on a paper plate. Provide an eyedropper and some vinegar and let children experiment with mixing the two compounds. What happens?

12. Begining Sound "V" Concentration Game
Use the patterns on Appendix page 404 to make a concentration game with objects that start with "V."

TOMATO
RADISH
CUCUMBER
CARROT
PEPPER
BROCCOLI

ACQUIRING READING SKILLS

Word List

vain	Verse
valiant	Very
van	Vest
vane	Vibrant
vase	Victory
vat	View
vault	Vine
veal	Violin
vegetable	Voice
veil	Vote
vent	

Book List

The Valentine Bears by Eve Bunting
The Valentine Star by Patricia Giff
Vegetable Garden by Douglas Florian
The Very Hungry Caterpillar by Eric Carle

Songs

She Waded in the Water (Tune: Battle Hymn)
She waded in the water and she got her feet all wet.
She waded in the water and she got her feet all wet.
She waded in the water and she got her feet all wet.
But she didn't get her (*clap, clap*) wet, (*clap*) yet. (*clap*)

She waded in the water and she got her ankles wet. (*repeat 3 times*)
But she didn't get her (*clap, clap*) wet, (*clap*) yet. (*clap*)

She waded in the water and she got her knees all wet…

She waded in the water and she got her thighs all wet…

She waded in the water and she finally got it wet…
She finally got her bathing suit wet!

Six White Ducks
Six white ducks that I
    once knew.
Fat ducks, skinny
    ducks, they were,
    too.
But the one little duck with
    feather on his back,
He ruled the others with a quack,
    quack, quack.

Down to the river they would go
Wibble, wobble, wibble, wobble, all
    in a row.
But the one little duck with the feather on
    his back,
He ruled the others with a quack, quack, quack.

The Wheels on the Bus
The wheels on the bus go round and round. (*move hands in
    circular motion*)
Round and round, round and round.
The wheels on the bus go round and round,
All around the town. (*extend arms up and out*)

A C Q U I R I N G   R E A D I N G   S K I L L S

The windshield wipers go swish, swish, swish. (*sway hands back and forth*)
The baby on the bus goes, "Wah, wah, wah." (*rub eyes*)
People on the bus go up and down. (*stand up, sit down*)
The horn on the bus goes beep, beep, beep. (*pretend to beep horn*)
The money on the bus goes clink, clink, clink. (*drop change in*)
The driver on the bus says, "Move on back." (*hitchhiking movement*)

Poems

There Was an old Woman

There was an old woman tossed in a blanket,
Seventeen times as high as the moon.
But where she was going, no mortal can tell,
For under her arm she carried a broom.
"Old woman, old woman, old woman," said I,
"Whither, oh wither, ah whither so high?"
"To sweep the cobwebs from the sky,
And I'll be with you by and by."

Weather

Whether the weather be fine,
Or whether the weather be not.
Whether the weather be cold,
Or whether the weather be hot.
We'll weather the weather
Whatever the weather,
Whether we like it or not.

Wee Willie Winkie

Wee Willie Winkie runs through the town,
Upstairs and downstairs in his nightgown.
Rapping at the window, crying through the lock,
"Are the children in their beds? For it's past eight o'clock!"

Windshield Wipers

The windshield wipers on our car
Are busy in the rain.
They swish and swing, clup-clup, clup-clup
Then back and forth again.

Three Wishes

I wish I had a yellow cat
To sit before the fire.
If only I could have just that
'Twould be my heart's desire.

I wish I had an open fire
To warm my yellow cat.
'Twould gratify my soul's desire
If only I had that.

I wish I had a little home
To hold my cat and fire,
And then I'm sure that I would have
My very heart's desire.

The March Wind

I come to work as well as play.
I'll tell you what I do.
I whistle all the live-long day,
"Whoo-oo-oo-oo! Whoo-oo!"

I toss the branches up and down,
And shake them to and fro.
I whirl the leaves in flocks of brown,
And send them high and low.

I strew the twigs upon the ground,
The frozen earth I sweep.
I blow the children round and round,
And wake the flowers from sleep.

Tongue Twister/ Alliterative Sentences and Phrases

How Much Wood Would a Woodchuck Chuck?

How much wood would a woodchuck chuck if a woodchuck could
   chuck wood?
He would chuck, he would, as much as he could,
And chuck as much wood as a woodchuck would if a woodchuck
   could chuck wood.

Say the sentences and phrases below three times quickly, if you can.

- Willful Willy whistled woeful woos while wading through the water.
- Will you, William?
- While we were walking, we were watching window washers wash Washington's windows with warm washing water.

Fingerplays/Action Rhymes

I Wiggle

I wiggle, wiggle, wiggle my fingers. (*wiggle fingers*)
I wiggle, wiggle, wiggle my toes. (*wiggle toes*)
I wiggle, wiggle, wiggle my shoulders. (*wiggle shoulders*)
I wiggle, wiggle, wiggle my nose. (*wiggle nose*)
Now no more wiggles are left in me, (*shade head*)
So I will be as still as I can be. (*sit still*)

Waving to My Friends

My friends are gaily waving, (*wave at someone*)
Waving, waving.
My friends are gaily waving, (*wave at someone else*)
And I am waving back.

Story: Mr. Wiggle and Mr. Waggle (Participation Story)

Directions: Have the children mimic your movements and recite the predictable parts of the story.

Mr. Wiggle and Mr. Waggle

This is Mr. Wiggle (hold up right hand, make a fist but keep the thumb pointing up—wiggle thumb) and this is Mr. Waggle (hold up left hand, make a fist but keep the thumb pointing up—wiggle thumb). Mr. Wiggle and Mr. Waggle live in houses on top of different hills and three hills apart. (Put thumbs inside of fists on both hands.)

One day, Mr. Wiggle decided to visit Mr. Waggle. He opened his door (open right fist), pop, came outside (raise thumb), pop, and closed his door (close fist), pop. Then he went down the hill and up the hill, and down the hill and up the hill, and down the hill and up the hill (move right thumb down and up in a wave fashion to go with text).

When he reached Mr. Waggle's house, he knocked on the door—knock, knock, knock (use right thumb to tap left fist). No one answered. So, Mr. Wiggle went down the hill and up the hill, and down the hill and up the hill, and down the hill and up the hill to his house (use wave motion to follow text). When he reached his house he opened the door (open fist of right hand), pop, went inside (place thumb in palm), pop, and closed the door (close fist), pop.

The next day Mr. Waggle decided to visit Mr. Wiggle. He opened his door (open fist), pop, came outside (raise thumb), pop, and closed his door (close fist), pop. Then he went down the hill and up the hill, and down the hill and up the hill, and down the hill and up the hill (move right thumb down and up in a wave fashion to go with text).

When he reached Mr. Wiggle's house he knocked on the door—knock, knock, knock (use left thumb to tap right fist). No one answered. So, Mr. Waggle went down the hill and up the hill, and down the hill and up the hill, and down the hill and up the hill to his house (use wave motion to follow text). When he reached his house, he opened the door (open fist of left hand), pop, went inside (place thumb in palm), pop, and closed the door (close fist), pop.

The next day Mr. Wiggle (shake right fist) decided to visit Mr. Waggle, and Mr. Waggle (shake left fist) decided to visit Mr. Wiggle at the same time. So, they opened their doors (open both fists), pop, went outside (raise thumbs), pop, and closed their doors (close fists), pop. And they went down the hill and up the hill, and down the hill and up the hill (wave motion to follow text), and they met on top of the hill.

They talked and laughed and visited (wiggle thumbs) until the sun went down. Then they went down the hill and up the hill, and down the hill and up the hill to their own homes (wave motion with both hands to text).

They opened their doors (open fists), pop, went inside (tuck thumbs inside), pop, and closed the doors (close fists), pop, and went to sleep. (Place your head on your hands.)

Small Group Enrichment

1. Mr. Wiggle and Mr. Waggle
Invite children to write a story about visiting a friend.

ACQUIRING READING SKILLS

2. Wacky Wild Things Snack

With the children, prepare the following recipe for a snack.
Ingredients

> 1½ cups (375 g) peanut butter
> 1½ cups (540 g) honey
> 2 cups (250 g) powdered milk
> 2 cups (300 g) powdered sugar

Mix ingredients to form a dough. Roll into balls. Decorate with coconut, dry cereal, marshmallows, pretzels, nuts, raisins, fruit pieces, chocolate chips, berries, etc.

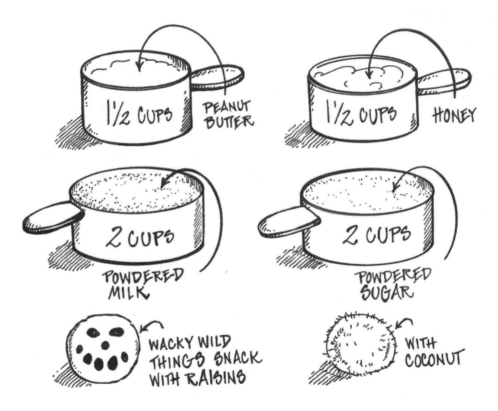

3. Wacky Wednesday

Read the book, *Wacky Wednesday* on Tuesday and let Wednesday turn into a wacky day at school. Send notes home to the parents in advance and ask them to let their children come to school on Wednesday dressed wacky (clothes on backward or wrong side out, two different shoes and so forth). You may even suggest hanging a bunch of bananas on the bedroom door so it is the first thing the children see—just like in the book. Then dress wacky yourself, switch things out of order in your room, and come up with some wacky activities such as drawing under the table instead of on top of the table. Have fun!

4. Window Art

Place art paper on the windows and allow children to create a tissue paper collage. It will look wonderful with the light coming through.

5. Weigh In

Provide scales and items to weigh.

6. Wish Pictures

Have children draw a picture that illustrates something they are wishing for.

7. Weather Watch

Make a weather chart and let children record the weather each day.

8. Water Works

Let the children wash the tables and chairs with water.

9. Wonderful Wigs

Provide wigs for the children to try on in the Dramatic Play Center. Old panty hose make a great braided hair wig. Cut the foot out of each leg. Cut each leg into three strips and braid. Tie braids with ribbons. Children put the waist on their heads and—bingo—they have braids.

10. Wolf Stories

Make a list of stories that have a wolf in them such as "The Three Little Pigs" and "Little Red Riding Hood." Rewrite the ending of one of the stories to change what happened to the wolf.

11. Wool on a Wheel

Check with local yarn stores to see if anyone is registered with them as a spinner. If so invite the spinner to come demonstrate the use of the spinning wheel. If you can't find a spinner you may still be able to obtain raw wool for the children to explore.

12. Whistle While We Work

Teach children how to whistle.

13. Wood Works

Pull out the construction table and let the children work with wood. They can sand it, hammer nails into it, and glue pieces together to create a wood sculpture.

14. Wagon Rides

Suggest the children take wagon rides on the playground.

ACQUIRING READING SKILLS

15. Weaving Wonders

Create a weaving loom by stapling five or six pieces of ¼" (0.5 cm) elastic to a piece of flat cardboard. Provide ribbon, yarn, and lace to weave.

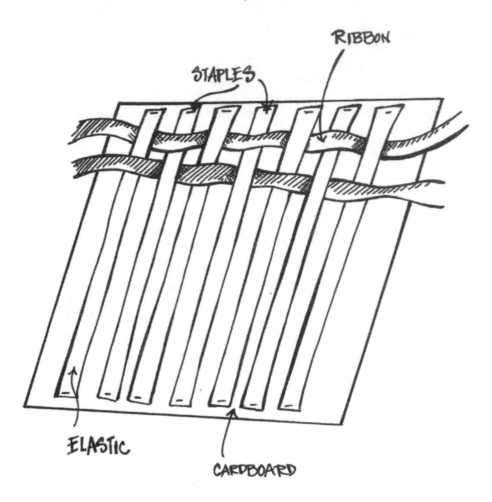

RIBBON

STAPLES

ELASTIC

CARDBOARD

16. Washing Walls

Provide some sponges and water and invite the children to wash the walls.

17. Beginning Sound "W" Concentration

Use the patterns on Appendix page 405 to make a concentration game with objects that begin with "W."

Word List

wade	we	wise
wag	weave	wish
wage	web	wit
wagon	weed	with
waist	week	wolf
wait	weird	wood
wake	well	wool
walk	went	word
wall	west	work
wand	wet	world
want	wife	worm
warm	wig	
wash	wild	
wasp	will	
waste	win	
watch	wind	
water	wing	
wave	wink	
wax	winter	
way	wipe	

Book List

I Wish That I Had Duck Feet by Theo LeSieg
Wacky Wednesday by Theo LeSieg
Whales by Gail Gibbons
The Wheels on the Bus by Paul O. Zelinsky
Where the Wild Things Are by Maurice Sendak
Whistle for Willie by Ezra Jack Keats
The Wind Blew by Pat Hutchins

There are very few words that begin with "X." The songs, stories, fingerplays, and poems in this section focus on the "X" sound in all locations: at the beginning of a word, in the middle of a word, and at the end of a word.

Songs

A-Hunting We Will Go

A-hunting we will go.
A-hunting we will go.
We'll catch a fox,
And put him in a box.
And then we'll let him go.

Poems

Tic Tac Toe (Pam Schiller)

Tic Tac Toe is a game I know.
You play it by making an X and an O.
I don't worry where you place your O,
Unless you have three in a row!

A Fox and an Ox

A fox and an ox
  Sitting in a box,
    Playing the sax
      All the live-long day.

    Said the fox to the ox,
      Sitting in a box,
       "It's a quarter to six,
      Let's be on our way."

I Say It with X's and O's (Pam Schiller)

I love you a little.
I love you a lot.
I say how much with Xs and Os.
When will I stop writing Xs and Os?
I think that is one thing that nobody
knows.

A FOX   AN OX   A BOX

Tongue Twisters/Alliterative Sentences and Phrases

Say the sentences and phrases below three times quickly, if you can.

- The fox bought socks for the ox.
- Ox socks.
- Ox and fox in a box.

Fingerplays/Action Rhymes

X Marks the Spot (Pam Schiller)
Make an X just like this, (make an X with fingers)
Mark the spot so you won't miss.
Stand back, take aim, (close one eye as if determining aim)
Toss the beanbag—win the game. (pretend to toss beanbag)

Story: What's in the Box? (Flannel Board Story)

Directions: Use a black sharpie pen to trace the patterns on Appendix pages 359-360 onto Pelon. Color them with crayons and cut them out. Use them with the flannel board to tell the story.

What's in the Box?
Look at this wonderful box. It's all wrapped up. It has pretty paper and a pretty bow. It's a present. I wonder what's inside. Do you wonder what's inside?

What do you think is in the box? Maybe it's a ball. Maybe it's a super hero with X-ray eyes. Maybe it's a xylophone.

If we could pick up the box, we'd know if it was heavy or light. If we could shake the box, we might hear something inside. We'd know if the thing inside makes a hard sound or a soft sound. But we can't shake this box so we just have to guess without many clues.
What do you think is in the box? (Let children guess)

Let's find out.
First we take off the bow. We'll put it right here. It's so pretty. Maybe we can use it again. Now let's take off the paper. If we are gentle and don't tear it, we can use the paper again, too.

X

OK! Are you ready to see what's inside? Look! It's a xylophone! Who can tell me what we do with a xylophone?

Small Group Enrichment

1. "What's in the Box?"
Place the story pieces in the language center and let children retell the story. Provide some pieces of Pelon and crayons so they can create some new items to be inside the box.

2. X-Rays
Obtain some X-rays from a local hospital or doctors office. Show children what they look like. You may want to tape them to your windows so that children can see the images better.

3. X Marks the Spot
Set up a Treasure Hunt. Tell children that clues can be found wherever an X marks the spot. Put an X on all your clues or close to your clues.

4. Play Tic Tac Toe
Play a game of Tic Tac Toe. This game is played with Xs and Os.

5. Find the Xs
Cut several Xs out of plastic or use magnetic letters. Bury the letters in the sand table. Challenge children to find the Xs.

6. Cross-Stitches
Provide some cross-stitch fabric and yarn and teach the children to make cross-stitches.

7. Circle the X Words
Make a list of several words. Challenge children to find and circle those that have an X in them.

8. Exit Search
Take a walk around the school in search of exit signs. How many did you find?

9. "X" Puzzles
Cut large Xs out of construction paper. Cut them into puzzle pieces and let the children work them.

10. XOXOXO

Teach the children how to sign a note with Xs for kisses and Os for hugs.

11. Xylophone

Encourage children to try tapping out a tune on a xylophone. If you don't have access to a xylophone, make a set of tone bottles to provide the same effect. Gather four glass jars all the same size. Fill the first jar ¼ full of water, the second jar ½ full, the third jar ¾ full, and the last jar full of water. Provide a dowel or other wooden stick to tap the jars. What do the children notice about the sounds?

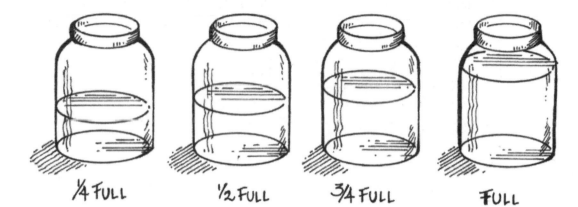

¼ FULL   ½ FULL   ¾ FULL   FULL

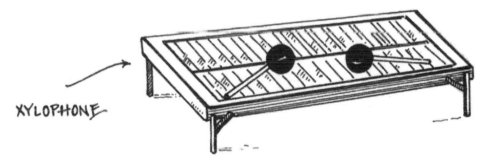

XYLOPHONE

12. "X" Sound Concentration

Use the patterns in Appendix page 406 to make a concentration game of objects with the "X" sound.

Word List

Words that begin with X	Words that have an x within	Words that end with X box
X-ray	axe	fax
Xerox	maximum	fix
xylophone	next	fox
	saxophone	mix
	taxi	ox
		sax
		six
		tax
		wax

Book List

Green Eggs and Ham by Dr. Suess
Tyrannosaurus by Janet Riechecky
Where the Wild Things Are by Maurice Sendak

Songs

The Yellow Rose of Texas (J.K.)

There's a Yellow Rose in Texas
That I am going to see.
No other fellow knows her.
No, not a one but me.
She cried so when I left her,
It like to broke my heart.
And if I ever find her,
We never more will part.

Chorus
She's the sweetest rose in Texas
That this man ever knew.
Her eyes are bright as diamonds;
They sparkle like the dew.
You may talk about your dearest May,
And sing of Rosa Lee.
But the Yellow Rose of Texas
Beats the belles of Tennessee.

Yankee Doodle

Father and I went down to camp
Along with Captain Gooding,
And there we saw the men and boys
As thick as hasty puddin.'

Chorus
Yankee Doodle keep it up,
Yankee Doodle Dandy.
Mind the music and the step,
And with the girls be handy.

And there was Captain Washington
Upon a strappin' stallion,
And all the men and boys around,
I guess there was a million.

Chorus

Yankee Doodle went to town

ACQUIRING READING SKILLS

Y

Ridin' on a pony.
Stuck a feather in his hat
And called it macaroni.

Chorus

The Grand Old Duke of York

The Grand Old Duke of York,
He had ten thousand men.
He marched them up the hill
And down the hill again.
And when you're up you up,
And when you're down you're down,
And when you're only half way up,
You're neither up nor down.

You Are My Sunshine

You are my sunshine,
My only sunshine.
You make me happy when skies are gray.
You'll never know dear how much I love you.
Please don't take my sunshine away.

Poems

Yellow (Pam Schiller/Tamera Bryant)

I like yellow.
I like it a lot.
I like yellow flowers.
They're great in a pot.

I like yellow dresses
And yellow paint messes.
I like yellow bows
And yellow paint on my toes.

I like yellow candy.
Bananas are dandy.
I even like Jell-O
As long as it's yellow.

Let's hear it for yellow.
It's the color to be.
It's happy and mellow,
Exactly like me.

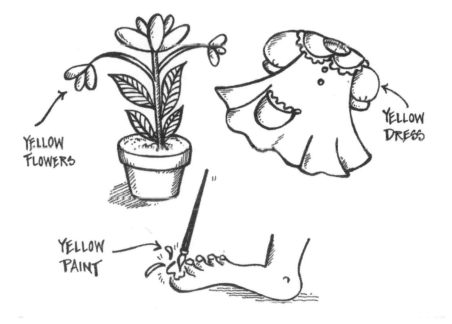

YELLOW FLOWERS

YELLOW DRESS

YELLOW PAINT

I Had a Little Yo-Yo (Tiffany Markle)
I had a little yo-yo.
It was my favorite toy.
I played with it quite often
When I was just a boy.
I used to know a trick or two,
You could even say a few.
But none that I remember now
Much less could even do.

You (Pam Schiller)
Deep in the heart of me
Nothing but you.
Find the best part of me
Constant and true.
Deep in the heart of me
Nothing but you.

Tongue Twisters/Alliterative Sentences and Phrases

Say the sentences and phrases below three times quickly, if you can.

- Yackety yaks yacking back
- Yellow yolks

Fingerplays/Action Rhymes

Yarn Trick (Pam Schiller)
Take a piece of yarn. (suit actions to words)
Tie it around your finger.
Now you won't forget
What you need to remember.

Story: A Yarn Tale (Group Story)

A Yarn Tale
Tell children that stories are sometimes called yarns. Give a ball of yarn to one of the children. That child begins a story, unrolling the yarn as she talks. She then hands the ball to the next child, who continues the story and the unrolling. Continue the process until everyone has had a turn or until the story comes to a natural end. How long is the unrolled yarn at the end of the story?

Small Group Enrichment
1. Yarn Designs
Give several pieces of yarn (yellow if you want) and encourage children to glue them into designs.

2. Yoga
Teach the children a couple of Yoga positions.

3. Yellow Collages
Provide yellow items for a collage. Offer tissue paper, sequins, paper scraps, buttons, beads, and so forth.

4. A Yard of Yarn
Give children 1 yard (1 m) of yarn and let them find things in the room that are one yard long.

5. Yam Plants
Grow a yam in your classroom. Cut the top off a yam. Stick toothpicks around its middle to suspend it on the top of a jar filled with water.

6. Yogurt Yummies
Invite children to mix 1 tablespoon (10 g) of trail mix to 3 tablespoons (75 g) of yogurt and enjoy a Yogurt Yummy.

7. Yo-Yo Fun.
Let children experiment with a yo-yo. If you know a trick or two, show children what you know. If you know a yo-yo wizard, invite him or her in to demonstrate.

8. Yodeling Yodelers
Introduce children to yodeling. If you happen to have any old Minnie Pearl records, let children listen to one of the best yodelers of all time.

9. Yolks, Yolks, and More Yolks
Make deviled eggs. Let children mash the yolks and add the relish and mayonnaise.

10. Yell for Us
Make up a class yell (cheer).

y

11. Yankee Doodle Hats

Fold newspaper into parade hats. Let children decorate. Be sure to provide the feathers.

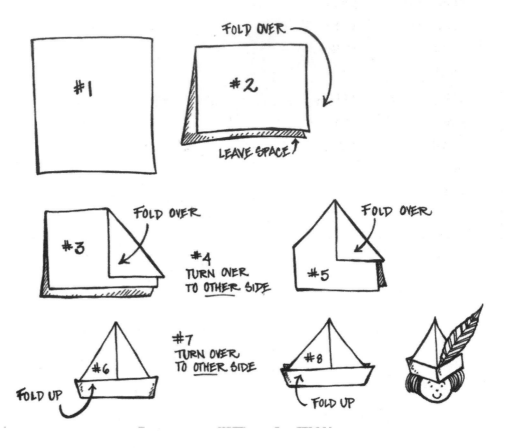

12. Yeah or Yuck

Play a game of Yeah or Yuck. Pose different statements to children and have them respond with their feelings about what you proposed. For example, spinach is good. They would say "Yeah" if they agree and "Yuck" if they disagree.

13. Beginning Sound "Y" Concentration Game

Use the patterns on Appendix page 407 to make a concentration game with objects that begin with "Y."

Word List

yak	yield
yam	yoke
yank	yolk
yard	you
yawn	young
year	your
yeast	yuck
yell	
yes	

Book List

It Could Always Be Worse: A Yiddish Folktale retold by Margot Zemach

Little Blue and Little Yellow by Leo Lionni

Yertle the Turtle and Other Stories by Dr. Suess

Yummers! by James Marshall

Songs

Zulu Warrior

I com a zimba, zimba, ziya,
I com a zimba, zimba, zee.
I com a zimba, zimba, ziya,
I com a zimba, zimba, zee.
See him there the Zulu warrior.
See him there the Zulu Chief,
Chief, Chief, Chief, Chief.

Repeat as a round with one group chanting "Chief, Chief, Chief…" and the other group singing the song.

My Dog Rags

I have a dog and his name is Rags.
He eats so much that his tummy sags.
His ears flip flop and his tail wig wags,
And when he walks he zig, zig, zags!

Oh, Do You Have a Zipper Coat? (Tune: Muffin Man)

Oh, do you have a zipper coat?
Zipper coat, zipper coat?
Oh, do you have a zipper coat?
Then stand and take a bow!

Repeat, asking for other "Z" items such as a zip code or zoo pass.

Zum Gali Gali

Zum gali gali gali (group 1 sings this chant for whole song)
Zum gali gali,
Zum gali gali gali,
Zum gali gali

Hebrew version:
Hechalutz le maan avoda. (group 2 sings either the English or Hebrew
   version of this song)
Avoda le maan hechalutz.
Ha shalom le maan ha amin.
Ha amin le maan ha shalom.

English version:
Pioneers all work as one.
Work as one all pioneers.
Peace shall be for all the world.
All the world shall be for peace.

Zulu Cradle-Song
Hush, thee, my baby,
Thy mother's o'er the mountains gone.
There she will dig the little garden patch,
And wood she will bring from the forest.
Hush, thee, my baby.

Poems

The Zebra (Pam Schiller)
The zebra looks just like a horse
Except for all those stripes, of
    course.

I wonder if she's black with
    stripes of snowy white—
Or is she snowy white with stripes as
    black as night?

The Zigzag Boy and Girl
I have a little zigzag boy
Who goes this way and that.
He never knows just where he put
His coat or shoe or hat.

I know a little zigzag girl
Who flutters here and there.
She never knows just where to find
Her brush to fix her hair.

If you are not a zigzag child,
You'll have no cause to say,
That you forgot, for you will know
Where things are put away.

ACQUIRING READING SKILLS

Tongue Twisters/Alliterative Sentences and Phrases

Zackary Zak
Zackary Zak zipped zippers zealously.
If Zackery Zak zipped zippers zealously,
How many zippers did Zackery Zak zip?

Fingerplays/Action Rhymes

My Zipper Suit (Traditional)
This zipper suit is bunny brown. (*hold arms out to side*)
The top zips up, the legs zip down. (*zip top up and the legs down*)
I wear it every day.
My Daddy brought it from downtown.
Zip it up, zip it down. (*run zippers up and*)
And hurry out to play. (*turn around*)

Zooty Za
Zooty za, zooty za,
Zooty za, za.

Thumbs up. (*suit actions to words*)
Zooty za, zooty za,
Zooty za, za.

Elbows back.
Zooty za, zooty za,
Zooty za, za.

Feet apart.
Zooty za, zooty za,
Zooty za, za.

Knees together.
Zooty za, zooty za,
Zooty za, za.

Bottoms up.
Zooty za, zooty za,
Zooty za, za.

Tongue out.
Zooty za, zooty za,
Zooty za, za.

Eyes shut.
Zooty za, zooty za,
Zooty za, za.

Turn around.
Zooty za, zooty za,
Zooty za, za.

Story: The Zebra on the Zyder Zee (Flannel Board Story)

Directions: Use a black sharpie pen to trace the patterns from Appendix pages 362-366 onto Pelon. Color with crayons and cut them out. Use them with the flannel board to present the story below.

The Zebra On the Zyder Zee (Pam Schiller)
The Zebra on the Zyder Zee
Wanted to sail across the sea.
He called to his friends 1, 2, 3,
"Come along and sail with me."

The Zebra on the Zyder Zee
Said "I'm lonesome, don't you see.
I want to sail across the sea,
But I simply must have company."

The first to come on the Zyder Zee
Was the Zebra's friend Sir Ronnee Ree.
He said, "I'll be your company
I'm dying to sail across the sea."

The next to come to the Zyder Zee
Was Elizabeth Holleque de Dundee.
She brought her little urchins three
And said, "Let's sail across the sea."

The Zebra on the Zyder Zee
Was just as happy as can be.
He was going to sail across the sea.
And the Zyder Zee had company.

ACQUIRING READING SKILLS

He hoisted the sail 1, 2, 3,
And the friends were off to see the sea.
Day and night and day times three,
The jolly mates sailed across the sea.

The little ship rocked on the sea.
The jolly mates ate bread and brie.
The little ones sipped cinnamon tea,
And the Zebra sailed the Zyder Zee.

At last, the journey across the sea
Came to an end at half past three.
The Zebra and his company
Had finally sailed across the sea.

The little ones and Ms. Dundee
Took the hand of Ronnee Ree.
And left the deck of the Zyder Zee
Saying good-bye to the deep blue sea.

Small Group Enrichment

1. Zillions of Zigzags

Give the children some children's pinking shears and let them cut some zigzag strips of paper.

2. Zip the Zipper

Provide several sizes and varieties of zippers for children to zip and unzip.

3. Walk a Zigzag Line

Make a zigzag line on the floor with masking tape. Challenge children to walk the line with a beanbag on their heads.

4. Trip to the Zoo

Take a field trip to the zoo.

5. Zoom

Read the book *Zoom* by Istvan Banyai. Show children how to draw a zoom picture. Fold a piece of 9" x 12" (22 cm x 30 cm) drawing paper into four sections. Have children draw an object in the first square and then a picture of where the object is sitting in the second square. Continue like the book. This activity will probably require some suggestions from an adult or an older child.

6. Do You Know Your Zip Code?

Have children bring their zip codes to school. Graph the zip codes. How many different zip codes are represented? Do a majority of the children live in the same zip code area?

7. Zigzag Art

Provide rickrack and glue and let the children create a zigzag picture.

8. Zap the Zone

Divide a piece of poster board into four areas or zones. Color each zone a different color. Place corresponding colored dots on several index cards. Turn the cards over like a deck of cards. Provide a beanbag and challenge children to draw a card and then toss the beanbag to land on the corresponding color zone on the poster board.

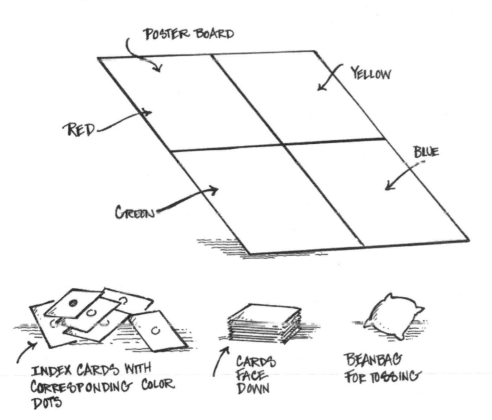

9. Zoo Time

Give the children plastic zoo animals and berry baskets to use for cages. Encourage them to build a zoo.

10. Zoom Lenses

Place magnifying glasses, binoculars, and camera lenses (if available) in the Science Center for investigation.

11. Circle 'round the Zero

Play Circle 'round the Zero. Children form a circle. One child is selected as IT. IT walks around the outside of the circle and stops behind a child. IT then does as the song directs—stands back to back with the selected child, then side by side and finally facing the child. When the song says tap your lovin' zero, IT taps her friend and the friend becomes the new IT.

> Circle 'round the zero.
> Find your lovin' zero.
> Back, back zero.
> Side, side zero.
> Front, front zero.
> Tap your lovin' zero.

12. Dee-Doo-Dah

Sing the song or listen to it on an album, CD, or cassette. How do you feel when you hear this song?

13. Zookeeper

Invite children to form a circle. The zookeeper stands in the center and points to various groups of children, calling out the name of an animal. The children must imitate the animal called out by making the appropriate noises and movements.

14 Beginning Sound "Z" Concentration

Use the patterns on the Appendix page 408 to make a concentration game of objects that begin with the "Z."

Word List	
zag	zinc
Zap	zip
Zebra	zone
Zero	zoo
Zest	zoom

Book List

If I Ran the Zoo by Dr. Suess
The Z Was Zapped by Chris Van Allsburg
Zella, Zack and Zodiak by Bill Peet
Zomo the Rabbit: A Trickster Tale From West Africa retold by Gerald McDermott
Zoom by Istvan Banyai

Brain Connections

● Between the fourth and eighth month of life, a neuron is assigned to every sound in the child's native language. This process is referred to as the creation of a native language map. The brain will continue to enhance discrimination of the sounds in this map for several years.

● If a child has a rich language experience prior to formal phonics instruction, it is likely that he or she will discriminate phonemes with both greater ease and greater accuracy.

ACQUIRING READING SKILLS

Appendix

Appendix Contents

Assessment Checklists

Patterns

Maze

Rebus

Sequence Cards

American Sign Language

Sound Word Cards

Recipes

Games

Glossary

References

Birth to Three Years

	Not Yet	Emerging	Accomplished
Recognizes specific books by cover.	☐	☐	☐
Pretends to read books.	☐	☐	☐
Understands that books are handled in particular ways.	☐	☐	☐
Enters into a book-sharing routine with primary caregivers.	☐	☐	☐
Demonstrates enjoyment of rhyming language and nonsense words.	☐	☐	☐
Labels objects in books.	☐	☐	☐
Listens to stories.	☐	☐	☐
Requests adult to read or write.	☐	☐	☐
Begins to notice specific print, such as letters in names.	☐	☐	☐
Uses increasingly purposeful scribbling.	☐	☐	☐
Distinguishes between drawing and writing.	☐	☐	☐
Produces some letter-like forms and scribbles with some features of writing.	☐	☐	☐

Three to Four Years

	Not Yet	Emerging	Accomplished
Knows that alphabet letters are a special category of visual graphics that can be individually named.	☐	☐	☐
Recognizes print in the local environment.	☐	☐	☐
Understands that different text forms are used for different functions of print (e.g., a grocery list is different than a menu).	☐	☐	☐
Recognizes separable and repeating sounds in language (e.g., in Peter, Peter, Pumpkin Eater).	☐	☐	☐
Uses new vocabulary and correct grammar in speech.	☐	☐	☐
Understands and follows oral directions.	☐	☐	☐
Is sensitive to sequences of events in stories.	☐	☐	☐
Shows an interest in books and reading.	☐	☐	☐
Connects information and events in a story to real-life experiences.	☐	☐	☐
Demonstrates understanding of meaning of a story by asking appropriate questions and making appropriate comments.	☐	☐	☐
Displays reading and writing attempts.	☐	☐	☐
Identifies several alphabet letters, especially those from own name.	☐	☐	☐
Writes (scribbles) message as part of playful activity.	☐	☐	☐
Recognizes beginning or rhyming sound in familiar words	☐	☐	☐

Fives

	Not Yet	Emerging	Accomplished
Knows the parts of a book and their function.	☐	☐	☐
Begins to track print when listening to a familiar text being read or when rereading own writing.	☐	☐	☐
"Reads" familiar texts emergently, i.e. not necessarily verbatim from the print alone.	☐	☐	☐
Recognizes and can name all uppercase and lowercase letters.	☐	☐	☐
Understands that the sequence of letters in a written word represents the sequence of sounds (phonemes) in a spoken word.	☐	☐	☐
Demonstrates some one-to-one letter sound correspondences.	☐	☐	☐
Recognizes common words by sight.	☐	☐	☐
Uses new vocabulary and grammatical constructions in own speech.	☐	☐	☐
Makes appropriate switches from oral to written language styles.	☐	☐	☐
Notices when simple sentences fail to make sense.	☐	☐	☐
Connects information and events in text to life and life experiences to text.	☐	☐	☐
Retells, reenacts, or dramatizes stories or parts of stories.	☐	☐	☐
Listens attentively to books the teacher reads to class.	☐	☐	☐
Names some book titles and authors.	☐	☐	☐
Demonstrates familiarity with genres of text (e.g., storybooks, poems, labels).	☐	☐	☐

	Not Yet	Emerging	Accomplished
Correctly answers questions about stories read aloud.	☐	☐	☐
Makes predictions based on illustrations or portions of stories.			
Demonstrates understanding that spoken words consist of sequences of phonemes.	☐	☐	☐
Given spoken sets such as "pan, pan, pen," can identify the first two as the same and the third as different.	☐	☐	☐
Given spoken sets such as "ran, pat, did," can identify the first two as sharing one same sound.	☐	☐	☐
Given spoken segments, can merge them into a meaningful target word.	☐	☐	☐
Given a spoken word, can produce another word that rhymes with it.	☐	☐	☐
Independently writes many uppercase and lowercase letters.	☐	☐	☐
Uses phonemic awareness and letter knowledge to spell independently.	☐	☐	☐
Writes (unconventionally) to express own meaning.	☐	☐	☐
Builds a repertoire of some conventionally spelled words.	☐	☐	☐
Shows awareness of distinction between "kid writing" and conventional writing.	☐	☐	☐
Writes own name (first and last) and the first names of some friends or classmates.	☐	☐	☐
Can write most letters and some words when they are dictated.	☐	☐	☐

Mama

Patterns: The Three Bears Rap (B)

Patterns: Smart Cookie (C)

little cookie   momma cookie

ginger snap cookie platter   sugar cookie sheet

pattern cookie sheet

ginger snap

sugar cookie

oatmeal cookie

Patterns: The Little Engine that Could (E)

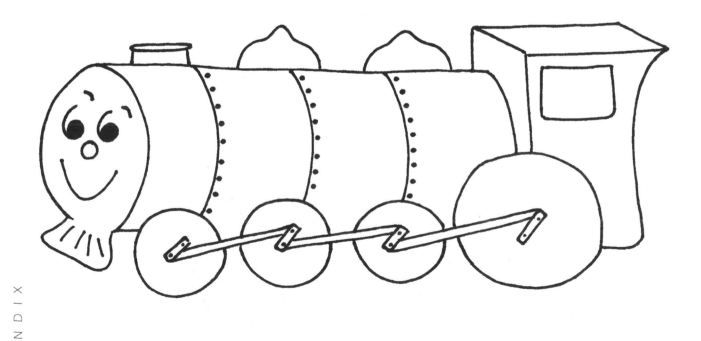

Patterns: The Gingerbread Man (G)

cat

cow

dog

farmer

Patterns: The House That Jack Built (J)

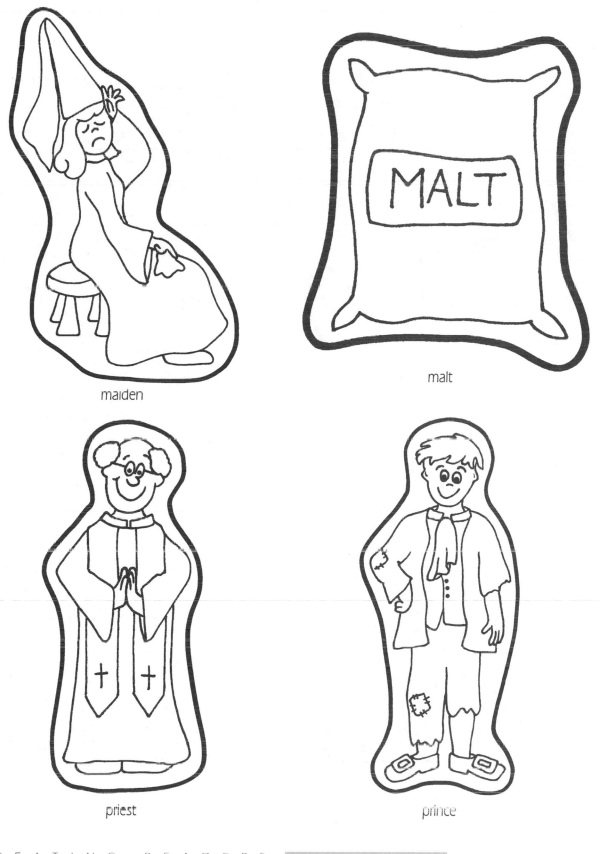

maiden

malt

priest

prince

rat

rooster

Patterns: Katy No-Pockets (K)

Katy

Joey

croc

baby croc

Patterns: Katy No-Pockets (K)

Patterns: Katy No-Pockets (K)

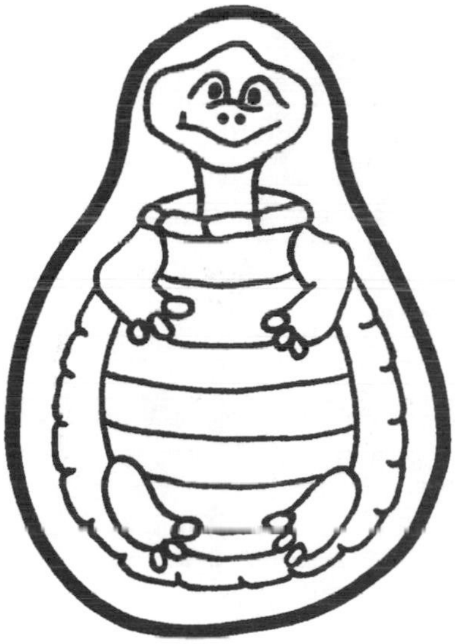

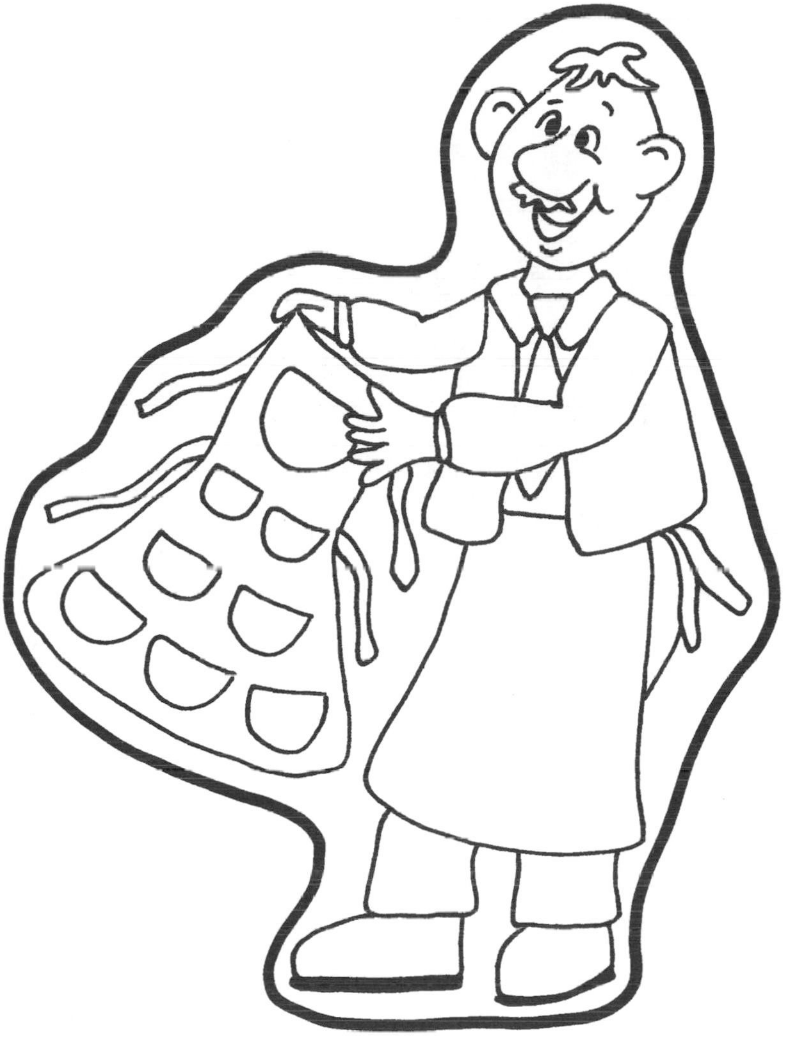

apron

pocket

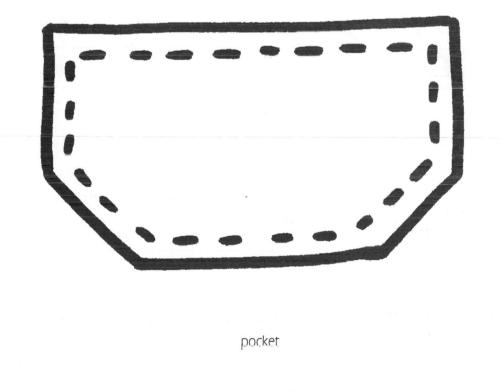

pocket

Patterns: This Old Man (M)

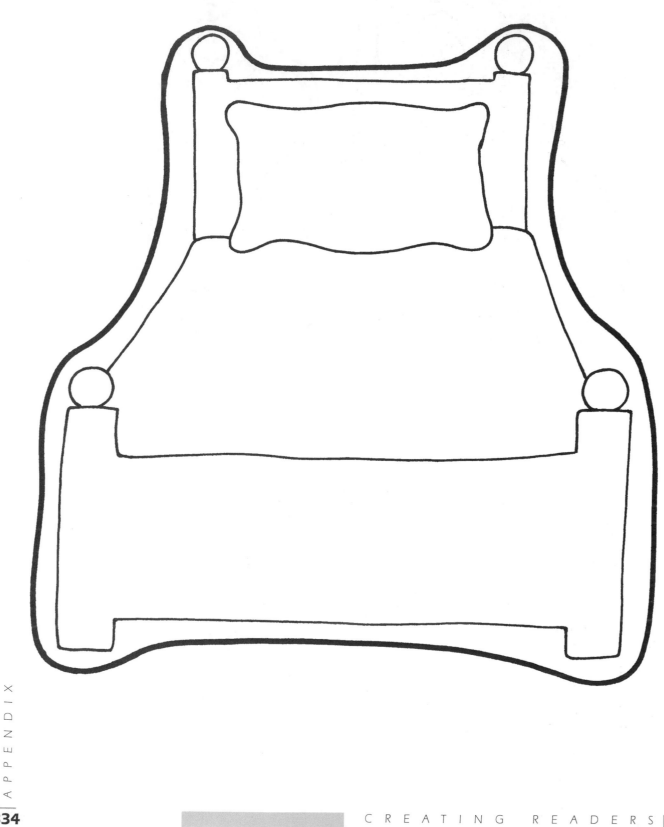

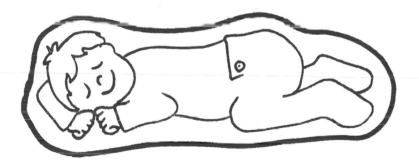

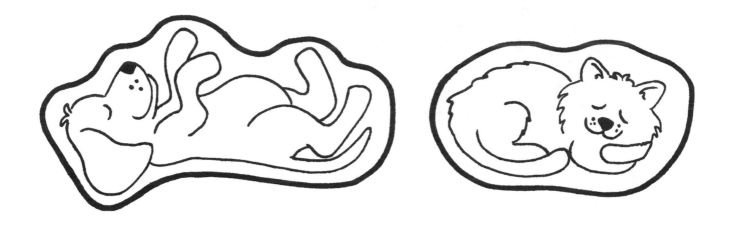

Patterns: I Know an Old Lady (O)

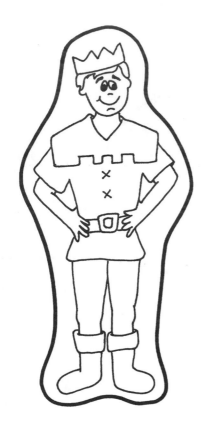

Patterns: The Princess and the Pea (P)

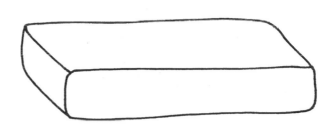

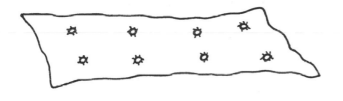

Patterns: The Quangle Wangle's Hat (Q)

(Enlarge the hat so the animals will all fit on the hat.)

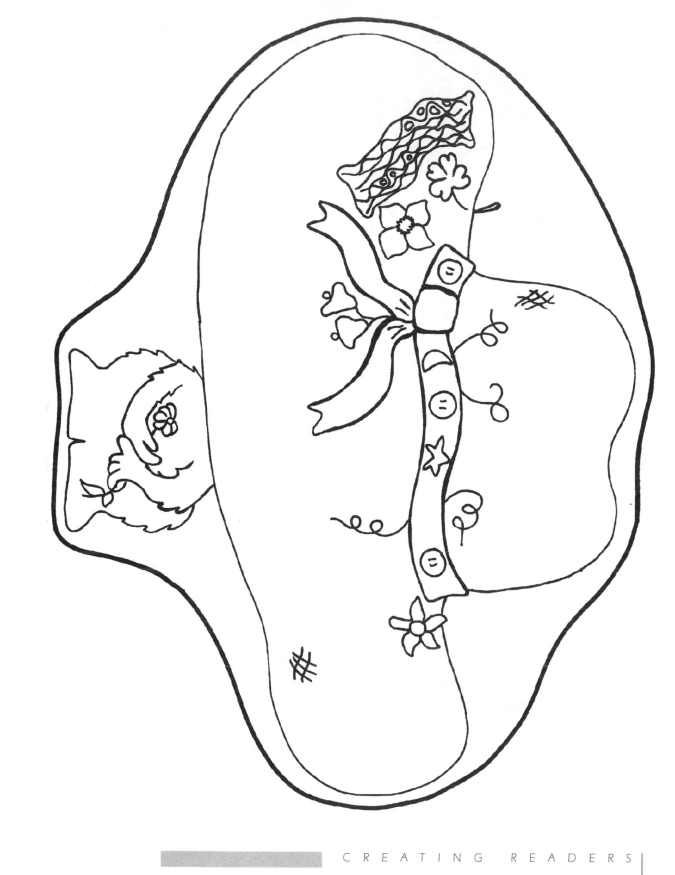

Patterns: The Quangle Wangle's Hat (Q)

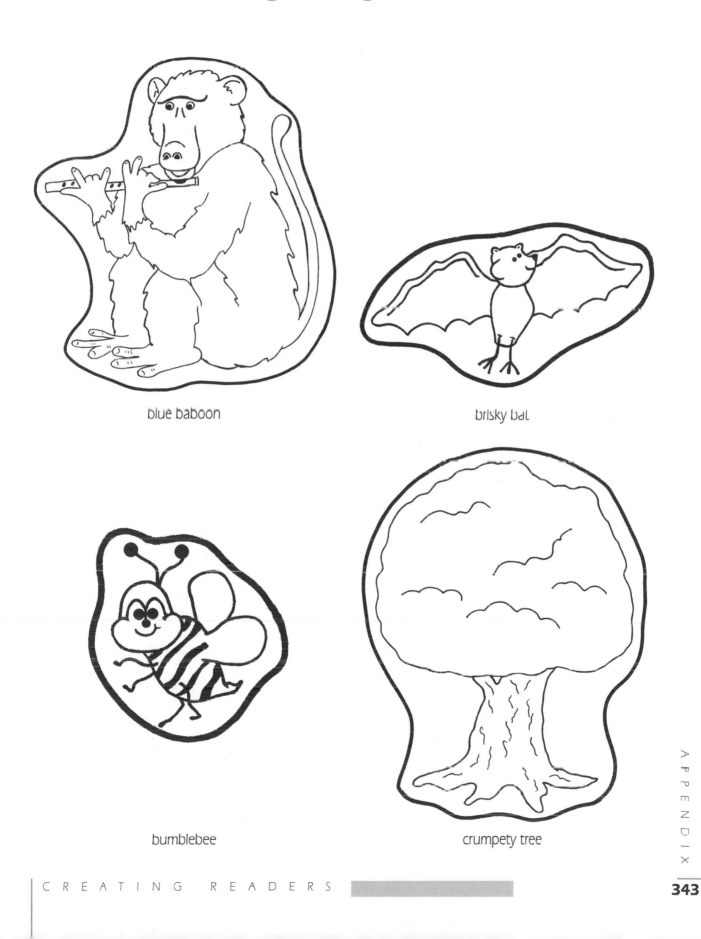

blue baboon

brisky bat

bumblebee

crumpety tree

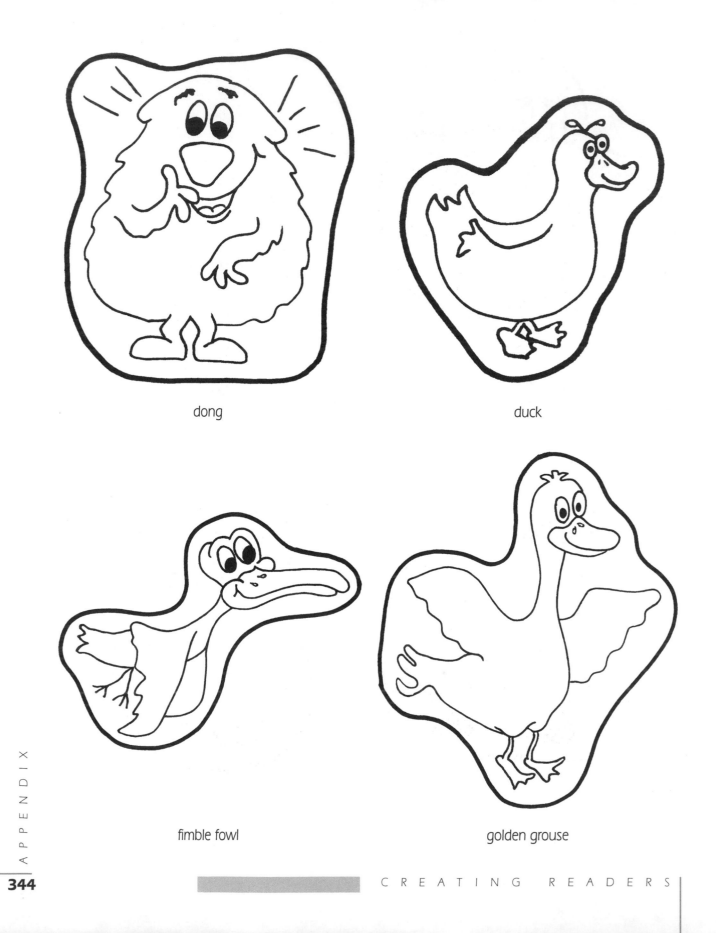

dong

duck

fimble fowl

golden grouse

Patterns: The Quangle Wangle's Hat (Q)

Mr. & Ms. Canary

olympian bear

orient calf

owl

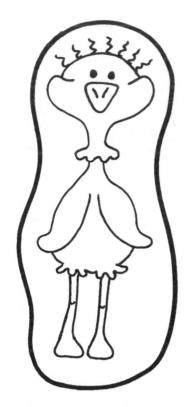

pobble

snail

stork

Patterns: The Little Red Hen (R)

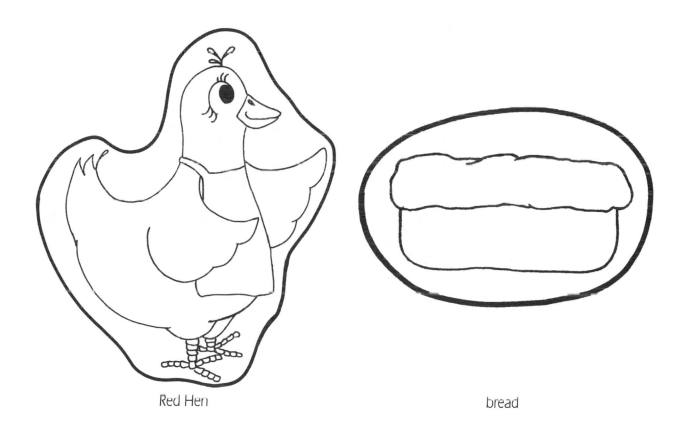

Red Hen

bread

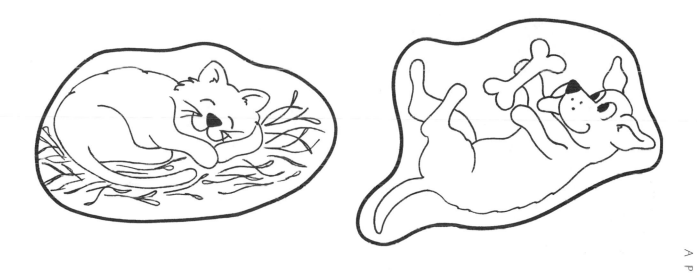

cat

dog

Patterns: The Little Red Hen (R)

pig

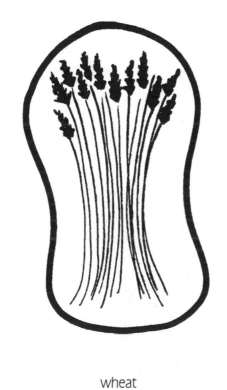

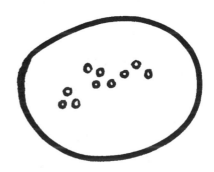

seed

wheat

Patterns: Santa's Workshop (S)

Patterns: Turkey-Lurkey (T)

Patterns: The First Umbrella (U)

Patterns: Valencia Valentine (V)

Patterns: Valencia Valentine (V)

Patterns: What's in the Box? (X)

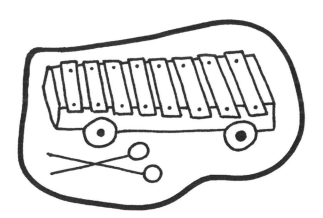

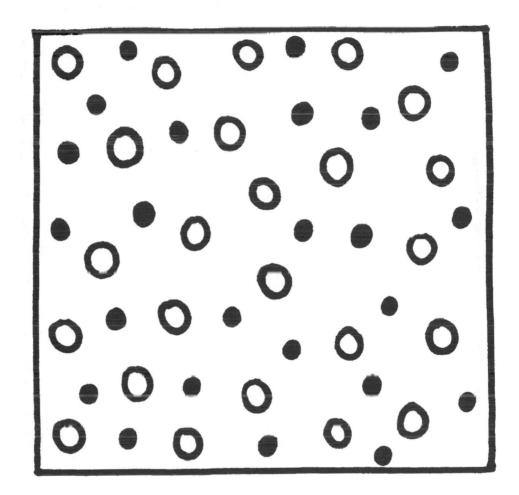

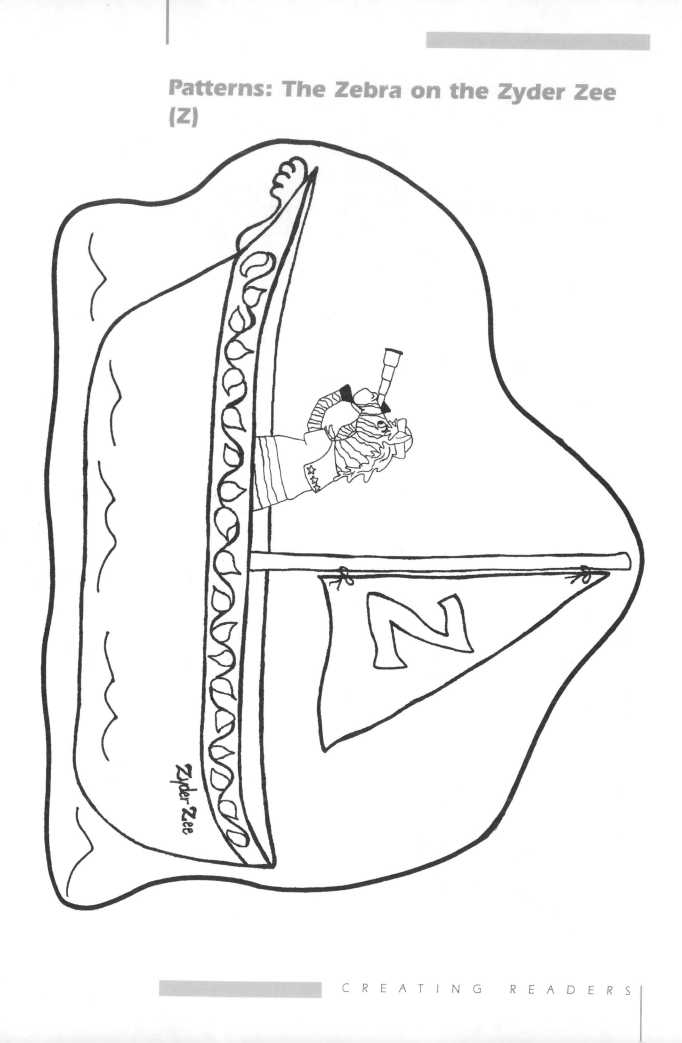

Zyder Zee

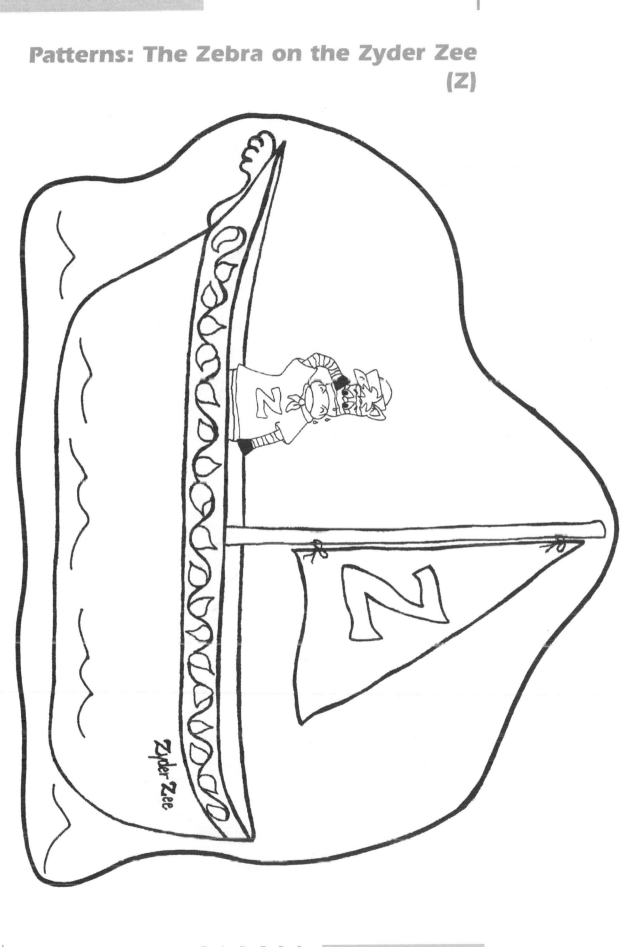

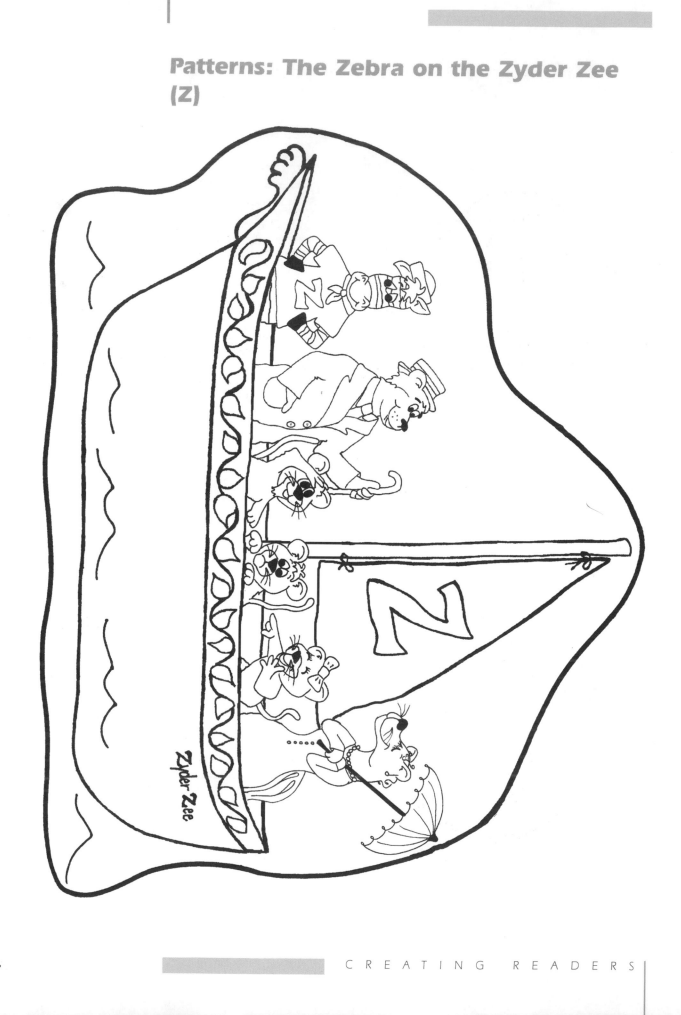

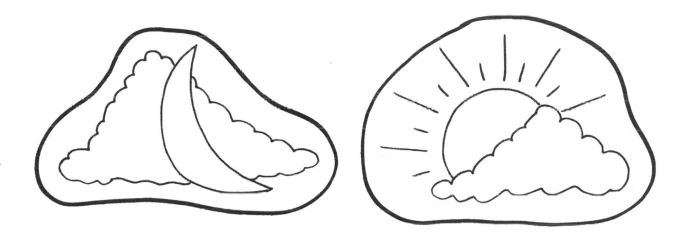

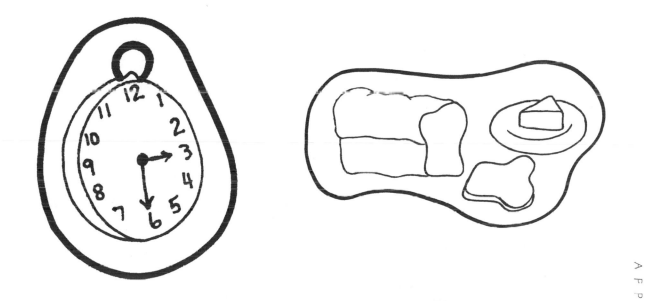

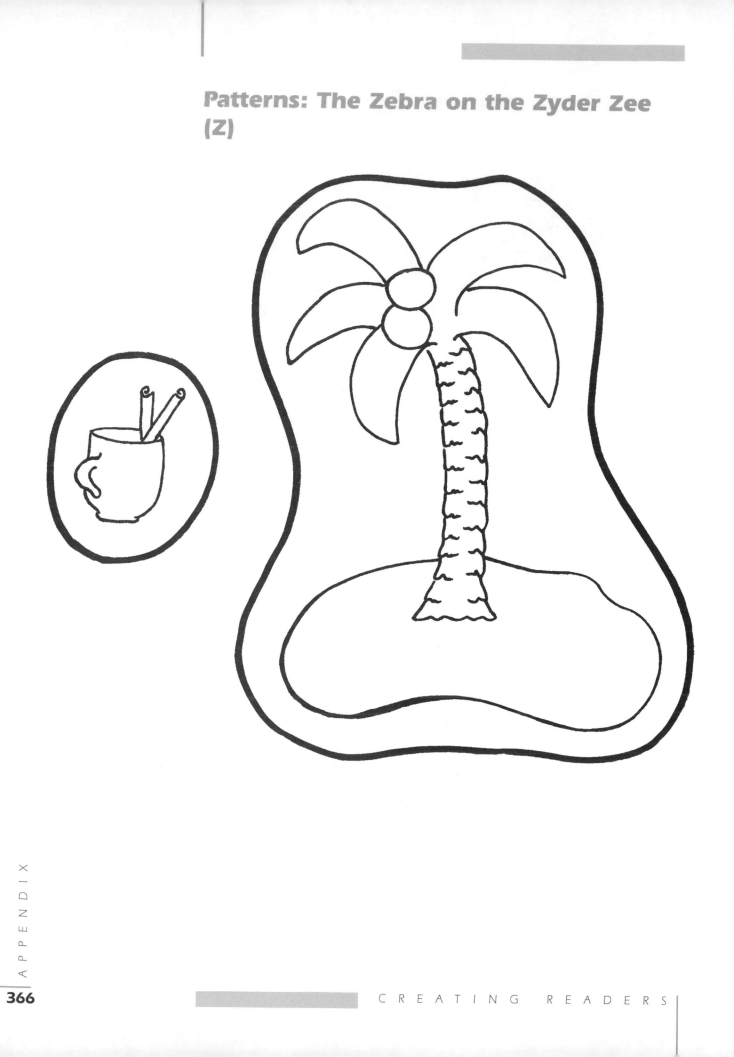

Patterns: Susie Moriar

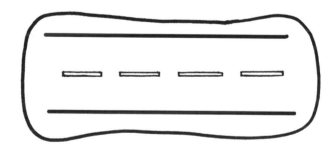

Patterns: Henny-Penny

Patterns: Henny-Penny

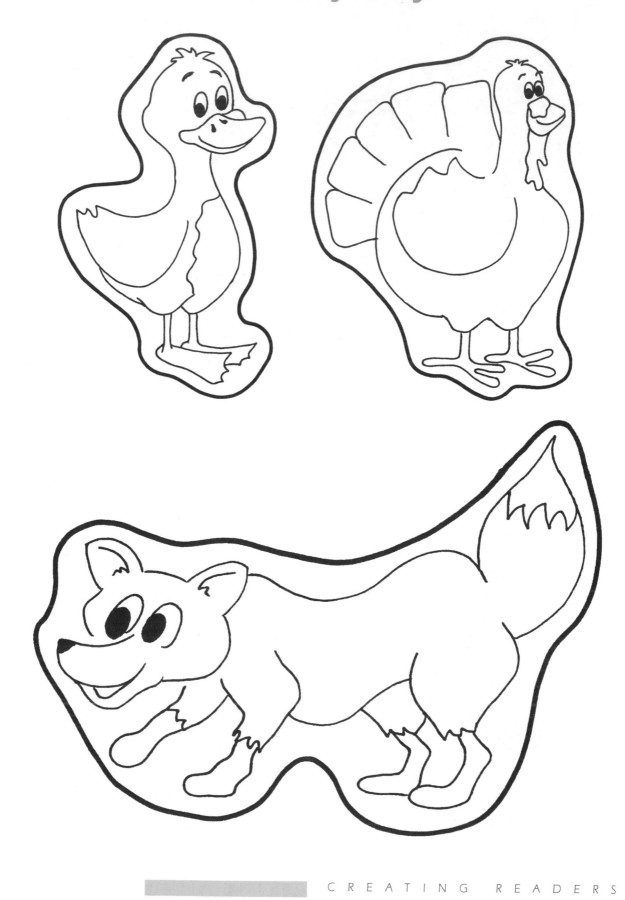

Patterns: Finger Puppets

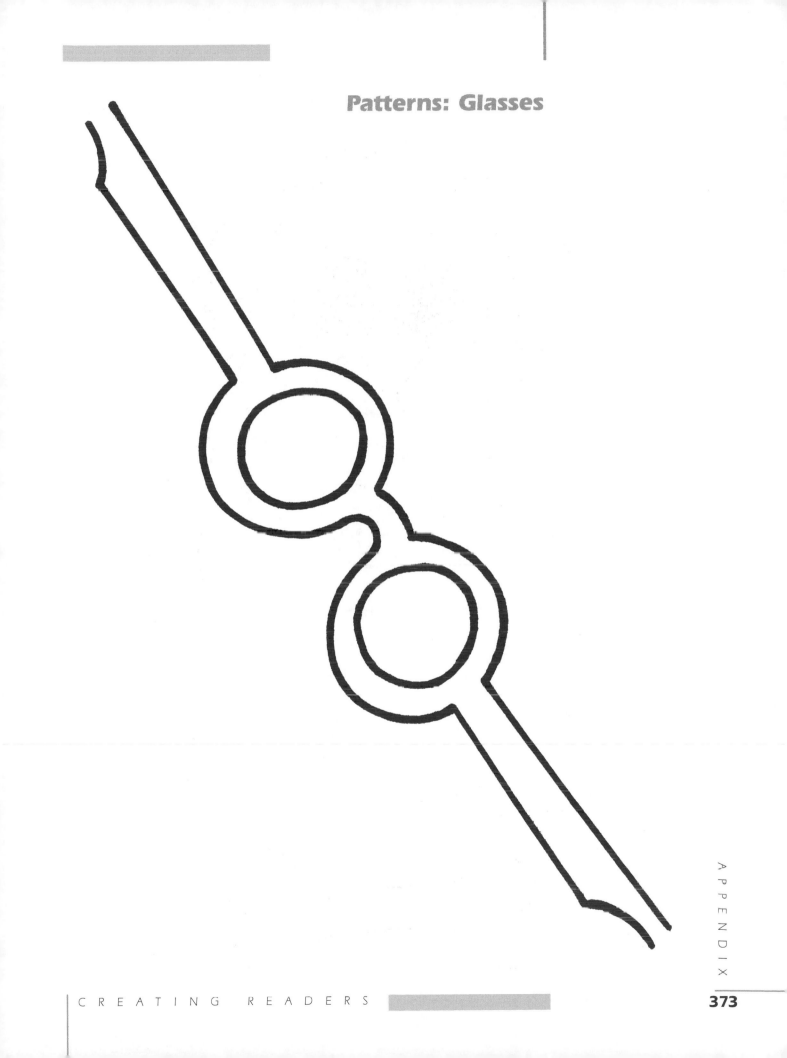

Patterns: Glove Puppets

Use Velcro to attach to gloves.

Patterns: Animal Sound Cards

A P P E N D I X

Patterns: Annie Mae Puzzle Doll

Maze

Rebus: Painting at the Easel

1

2

3

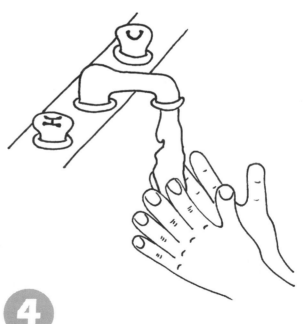

4

Rebus: Movement Activity

pineapple chunks

Eat

banana slices

stir salad

Fruit Salad

T. apples

T. oranges

Sequence Cards: The Three Bears

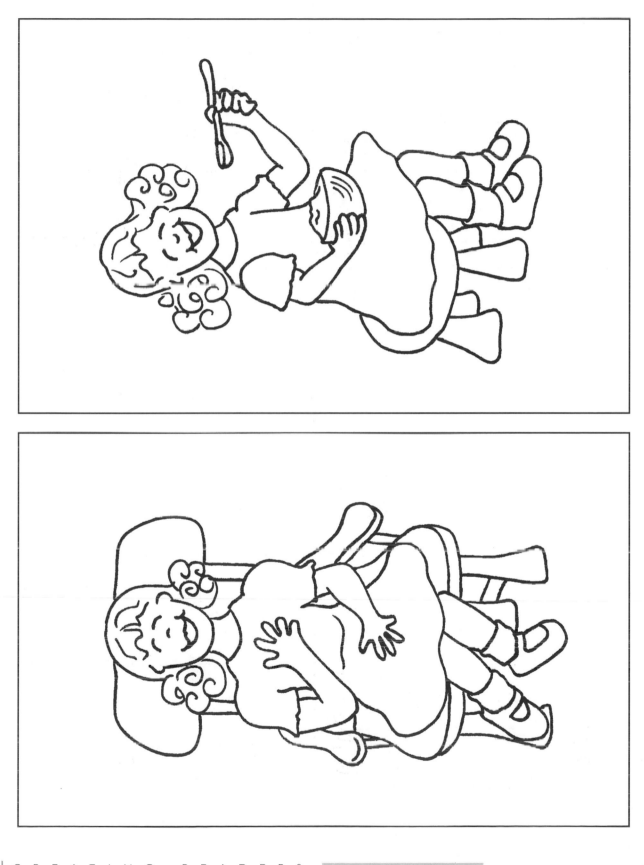

Sequence Cards: The Three Pigs

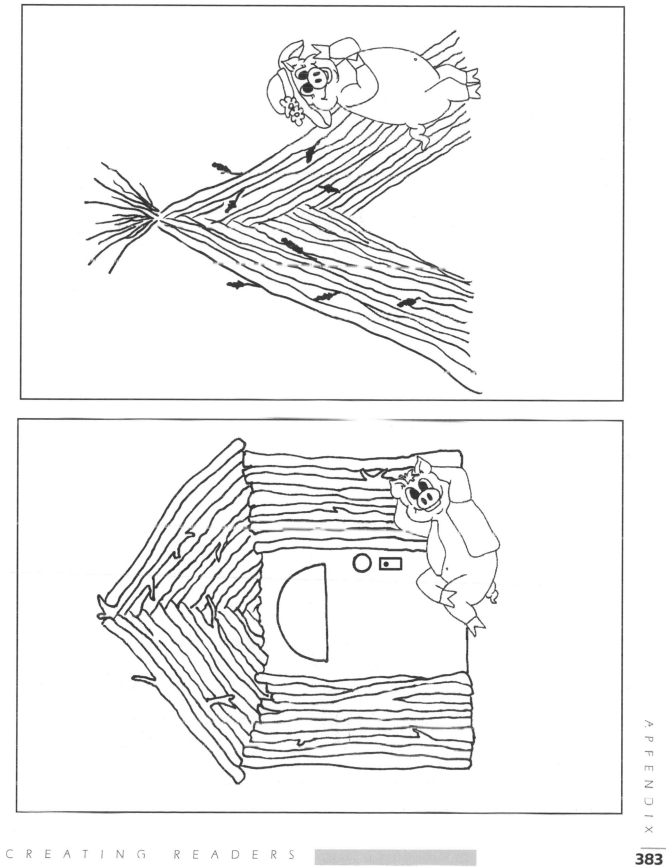

Sequence Cards: The Three Pigs

Brother

Finished

Friend

More

No

Sister

Stop

Thank You

Yes

Concentration game patterns can be used in a variety of ways.

Concentration Games

Make two copies of each page. Color, cut, and laminate the cards. Encourage children to lay all the cards facedown, then turn them over two at a time to find matching pairs.

Matching Games

Make two copies of each page. Color, cut, and laminate the cards. Invite children to sort the cards into matching pairs.

Make two copies of each page. Color, cut, and laminate. Punch a hole in the top of each card, tie a piece of yarn through each card, and hang from a clothes hanger. Provide clothepins for children to clip onto matching cards.

Beginning Sound Word "B" Concentration

Beginning Sound Word "C" Concentration

Beginning Sound Word "D" Concentration

Beginning Sound Word "F" Concentration

Beginning Sound Word "G" Concentration

Beginning Sound Word "H" Concentration

Beginning Sound Word "J" Concentration

Beginning Sound Word "K" Concentration

Beginning Sound Word "L" Concentration

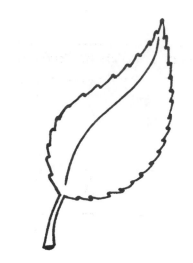

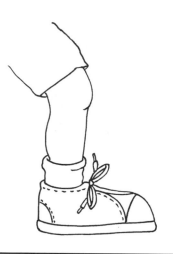

Beginning Sound Word "M" Concentration

Beginning Sound Word "N" Concentration

Beginning Sound Word "Q" Concentration

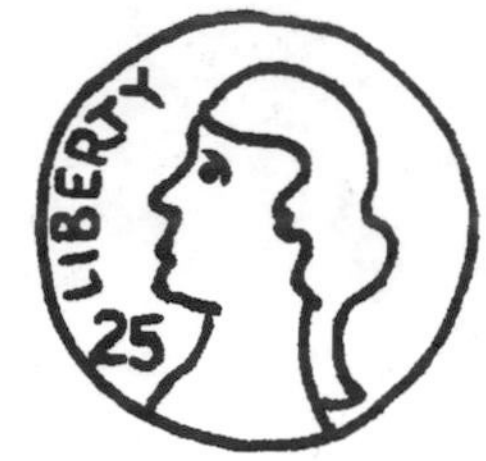

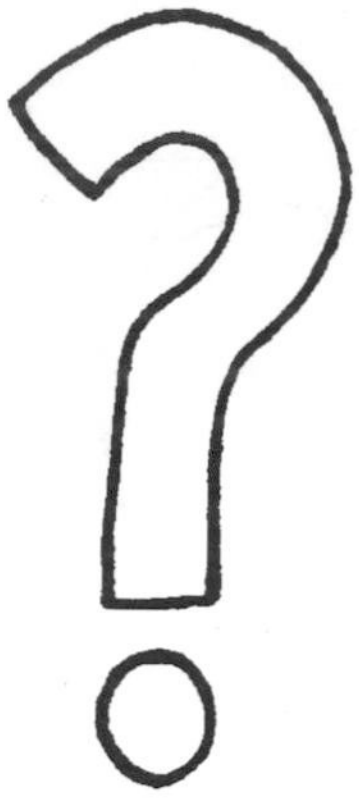

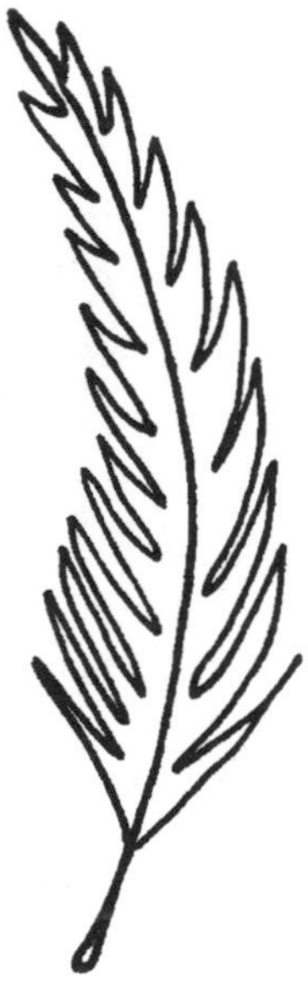

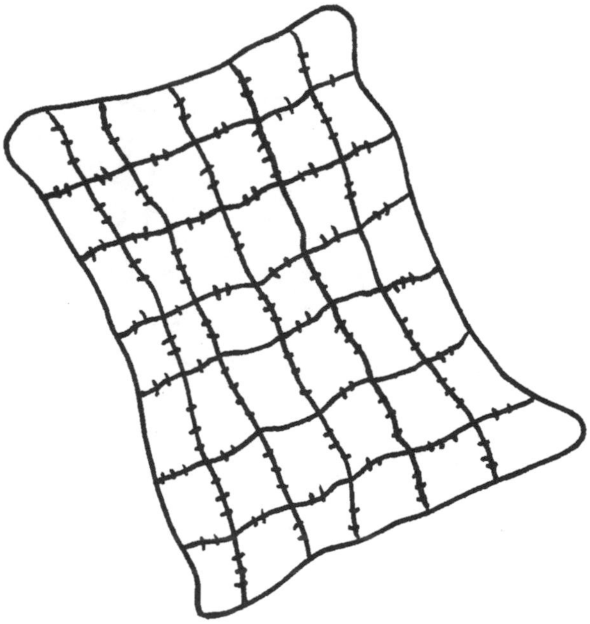

Beginning Sound Word "S" Concentration

Beginning Sound Word "T" Concentration

Beginning Sound Word "W" Concentration

Sound Word "X" Concentration

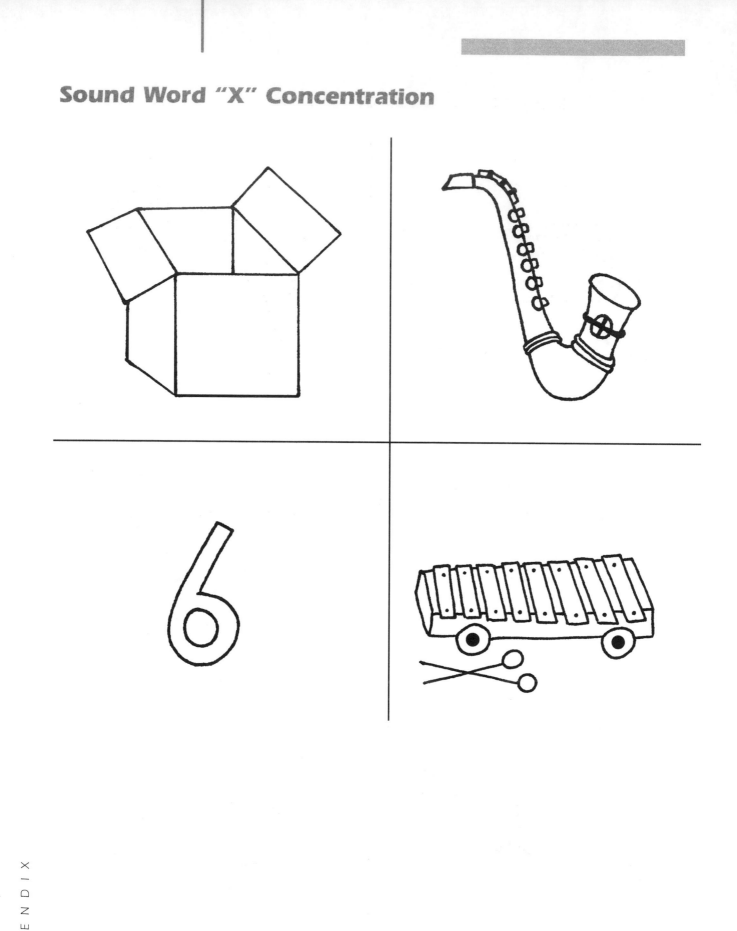

Beginning Sound Word "Y" Concentration

Beginning Sound Word "Z" Concentration

Concentration Patterns: Rhyming Objects

Sound Patterns

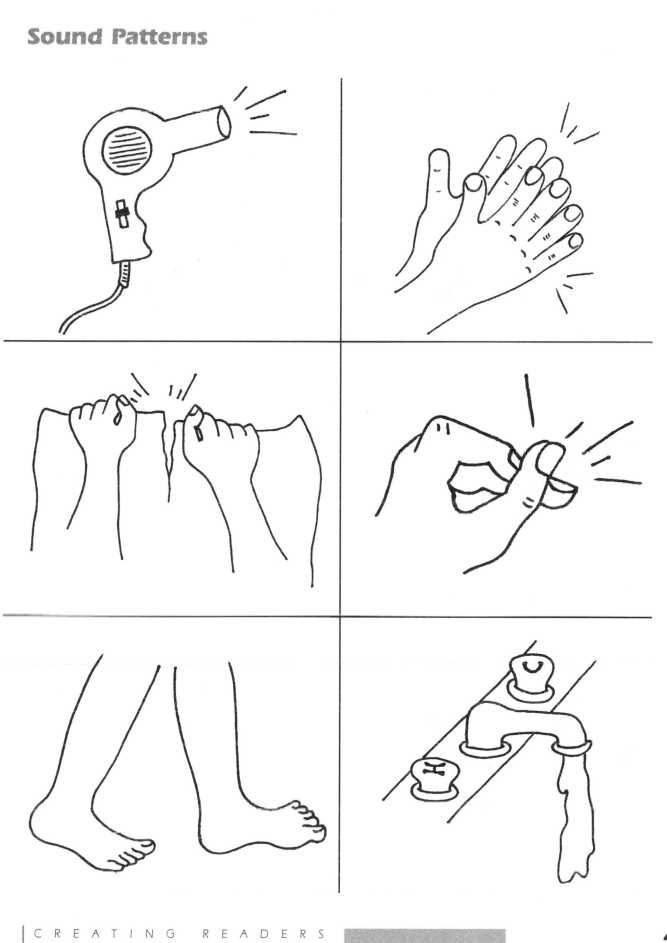

Recipes*

*Use caution when children are helping with recipes, especially when sharp utensils, electric appliances, and hot pans are a necessary part of the recipe. In addition, check for allergies before serving food, especially nuts, dairy products, and fruit.

Goop, Gak, Fingerpaint, and Other Non-Edible Recipes

Bubble Soap

Materials
1 teaspoon (5 ml) glycerin
½ cup (120 ml) liquid detergent
½ cup (120 ml) water
measuring cups and spoons
mixing bowl and spoon

Directions
Mix glycerin with liquid detergent and water. Gather bubble wands to make bubbles galore!

Fingerpaint Recipe #1

Mix 1 tablespoon of liquid starch with 1 teaspoon of dry tempera paint directly onto fingerpaint paper. Invite children to mix the two ingredients.

Fingerpaint Recipe #2

Materials
large mixing bowl and spoon
⅓ cup of cornstarch
cold water
measuring cup
hot water
1 envelope plain gelatin, such as Knox
½ cup of Ivory Flakes (or Ivory Snow)
containers
powdered tempera paint

Directions

Dissolve ⅓ cup cornstarch in ¾ cup cold water. Add 2 cups of hot water to cornstarch mixture and cook. Stir until the mixture is clear. Dissolve 1 envelope plain gelatin in ¼ cup cold water. Add gelatin mixture to cornstarch mixture and stir to blend. Add Ivory Flakes or Ivory Snow. Divide into containers. Add desired color of powdered tempera to each container.

Fingerpaint Recipe #3

Materials

1½ cups laundry starch
cold water
large mixing bowl and spoon
1 quart boiling water
1½ cup soap flakes
¼ cup talcum
containers
powdered tempera

Directions

Add just enough cold water to the laundry starch to make a creamy paste. Add boiling water and cook until mixture becomes transparent or glossy looking. Stir continually. Add talcum and allow mixture to cool. Add soap flakes and stir until they are evenly distributed. Pour into containers and add powdered tempera to color.

Salt Paint

Mix 1 teaspoon of salt into fingerpaint and let children enjoy a tactile fingerpainting experience.

Goop

Materials

2 cups (500 g) salt
1 cup (240 ml) water
1 cup (125 g) cornstarch
measuring cups
saucepan
mixing spoon
stove or hot plate
plastic bag or covered container

Directions

Cook salt and ½ cup (120 ml) of water for 4-5 minutes. Remove from heat. Add cornstarch and ½ cup (120 ml) water. Return to heat. Stir until mixture thickens. Store in plastic bag or covered container.

Gak

Materials

2 cups (480 ml) glue
1½ cups (360 ml) tap water
food coloring
2 teaspoons (10 g) borax
1 cup (240 ml) hot water
2 bowls
spoon
tray
plastic bag

Directions

Combine glue, tap water, and food coloring in a bowl. In a larger bowl, dissolve the borax in 1 cup of hot water. Slowly add the glue mixture to the dissolved borax. The mixture will quickly coagulate and be a little difficult to mix. After mixing well and removing all pockets of glue, pour off any excess water. Let stand for a few minutes and then dump onto a tray. Dry for 10 minutes. Store in a plastic bag. Place in the refrigerator to prolong life.

Edible Recipes

Apple Cider

Materials

32 oz. (4 cups or 1 L) apple juice
1 teaspoon (5 g) cinnamon
¼ cup (60 ml) lemon juice
2 tablespoons (30 ml) honey
measuring cups and spoons
large saucepan
mixing spoon
stove or hot plate

Directions

Mix, heat, and serve.

Applesauce

Materials
6 apples
½ cup (120 ml) water
⅛ teaspoon (0.5 g) cinnamon
1 teaspoon (5 ml) lemon juice
sugar to taste
cutting board and knife
large saucepan
stove or hot plate

Directions
Peel, core, and cut up apples. Put in large saucepan. Add water, sugar, and lemon juice. Cook until tender. Add cinnamon. Press through a colander.

Baggie Ice Cream (one serving)

Materials
½ cup (120 ml) milk
1 tablespoon (20 g) sugar
¼ teaspoon (1 ml) vanilla
small resealable plastic bag
large resealable plastic bag
3 tablespoons (60 g) rock salt
measuring cups and spoons

Directions
Place the milk, sugar, and vanilla in a small plastic bag and seal. Fill a large plastic bag with rock salt and ice. Put the small bag into the larger bag. Seal and shake. Makes one recipe for each child.

No-Bake Cookies

Materials
½ cup (80 g) raisins
½ cup (75 g) chopped dates
2 tablespoons (30 ml) honey
graham crackers
mixing bowl and spoon
resealable plastic bag
rolling pin

Directions

Pour raisins, dates, and honey into mixing bowl. Put several graham crackers in a plastic bag. Crush them with a rolling pin. Add to honey-fruit mixture until the mixture is dry enough to roll into balls.

Haystacks

Materials

small package of butterscotch chips
small package of chocolate chips
package of Chinese noodles
large saucepan
mixing spoon
stove or hot plate

Directions

Combine one small package of butterscotch chips and one small package of chocolate chips. Melt over low heat. Add one package of Chinese noodles. When cool enough to touch, shape into haystacks. Let set.

Letter Pretzel Cookies

Materials

1½ sticks (150 g) margarine, at room temperature
½ cups (125 g) sugar
1 teaspoon (5 ml) vanilla
1 ¾ cups (220 g) enriched all-purpose flour
2 tablespoons (30 ml) milk
measuring cups and spoons
mixing bowl and spoon
oven

Directions

Beat margarine and sugar until blended. Add vanilla, then the flour and milk. Chill. Divide dough into four parts. Divide each part into 8 pieces. Roll each piece into an 8" (20 cm) strand. Twist into letter shapes. Bake at 375° for 8-10 minutes.

Pancakes

Materials

1¼ cups (150 g) sifted flour
1½ teaspoons (8 g) baking powder
2 tablespoons (40 g) sugar

¾ teaspoon (5 g) salt
1 egg
1¼ cups (300 ml) milk
3 tablespoons (45 ml) oil
maple syrup
sifter
large and small mixing bowls
mixing spoons
griddle or frying pan
stove or hot plate

Directions

Sift flour, baking powder, sugar, and salt into the large mixing bowl. In a smaller bowl, beat the egg, then add the milk and oil. Stir liquid into flour mixture until dry ingredients are wet. Cook on griddle or frying pan.

Painted Cookies

Materials

2 ½ cups (310 grams) all purpose flour
1 teaspoon (5 g) baking soda
1 teaspoon (5 g) cream of tartar
1 cup (250 g) margarine
1½ cups (225 g) sifted powdered sugar
1 egg
¼ teaspoon (1 ml) orange extract
sifter
large mixing bowl and spoon (or electric mixer)
cookie sheet

Directions

Sift dry ingredients together. Cream margarine and sugar in large mixing bowl. Stir in egg and extract. Blend in dry ingredients. Cover and chill 2-3 hours. Divide in half. On a lightly floured board, roll to ¼" (6 mm) thickness. Cut into shapes. Place on ungreased cookie sheet. Decorate with Cookie Paint. Bake at 375°F (190°C) for 8-10 minutes. Makes about three dozen.

Cookie Paint

Place small amounts of evaporated milk into separate custard cups. Tint with food coloring. Paint on cookies with small brush.

Peanut Butter

Materials

1½ tablespoons (23 ml) vegetable oil
1 cup (125 g) roasted peanuts
½ teaspoon (3 g) salt
blender

Directions

Mix in electric blender. Blend to desired smoothness.

Peanut Butter Balls

Materials

½ cup (320 g) peanut butter
½ cup (120 ml) honey
1 cup (125 g) nonfat powdered milk
measuring cups
mixing bowl and spoon
refrigerator

Directions

Mix well. Squeeze and pull until shiny and soft. Roll into balls and chill to set. Yummy!

Gelatin Wobblers

Materials

4 oz. (110 grams) package of gelatin
1½ (360 ml) cups boiling water
stove or hot plate
mixing bowl and spoon
molds
oil
refrigerator

Directions

Dissolve gelatin in boiling water. Pour into lightly oiled molds and refrigerate for 3 hours.

Games

The Farmer in the Dell

The children all stand in a circle facing the center, except for one child who stands in the middle and is the "farmer." The children in the circle join hands and walk or skip in a circle around the farmer while singing the song below. The "farmer" chooses a "wife" from the children in the circle to join him in the middle; the "wife" chooses a "child," etc. The child chosen to be the "cheese" stands alone (the "farmer," his "wife," etc. all rejoin the circle) and becomes the "farmer" in the next round of "The Farmer in the Dell."

> The farmer in the dell,
> The farmer in the dell,
> High-ho the derry-o,
> The farmer in the dell.
>
> The farmer takes a wife…
> The wife takes a child…
> The child takes a nurse…
> The nurse takes a dog…
> The dog takes a cat…
> The cat takes a rat…
> The rat takes the cheese…
> The cheese stands alone…

Leap Frog

At least two children are needed to play this game. One child crouches down on the ground like a frog (knees bent and hands on the ground between and a little in front of his feet). The next child crouches down as well and then leaps and puts her legs on either side of the first child and her hands on the first child's back. Then she leaps onto the ground in front of the first child. The first child is now behind the second child and he leaps over her in the same way. If you are playing with many children, they can line up so that one child can leap over several "frogs" in one turn, landing on the ground between each frog.

Glossary

Alliteration — The repetition of an initial letter in a group of words.

Auditory Memory — The ability to recall sounds, words, and information heard.

Auditory Perception — The ability to hear likenesses and differences in sounds (beginning sounds, rhyming sounds, ending sounds).

Classification — The ability to categorize items or objects by like or common criteria.

Comprehension — The act of understanding. An ability to grasp the meaning and relevance of something.

Conceptual Development — The process of developing new ideas by matching information to established patterns and expanding those patterns to accommodate new information.

Decoding Skills — The ability to sound out letters.

Emergent Literacy — A term used to describe the beginnings of oral and written language proficiency.

Emergent Writing — Writing-related activities and behaviors that precede a child's understanding of conventional print.

Invented Spelling — Unconventional writing based on a young child's beginning use of letter sounds.

Left-to-Right Progression — The natural eye sweep needed for reading.

Literacy — Reading, writing, and comprehending text.

Motor Coordination — Use and development of the large and small muscles. Large muscle development precedes small muscle development. Small muscle development will be needed for holding and controlling a pen or pencil.

Onomatopoeia — Words that sound like what they name or describe.

Phonemes — Small units of speech that correspond to letters of an alphabetic writing system.

Phonemic Awareness	An awareness that language is broken down into small units called phonemes. For example, the word dog is composed of "d" and "og."
Phonological Awareness	An appreciation for sounds and meaning of spoken words. For example, cake and brake have similar sounds, stop and start have the same beginning sounds, and dinosaur has three syllables.
Phonics	The use of sound-symbol relationship in the teaching of reading.
Phonology	The aspects of language related to the sounds of language.
Readiness	Prepared for advanced instruction.
Segmentation	The breaking down of words into phonemes.
Syllable	A unit of spoken language.
Syntax	Language structure related to the way in which words go together to create phrases, clauses, and sentences.
Visual Memory	The ability to retain and recall visual images of shapes and letters.
Visual Motor Coordination	Coordination of the eye and arms, hands, and fingers.
Visual Perception	Ability to see likenesses and differences in size, shape, and color.
Whole/Part Relationships	The understanding of concepts expressed through language.

References

Adams, M. 1990. *Beginning to Read.* Cambridge, MA: MIT Press.

Adams, M., B. Foorman, I. Lundberg & T. Beeler. 1998. *Phonemic Awareness in Young Children.* Baltimore: Paul H. Brookes Pub.

Burns, M., P. Griffin, & C.E. Snow, (eds.). 1999. *Starting Out Right: A Guide to Promoting Children's Reading Success.* Washington, DC: National Academy Press.

Neuman, S., C. Copple & S. Bredekamp. 1999. *Learning to Read and Write.* Washington, DC: National Association for the Education of Young Children (NAEYC).

Schickedanz, J.A. 1999. *Much More Than the ABCs: The Early Stages of Reading and Writing.* Washington, DC: National Association for the Education of Young Children (NAEYC).

Totline Staff. 1994. *1001 Rhymes and Fingerplays for Working With Young Children.* Everett, Washington: Warren Publishing House, Inc.

Griffin, P. & M. Burns, (eds.). 1998. *Preventing Reading Difficulties in Young Children.* Washington, DC: National Academy Press.

Index

T

X

Y

Z